Cults, Sects, and the New Age

Rev. James J. LeBar

Introductory Comments by
Cardinal John J. O'Connor
and Cardinal John J. Krol

Contributing Authors:
Rev. Wm. Kent Burtner, O.P.
Rev. Walter Debold
Rev. James E. McGuire, S.T.D.

Our Sunday Visitor Publishing Division
Our Sunday Visitor, Inc.
Huntington, Indiana 46750

Nihil Obstat:
Edward J. Montano, S.T.D.
Censor Librorum

Imprimatur:
Patrick J. Sheridan
Vicar-General, Archdiocese of New York
February 4, 1989

The nihil obstat and imprimatur are official declarations that a book or pamphlet is free of doctrinal or moral error. No implication is contained therein that those who have granted the nihil obstat and imprimatur agree with the contents, opinions or statements expressed.

Our Sunday Visitor Publishing Division
Our Sunday Visitor, Inc.
200 Noll Plaza
Huntington, Indiana 46750

ISBN: 0-87973-431-0
LCCCN: 88-63530

PRINTED IN THE UNITED STATES OF AMERICA

Cover design by Steve A. Windmiller

431

This book is respectfully dedicated to

TERENCE CARDINAL COOKE
Archbishop of New York
1968-1983

who recognized the problem of the cults very early, and did not stand by idly and wait for someone else to act. It was through his suggestion that I first became involved in the study of this problem. It was through his active support and cooperation that the Church of New York became a leader in the spiritual warfare for the minds of people.

It will forever be to his memory that he sought information and knowledge on this emerging phenomenon and then provided assistance not only to the Church in New York, but to the entire country when the need arose. He did not back down when opposition came forth, and his constant support was an inspiration to continue the search for an answer to the problem of the cults, sects, and new religions.

Rev. James J. LeBar
January 8, 1989
Feast of the Epiphany

Acknowledgments

The authors are deeply indebted to the many people who provided information, suggestions, insights, etc., to make this work possible. Special thanks goes to Jackie Eckert, project editor at Our Sunday Visitor. The author would also like to thank the various publishers and individuals from whose works, copyrighted and otherwise, material was excerpted and used in this book. The names of said publishers and individuals are cited throughout this work wherever their material appears. If any materials have been used inadvertently without proper credit, please notify Our Sunday Visitor in writing so that future printings can be corrected.

Table of Contents

Preface

Thank God for good scholars, especially when they are pastorally oriented. *Cults, Sects, and the New Age* is the first work I have seen that answers the puzzling and sometimes terrifying questions confronting parents, teachers, bishops and others, including the young.

In this past decade alone, more than 2,500 "new" religious cults have appeared in the United States. They have promised happiness, contentment, and purpose in life to the hundreds of thousands of young people they have attracted. Some cults appeal particularly to the highly idealistic who want to change the world. The mystically inclined are attracted to those cults which offer guru-style meditation. A substantial number of young (and older) people looking for absolute religious certitude find it in the fundamentalist Bible studies that characterize some cults; many of these cults are strongly "pentecostal," as well.

The greater number of cults ("new religions" or "sects") initially emerged in our culture quietly and unobtrusively, then seemed to burst suddenly into the limelight. Many were and are Christian in basic teaching and practice, rooted, if very literally, in the Scriptures. Many more are God-centered, if not specifically Christian. But a substantial number are purely "naturalistic," colored with animism, tinged with colorations of Zen, or attuned to the elements: fire, water, earth, air, sun, moon and stars.

And now Satanism is having its day, Satanism and witchcraft and the indescribably obscene. Books and magazines on the "occult" have proliferated. Even murder and suicide have been attributed to their influence.

What constitutes the various cults? What makes some of them so successful? Who are the people behind the cults, directing the movements they engender?

Four scholarly and pastoral American priests (one, Father James J. LeBar, I am proud to call a New Yorker) go a long way toward answering such questions. They have been studying these cults and movements for many years, consulting representatives of other traditional religious persuasions, as well. They are clear about the dangers to all established religious bodies, the integrity of family life and society at large.

This is a straightforward, unsentimental look at cults. At the same time it is a gentle book. It offers hope and encouragement to those who have seen their young ones become involved in the kind of cult that has transformed their lives in a tragic manner, tearing apart their ties with their families, bringing them to reject their once-revered religious practices, and even seeming to convert them into "robots." Of equal importance, the authors give sound practical advice for responding effectively to the blandishments of the cults.

In 1986, the Vatican Secretariat for Promoting Christian Unity called specifically for the kind of study and pastoral sensitivity this book reflects when it issued its own statement on the subject: "Sects and New Religious Movements." Our four American priests have answered the call, and given us very much what we have needed to address the growing problems of cults in our day.

JOHN CARDINAL O'CONNOR
Archbishop of New York

Introduction

The Fathers of the Second Vatican Council opened a new era of reconciliation and the possible reunification of disparate Christian Churches when they encouraged dialogue and serious study of the essential differences between these churches and the Roman Catholic Church. Jewish and Protestant faithful as well as the clergy, the rabbis and the scholars of these traditions were generally pleased by this marvelous initiative on the part of Pope John XXIII and the Fathers of Vatican II.

Twenty-one years after the Council ended, a new question of religious freedom and serious scholarly dialogue has been raised on the international level. That question is quite simply: how should the mainline or conventional religious traditions speak with the so-called "new religious movements, sects, and cults"? This is a question that Jewish, Roman Catholic, Protestant, and Orthodox clergy and laity have been facing in growing numbers since 1966.

For two thousand years, one of the great treasures of the Roman Catholic Church's deposit of faith has been the centrality of the Church's Magisterium, the ultimate, authoritative teaching voice of the People of God spoken through the Pope and the College of Bishops. Vatican II was one manner of teaching, an extraordinary, solemn exercise of the apostolic voices of the Church. Vatican II re-stated many of the fundamental revealed truths of Catholic dogma and doctrine in a decidedly pastoral context.

Far less solemn but definitely important was the Vatican's recent statement on "New Religious Movements, Sects and Cults," of the Secretariat for Promoting Christian Unity, a pastoral teaching voice that seeks to understand the ideologies and emotional appeal these groups are exerting upon today's international youth. In the interest of preserving religious free-

9

dom and the dialogue called for by the Council, this document encourages that all people be properly and fully informed about these "new religions."

The Magisterium is here encouraging a studied and realistic awareness and analysis of the challenges to faith and family stability posed by the emergence of these groups. This is clearly a responsible and proper exercise of the Church's authentic teaching office.

The book which follows, written by four American priests, is a comprehensive response to the Vatican's statement that a full understanding and analysis of the so-called new religious movements is necessary. Based on their personal experiences with many people of various religious backgrounds and professions, this book offers valuable information and insights on how to deal with these groups.

The Fathers of Vatican II were very precise and careful to point out that elements of the true faith do exist in a limited way in other religious traditions outside Catholicism. The present question regarding new religious movements, sects, and cults must undergo the same deliberate and scholarly examination process undertaken by the Magisterium in dialoguing with the conventional or mainline denominations. The work of these priests will help the effort to continue such a process in an informed manner. It is to be hoped that more research writing will be forthcoming from a wide range of religious observers and commentators.

JOHN CARDINAL KROL
Archbishop of Philadelphia (retired)

I

What Are We Talking About?

Freedom is a precious gift. The freedom to believe in God (or not to) and to worship as one desires is part of that precious gift.

When the founding fathers of the United States set forth their Declaration of Independence, they said:

> We hold these Truths to be self evident, that all men are created equal, that they are endowed by their Creator with certain inalienable Rights, that among these are Life, Liberty, and the Pursuit of Happiness. . . .

Based on this first principle, the Constitution of the United states was ratified, and then amended to add the Bill of Rights, ten statements of basic rights of freedom of the American people, the first of which states:

> Congress shall make no law respecting an establishment of religion, or prohibiting the free exercise

thereof; or abridging the freedom of speech, or of the press;. . .

As originally intended by the founding fathers of the United States, the judicial purpose of the Constitution and the Bill of Rights was a restatement of the Judeo-Christian principle: "The purpose of law is to restrain evil; it is not a device to restructure man or human institutions." In recent years the history of the American people has seen this principle develop into two diverse concepts. In judicial practice there has been an increasing use of the term "separation of church and state," which many other countries, in seeking to divest themselves of "religion" in their lives, seek to emulate. In the legislative arena, we have certain permissible co-existence procedures for church and state as long as there is no "excessive entanglement." For example, the United States Supreme Court has allowed the placement of Christmas crèche scenes in Scarsdale, New York and Providence, Rhode Island, but it has not allowed teachers of secular subjects from public school systems to go into Catholic parochial schools. We may have prayers in Congress, but we are not allowed to have prayer in public school classrooms. There are chaplains in the armed forces and in federal, state, and city institutions for the imprisoned, handicapped and the sick, recognizing the obligation of the state to provide for the freedom of worship of people in those particular situations. On the other hand, some nursing orders of sisters are prohibited from ministering to the poor and handicapped. State funding is withheld unless the sisters divest themselves of any religious affiliation.

The United Nations Declaration of Human Rights brings the principles so familiar to Americans to the entire world:

> Everyone shall have the right to freedom of thought, conscience, and religion, and the freedom to manifest one's religion or belief (Article 13).

The Church itself, in the Second Vatican Council, while professing the truth of the Catholic Faith, still recognizes the basic right of every individual to religious freedom, and will not force Catholic belief and practice on anyone:

> The Vatican Council declares that the human person has a right to religious freedom. Freedom of this kind means that all men should be immune from coercion on the part of individuals, social groups and every human power so that, within due limits no-

body is forced to act against his convictions in religious matters in private or in public, alone or in association with others. The Council further declares that the right to religious freedom is based on the very dignity of the human person as known through the revealed word of God and by reason itself. This right of the human person to religious freedom must be given such recognition in the constitutional order of society as will make it a civil right (*Decree on Religious Liberty*, 1965, No. 2).

In the second half of the twentieth century, particularly in the 60s and 70s, many new religious movements sprang up, seemingly out of nowhere, attracting great numbers of followers in the United States.

Because of our high regard for freedom and human rights, no one paid much attention to these movements, despite their increasing influence on people. New cultures seem to see things differently, and while there was a new appreciation of freedom after the Second World War, its true meaning seemed to disappear after some years. It was replaced with a rather selfish and self-serving idea which stressed "I'm free to do whatever I want — no matter whom it may affect."

As society became more tolerant and compromising, many people lost the memory of an important fact: freedom is not something automatic, it must be protected and defended.

During the 60s and 70s society sought freedoms in every direction and in every facet of life. Certainty, dogmatic truths, morality, and the rights of others, all took second place to the "FREEDOM" of the individual to have WHAT he wanted, WHEN he wanted, and HOW he wanted it.

San Francisco, Berkeley, and the West Coast universities soon became the center of the "me only" attitude. The Hippie culture, the Jesus people, and later on, the Church of Satan all had their beginnings in California. Perhaps in a sense, these groups could be considered the foundation stones of the cult phenomenon as they prepared the youth culture for the abandonment of tradition and lawful order (as the Hippies did), a self-centered concept of God (as the Jesus people proclaimed), and the ultimate disregard of morality in the Judeo-Christian sense (as the Church of Satan manifested).

Joseph Cardinal Ratzinger, president of the Congregation of the Doctrine of the Faith, identifies Herbert Marcuse, of the University of California at San Diego, as a major contributor

13

to the cultual revolution and intellectual upheaval of the 1960s (cf. *Ratzinger Report*, St. Ignatius Press, 1985, p. 178).

In his writings and associations with Columbia and Harvard Universities, and the Russian Institutes as well, Marcuse was a strong advocate of the Liberation-from-God's Authority policy — which sparked the student revolts at the California universities, and Columbia University in New York City.

Into all this societal upheaval came the cults. Little known at first, seemingly harmless to society, and offering an answer to world conditions, one group after another proclaimed themselves to have the ONLY answer and the TRUE answer. Most of the groups we call cults did not begin in San Francisco, but they found a fertile spawning ground there.

As people moved out of the hippie culture and through the Jesus people era, those who came next were apt to seek what was in turn, new in their time period, and that new phenomenon was the cult, and to be more precise, the pseudo-religious cult.

A dictionary defintion of "cult" produces three elements:

1. System of religious worship or ritual;
2. Devoted attachment to, or extravagant admiration for, a person, principle, etc., especially when regarded as a fad.
3. A group of followers; sect.

In the twentieth century the term has taken on a new and more particularized definition that must now be delineated not in few words, but rather according to topical criteria.

The following characteristics, when found in a particular group, are sufficient to call the group a cult, and more accurately, a pseudo-religious cult (one which purports to be religious, but in effect is not).

First there must be a charismatic leader (male or female) who directs the group and seeks to draw all attention to himself or herself rather than to God. The leader is generally living, but there are some groups whose original leader has died and which carry on nonetheless because the successors continue to follow the same methodology.

Second, deceitful practices and a hidden agenda are identifiable in the recruitment process. Usually the name of the group is not disclosed in the beginning, and the prospective recruit is given a rosy picture of idealistic young people working together for a better world. No mention is made of turning over one's possessions or of maintaining total obedience to the leader through the subordinates.

Third, the initiation or conversion process is very rapid and there is no opportunity for the recruit to evaluate what's happening, and to discover if it is really what he expected. Most cult groups will not permit their recruits to visit with parents or friends, and keep the recruit in the company of a committed member during the entire indoctrination time. On more than one occasion former members have told of being accompanied even to the bathroom by their cult "shadow" during their indoctrination.

The *fourth* item has to do with departure from the group. When there is great difficulty in making a move out of the group because guilt complexes are placed on individuals, we have another sign. Threats of spiritual and bodily harm are often put upon all members to dissuade them from leaving. Members from the Unification Church were told, for example, that their ancestors would fall from heaven if they departed the group.

A *fifth* situation that marks the cult concerns the use of monies collected by the membership. There is great secrecy concerning the disposition of these funds and a lack of visible signs that these funds are used as the donor intended. Evidence suggests that the typical cult leader lives in great splendor, often having several residences and means of transportation, while the general members live in shabby surroundings, and sometimes have no fixed abode at all.

Based on the above characteristics, a working definition of "cult" can be established. This definition was developed and is used by the Interfaith Coalition of Concern about Cults (ICCC), a cult-watching organization founded by four major faith groups in New York City at the time of the Unification Church mass wedding in 1982. The ICCC defines a cult in this manner:

> A destructive cult has a self-appointed messianic leader who focuses followers' veneration upon him or herself, claims divine selection, and exercises autocratic control over members' lives. Deception and misrepresentation is used for purposes of recruitment, retention and fund-raising. Techniques are used that are aimed at controlling individual thought and personal privacy, frequently leading to a coerced reconstitution of personality.

It is important to recognize at the outset that there are many religious groups founded in the past century that are not cults and should not be categorized as such merely because they started up recently and are in juxtaposition with the ordinary way of doing things.

For this reason, it might be helpful to examine, from the opposite point of view, the before-mentioned characteristics and see what is not a cult, even though it might seem so on the surface.

Here are some general principles to use in this examination:

First, presuming that its leadership does lead people to God, even if it might be through a charismatic leader, does the group have an accountability system to prevent the improper assumption of roles by an individual or a group of people?

Second, is it completely honest in the presentation of its program to prospective members, so that both the pleasing elements and the challenging ones are apparent? Does a recruit have an opportunity to study the group from many aspects, including what is expected of the person who joins?

Third, is every opportunity given the individual to evaluate carefully his or her position beforehand? Is there a period of time for the recruit to study not only the teachings of the group, but also its methods and lifestyle? Can the recruit talk with present members and former ones equally without the leaders of the group hovering nearby within hearing distance?

Fourth, is there a history of former members who have left willingly or have they been removed unwillingly? Have these former members good things to say about the group even though they personally found it not to their liking?

Fifth, is there visible evidence that the particular group is fulfilling its mandate (whatever mission they have assigned to themselves) in an open and honest manner so that those who give funds to the cause can see what's being done?

In light of the above-listed characteristics, we can consider, for example that a person unfamiliar with mysticism and eastern traditions might see in Buddhism or Hinduism some of the cult characteristics, and unless that person applied the second set of questions, could make an erroneous decision and identify these groups as cults (which they are not). Someone else might look at one of our Catholic religious communities of strict observance and declare it a cult, based on an improper application of the principles mentioned before.

To identify the specific practices that make a cult dangerous and destructive is not difficult. Applying them to a particular group, however, is often an elusive task, for one finds out rather early that the cults and society do not speak the same language. Utilizing a practice known as heavenly deception or divine deceit, a group will alter the meaning of words that have significent meaning to society. A cult member will say "yes" when actually meaning "no," and often use the word "father" to mean not the earthly parent, or the heavenly Father, but the spiritual parent or cult leader.

A cult can be recognized when the following characteristics are manifested by observation of the group and by the reports of former members, or parents of present members:

   a) an inordinate preoccupation with fund raising;
   b) the use of mind control and mind manipulation methods in recruitment and training, which produces a severe change of personality;
   c) sudden and complete separation from friends, family, and anyone else who could change a person's mind;
   d) a deep rooted hatred for anyone outside the group;
   e) the exacting of total obedience from the recruit to the leader of even the lowest level;
   f) the giving up of the right to leave the group.

These ideas, culled from the general principles outlined earlier, bring the cult problem into clear focus, and make it a concern for all church and civic leaders. Any cult leader may have a hidden agenda which could include taking over either a particular church or civic entity, be it neighborhood, town, state, or even the nation. Often this program is done in the name of God as one whose mission is to save the world.

Defining a cult has become more difficult in recent years because of the rapid proliferation of groups. Originally, a pseudo-religious group meeting the before-mentioned criteria was easily seen to be a "cult." However, it soon became obvious that religion was not the only area invaded by the mind snatchers. Human potential programs have been seen in their more sinister light, and are considered cults. Other entrepreneurs saw the success of the cultic methodology and applied it to non-religious programs. Thus came the therapy cults, the political cults, and even the business cults. All of these groups found success and acceptance because they appealed to a certain aspiration of people. Thus with the exception of the fundraising criterion, these latter cult groups fit into the same schema. And the leader is also charismatic and enthusiastic, but no mention is made of God.

Considering the success of so many cults, it was only a matter of time too, before power seeking individuals noticed the hunger of people for Bible study and leadership. From this seemingly beneficial goal came groups who stressed Bible study and biblical leadership. These groups produced intense bible courses and a way of life that have given it the title of "Shepherding/Discipleship." By comparison, Shepherding/ Discipleship makes the fundamentalist churches seem meek and mild.

To distinguish a small, free, Bible church from the shepherding movement is extremely difficult because often the membership, and sometimes even the pastor, is not aware that certain members have joined the church with a hidden agenda, namely "sheep stealing," whereby they will work their way into the group, and then turn the entire group over to a shepherding leader. Thus we have again, what seems at first glance to be a good effort to follow the Bible and the teachings of Jesus, actually turn into destructive cultism.

The last element that complicates the "cult problem" of the present time is actually the antithesis of all that has been said already. While it too has been present throughout the world for centuries, its particularly dangerous potential for drawing people has only recently become apparent.

This part of our problem is the "occult," and in particular the worship of the devil, commonly called satanism. Together with it comes the growing practice of witchcraft, although some will assert that there is no connection between the two. It is important to understand that both of these latter categories need separate attention, whether or not they are in fact, connected. There are many unique problems associated with each.

Thus, a definition of cult becomes even more difficult when it attempts to embrace all these categories. We need to look more at the procedures (practices) and methodology for our definition. We must not fall into the trap of thinking any group doctrinally or morally different from our way of life is automatically a cult. Perhaps it is, but then again. . . maybe not.

The cults are a problem in modern society precisely because of this ambiguity and confusion. Our concern here are the destructive, pseudo-religious cults which deprive a person of freedom: freedom of thought, freedom of worship, freedom of choice. When we realize too, that these same groups add to this, indoctrination procedures filled with deception, manipulation and control to an excessive degree, the urgent need to counter the cults, sects and new religions is easily perceived.

II

Causes of the Problem

Critics of those who oppose the cults in today's society offer the argument that traditional churches are losing membership and that is why cults need to be rendered harmless. Other critics accuse the churches of stifling the freedom they are pretending to protect. Some cult leaders accuse the churches of unecumenical activity, or of not having the truth which people seek, and of having failed society itself.

In a class by themselves are those critics who profess that there is no cult problem at all, and that the whole anti-cult movement is itself a cult.

Typical of this class are Professors Bromley and Schupe. David Bromley is Professor and Chairman of the Department of Sociology and Anthropology at Virginia Commonwealth University. Anson Schupe is Associate Professor of Sociology and Associate Director of the Center for Social Research at the University of Texas at Arlington. Together they wrote *Strange Gods: The Great American Cult Scare* in 1979, in which they state:

In this book we insist, on the basis of hard, reliable evidence, that much of the controversy over so-called cults is a hoax, a "scare" in the truest sense of the word. There is no avalanche of rapidly growing cults. . . . There is no mysterious brainwashing process used to trap and enslave millions of young Americans. . . .There is no convincing evidence that all new religions are out merely to rip off every available dollar from the American public. . . . There is no compelling reason to believe that all modern gurus and spiritual leaders are complete charlatans. Finally, there is no bona fide mental health therapy called deprogramming that works as its practitioners and promoters claim. If anything, the logic behind deprogramming smacks of the same medieval thinking behind the seventeenth century Salem witch trials in colonial America (p.4).

In fairness to these authors, it should be noted that they acknowledge that cult related problems do exist, but they dismiss them almost immediately as mere rhetoric and totally useless:

Yet this cult hoax is not the result of hallucination. Nor is it sheer fabrication by the people who have been most anxious to promote it. It is not a deliberate fraud, but it is a deliberate attempt to horrify and scare us. Stories are spread by a number of Americans who sincerely believe them and genuinely feel that they have been victimized. At least some of their complaints are not groundless. . . . These new religions are at odds with the values, lifestyles and aspirations of the majority of contemporary Americans. Virtually all of the groups do condemn and reject the way most of us live. They do seek to recruit and reshape anyone who will listen to them (ibid.).

Thomas Robbins is another sociologist of religion. He takes a slightly different approach. He acknowledges that cults pose a problem, but he sees it as a natural progression in a secular world, and that evils attributed to the cults are actually a part of society and are manifested in many places in addition to the cults themselves. According to Robbins, cults should be left alone to practice their own form of religion. Unfortunately, these three professors and others ignore the reality of experience as well as the facts of life.

There are many new religious groups around that have taken young people from their families and a normal way of life, and transformed them into completely different people. There has been an exceedingly high number of people who come out of the cults — albeit quite unwillingly through deprogramming in many cases — who want nothing to do with the group and speak out clearly on the evils of the group.

If there had been only one or two, or even a dozen people speaking out on the evils of the group after leaving it, we might dismiss them as malcontents or misguided people deceived into leaving the group. But when the overwhelming majority of people leaving the cults — for whatever reason — speak the same story, relate the same techniques, and in some cases detail the same horrors of cult life, the truth itself is there to be perceived.

One cannot wish the problem away. One cannot merely state it does not exist, and have it vanish. It is also difficult to apply ecumenical principles and standards of fair play to such groups when they in turn manipulate principles and standards to their own advantage whenever possible.

The problem of the cults with their continuous seduction and indoctrination of young people (and others) remains with us. If we are to solve the cult problem effectively we need to understand why we have the problem, and its root causes.

One reason the cults pose a problem in society today is because they continue to attract members. There are no cults in public knowledge that actually kidnap recruits and secrete them away against their wills. Every individual who becomes involved in a cult has made at least one free choice along the way. The first choice may have been completely innocent. It may have been the acceptance of an invitation to dinner, or the acceptance of an offer to accompany a friend to bible study, or to a personality workshop. This sets the process in motion. Later on, politeness, or an unwillingness to offend a gracious host or teacher, may keep the potential recruit coming back repeatedly. Finally, when the direct overture is made to join the group, peer pressure and fear cloud the recruit's capability for decision-making.

Circumstances of this kind describe the visible process. We must look deeper, however, to find other elements that further influence the potential member, elements that can be identified as factors contributing to decisions made by the recruit, in the process.

Our consideration of these additional influences must be looked at in two parts. We need to examine society, and our Church. (Much of what is said about the Roman Catholic Church can be applied to other churches as well.) This examination needs to disclose the elements that affect a person's life both spiritually and materially. In an honest and sincere manner we need to diagnose the symptoms of the disease before we can treat it. We must not make the mistake merely of eliminating the symptoms. We need to root out the disease.

Society

Society today continuously faces a polarization of East and West. The two major super powers have frequently been on the brink of confrontation. Communists are constantly repressing their people, and striking out at the United States with accusations of war mongering, nuclear build-up, and unwarranted intervention in the affairs of other nations. At the same time, the communist ideology is a constant source of unrest in many countries. Eventually, through lies, confusion, deception, and the winning over of many people, especially the young, the communists are able to take over one country after another. Oftentimes they succeed because a particular country has never experienced the freedoms so cherished by Americans. The insurrectionists can influence the poor people, many of whom are oppressed in one way or another. And they also deceive them into thinking the Communist way is so much better that they are willing to fight for it.

The East-West confrontation, however, is not the only problem of society. In the free world, society has adopted an attitude of comfort, convenience and pleasure. In the desire for its own comfort, society has abandoned traditional principles of respect, reverence and care for others. This "me-first" attitude has caused people to disregard the moral principles upon which society is based. When moral principles are removed, permissiveness rushes in to fill the vacuum, and anything goes. The result has been the emergence of the drug culture, the rise of alcoholism, and the abandonment of sexual mores.

One recent author sees an even more sinister plan here. Do away with sin, then there is no need for observing any law. Do away with law and there is no need to restrict one's desires.

Without sin and without law, we in effect destroy God. And without God there is no ultimate basis for morality.

Is the root cause of the cult phenomenon, therefore, to be found in society? Has society failed its youth in not providing the framework for a worthwhile life? Not totally, of course, for the vast majority of young people do grow up into fine citizens, perhaps lacking some virtue, but trying hard. And although the remainder (those who do not) is a small percentage, it nevertheless rates attention. Because such attention is lacking, the cults have easily moved into the vacuum.

The Church

The Catholic Church faces a crisis today. In the United States in particular, large numbers of Catholics have left the Church and joined Fundamentalist churches such as the Assembly of God, the Missionary Alliance, or the Seventh Day Adventists. Others have just stopped attending Mass and become inactive.

Approximately 40% of young people who join cults are from Catholic backgrounds. The level of teenage suicide is as high for Catholic youth as for any other religious group.

In assessing and dealing with the root causes of this situation, it is very important to recognize that the practices and procedures of the Catholic Church have a long and successful history, and their value must not be dismissed out of hand.

The early Church began with an enthusiastic evangelization program at the time of the Apostles, and eventually brought Christianity to the entire known world at the time. It withstood heresies in the early centuries and schisms later on. It produced great educational systems, and a care-giver system second to none in the fields of health, medicine, and care of the poor. Great religious orders and communities were founded to serve these apostolates. Thousands of dedicated people flocked to these communities to continue the work of Christ by serving the community. This religious and social mission of the Church was carried out even when the Church administration at the highest level was undergoing difficult times.

Consider, for example, what happened in the fourth century. Arius was a priest, a native of Libya who was attached to the Church in Alexandria. He denied the divinity of Christ and was excommunicated by the bishop. In the Council of Nicea, the divinity of Jesus was affirmed; Arius was condemned again. Despite the condemnation, many bishops were appointed who favored the interpretation of Arius. In due time 75% of the Church leadership followed Arius. Truth prevailed, however, and eventually Arius and his teachings were definitively condemned. Toward the end of the century, Arianism declined rapidly.

In the eleventh century, at the time of the division between Constantinople and Rome (1054), the Church had to accommodate itself to the reality of schism. Of necessity, it had to acknowledge and recognize diversity in rituals of worship and customs of religious life as factors to be dealt with in a careful manner because of the schism with Constantinople.

As the Faith spread throughout Europe during the Middle Ages, the Church moved to intensify its educational efforts among the people in secular as well as religious matters. Traditions in the Church last for a long time, and at times efficiency of operation suffered when society changed and the Church did not. For example, the Church preserved its liturgy by retaining the Latin language (in the Roman Rite). But as modern languages developed and people no longer understood Latin, many no longer understand what was happening in the liturgy. The liturgy became, for many, a ritual of habit because of this. Often, those who were called to special service and to a life of religious practice, felt obligated to join a convent or monastery. In this specialized environment they were then able to understand the liturgy and practices of the Church.

Twenty ecumenical councils have been summoned in the history of the Church to help keep the Church in closer touch with the world. The latest of these councils, Vatican II (held from 1962 through 1965), has resulted in a great renewal of the Church. Unfortunately, the deterioration of society described earlier, affected the people of the Church as well, and much of what was intended by the council has been misread and misdirected by a small, but vocal minority of members.

What this brought about, however, was great confusion in the minds of ordinary people. Modern means of communication made opinions of theologians and others available to everyone almost instantly. A curious situation arose also when priests or religious had a disagreement with the Church or one of its teachings. Instead of seeking to solve it privately, the problem was often brought to the media and discussed in public, often with a bias in favor of the individual.

In the time since Vatican Council II, no matter what pronouncement came from the Holy See, there were people to oppose it. The new mores of society saw nothing wrong in extra-marital activity, in the limitation of child-bearing, or in expressing one's own opinion and rallying support for a dissenting position in doctrine or morality. Theologians openly oppose the Church, but instead of leaving it, as would have happened in earlier centuries, they stay on and defy the Church to ask them to leave. The effect of all this controversy and disturbance has been devastating to the Church as thousands of priests and religious renounced their vows and way of life, returning to the secular life. Some sought legitimate dispensation, but others would not follow the process, did not wish to wait, or in some cases, just felt the Church had no business telling them how to live. Many religious communities underwent change according to the spirit of renewal. In many instances the changes all but destroyed the community as it had been known for years, sometimes for centuries.

When ordinary people saw all this happening, they too were confused and often crushed when a priest or sister they knew well departed the ministry, often marrying without the blessing of the Church. Parents found that their children were not educated in the Faith as they themselves had been in the Catholic schools or the CCD program.

These children have since grown up not knowing the traditions of the Church. Today, as adults, they have no knowledge at all of the teachings and doctrines of the Church (though they do not realize it).

As indicated earlier, Catholics, young and old alike, do not live in a vacuum. The trends of society and the advances in technology leave their mark on the believer as well as the unbeliever. Radio and television, records and tapes, newspapers and magazines, all have been promoting and intensifying the pleasure culture for the past quarter century. The more technology has been able to give explanations for previously unknown phenomena, and bring about new healings through medicine, the less people turned to the Church to give them the answers they needed. This does not imply that the Church has not been responsive to the needs of people in recent years. It has been valiantly trying to continue to teach the Good News to its membership through the Catholic school system and the CCD programs. The work of the missionaries at home and abroad continue to seek out new people to hear the Word of God and profess the faith.

Five of the most visible problems are identified as follows:

1. Almost every diocese in the United States reports a decline in Mass attendance.

2. Father Alvin Illig, Director of the Paulist National Evangelization Program comments on the lack of converts in the Church today:

> For the second year in a row, the number of adult converts in the United States has decreased. In 1983 there were 95,346 adult converts; in 1984 there were 91,750 converts; and in 1985 there were 87,996 converts. In two years the number of converts has plummeted 7.7% or by 7,350 converts. We are at the lowest ratio of converts to active Catholics in the recorded history of the Church in America: 1.6 adult converts to 1,000 active Catholics. In 1950, for instance, there were 4.3 converts to 1,000 active Catholics (circular letter to priests, 1986).

3. A very large percentage of Confirmation candidates regard reception of the sacrament as the completion of their religious education instead of the beginning of an active life in the Church.

4. There are many people, sisters especially, who are no longer content to serve the Church as teachers of the young.

5. Even among those who attend Mass regularly, the Church has difficulty generating enthusiasm for active participation. We can get people to cheer and chant at a football game or other rally, but we have generally been unable to get average Sunday congregations to be enthusiastic in prayer and song.

We could go on with probably a hundred more items and still not touch the surface of the problem.

* * *

After a ministry of more than twenty-five years as a priest (and six as a seminarian), I have seen first-hand much of the Church's apostolate both before and after the Second Vatican Council. Through the ministries of parish priest, scout chaplain, and school teacher, I have come face to face with young people and their problems. As a coordinator for the Archdiocesan Office of Communications for nine years, I also had a chance to study the workings of the Church and, at times, act as spokesman on specific issues. As a television producer, I had opportunities to prepare programs to bring the Gospel message of Jesus Christ to the general public in various formats.

However, it is as a specialist intensively involved in the field of pseudo-religious cults for the past eleven years, and as a mental health facility chaplain for the past seven years, that I have come to hear the personal stories of people (and their families) caught up in the cults. It is this factual, first-hand knowledge of the cults that puts the problems in correct perspective.

The basic statement of every Catholic ex-cultist I have counseled has always been the same: "The Catholic Church did not mean anything to me. The cult group seemed like a good thing so I went to them." Some parents have admitted to me that they were not regular church-goers, but others were quite active. In earlier years, some parents reported they sought out the advice of priests, but received little, if any, help. Others reported that they received advice such as, "Well, at least your son is involved in some Christian organization. He's getting God."

The basic premise that I put forth as the underlying reason for the success of the cults with our Catholic youth is simple but vital: IN LARGE PART THE CURRENT GENERATION OF YOUNG PEOPLE HAVE NO FAITH. And we might extend that somewhat to include adults as well, many of whom are teaching today's youth.

To support this premise, consider the following testimonies of former cult members:

> — I went to the priest and he told me it was okay to join.
> — I never really knew Jesus as a person interested in me.
> — I went to twelve years of Catholic School and never had a priest, brother, or sister who knew me personally.
> — I never learned the beauty or the reality of the Bible.

This is not surprising when you consider these commonly reported incidents:

> — Parents send their children to Catholic school and CCD, but do not take them to Mass. Sometimes when pastors insist children attend Mass weekly, parents remove the children from the program.
> — Seminary faculties in many areas have indicated that many seeking admission to the seminary do not know even the basics of the Catholic Faith.
> — Children can recite TV commercials and

Sesame Street jingles before they enter school. But few children know even their basic prayers when they enter school.

— Many children have never had the opportunity to know Jesus in the Holy Eucharist through Holy Hours, Benediction, or similar devotions.

— Children see no problem, having missed Mass the week before, of receiving Holy Communion the next time they are at Mass.

On a broader scale, there is considerable evidence of the lack of faith throughout the Catholic population of today:

— Divorce and remarriage are not seen as anything wrong. "God understands our situation" is the common retort.

— Prospective marriage partners often do not want to educate the children in the Catholic Faith. "Let the children decide which religion he or she wants when of age" is a common reasoning.

— When preparing for marriage, the Catholic person will often forego a Catholic ceremony, and while not leaving the Catholic Church officially, will attend the Church of the spouse on a regular basis.

Evidence that a real faith — one to protect, defend, and practice — really exists, is difficult to discern. Most of the young people I have interviewed as they come out of the cult have had only a cultural exposure to Catholicism, usually interpreted to mean Baptism, attendance at Mass on special occasions, and perhaps religious education sufficient for First Communion, but not necessarily Confirmation. This was not difficult to put aside, especially when the cult recruiter offered something seemingly better.

Two examples will suffice to show the extent of the problem based on my own direct experience and observation:

A) A high school student announced to his mother, active in CCD work, that he had become a Satanist. When asked why, he boldly proclaimed that all he had learned was that God had a lot of rules you had to follow. Catholicism would give a reward in the next life if he followed a rigid path of goodness. But this life would be full of pain, sorrow, and difficulties. Worship of Satan promises pleasure and "anything goes" in this life. And since he is not sure that God even exists, he prefers to follow the path of Satan and pleasure.

B) A very fine Protestant woman married a widower who had two Catholic boys from his first marriage. They had five children of their own. As she promised, she raised the original two boys Catholic, even after her husband died. She married again, this time to a Protestant man. The boys grew up and married. The Catholic boys married Protestant girls and now attend the Protestant Church. The Protestant boys married Catholic girls and sometimes attend the Catholic Church. In addition, her only daughter recently married a Moslem. None of them has officially changed his religion, nor do they see anything improper in attending another church, even on a regular basis. Convenience is accepted as the measure of action. One takes the path of least resistance.

The lack of existence of a real, vibrant faith in our young people is further evidenced even in those who are active in parish and school. There is prevalent today, a certain activism that is not connected to religious practice or faith. Parish altar boys will be faithful and dependable in their assignments, but see nothing wrong in not attending Mass when they do not have to serve. Confirmation projects that teach Christian service are faithfully executed until it is time for the reception of the Sacrament, and then in so many cases, the interest and service ceases. (While these projects are by no means lifelong commitments, one would expect a good percentage of the students to have experienced something they would want to continue, for a while, at least.) Even among those who after Confirmation continue to give service at the altar and to the needy, there comes a time when it seems as if all that they have learned and experienced in previous years is thrown out. Nothing replaces it.

A quick examination of volunteer service among many religious and charitable organizations in which people are involved will show three significant factors that support the premise that faith is missing among the youth. The predominant age of the volunteer is over 45. Secondly, the background of most volunteers stems from pre-Vatican II times where a deeply instilled FAITH was the order of the day. Younger volunteers choose youth oriented programs and are active only while their own children are involved. When their children's interests change, the adults withdraw. This is understandable in a sense. But when the next level of parents should be moving up to take their places, we find them noticeably missing. The "me-first" attitude of each generation affects the next generation level in an increasing proportion.

Volunteer services that bring instant gratification and success are popular, but the tasks that require great effort and little tangible results often go undone because volunteers do not step in. The thought that one can do these things for the love of God is not even considered.

Thirdly, many volunteers cannot see the value of spiritual activities involving the elderly, homebound, or handicapped people. They are unable to appreciate the comfort and solace that comes from bringing Holy Communion to these people. In many cases, when church leaders attempt to spiritualize the ministry for young adult volunteers, little interest is aroused. The volunteers who do take part in the spiritual activities and appreciate the spiritual formation programs are the older adults, and encouragingly, many teenagers.

For the reasons inherent in the examples just cited, it is apparent that lack of faith, as it exists in our younger generation, actually deprives them of the joy and satisfaction of doing something worthwhile for Christ.

So many people have a low sense of self-worth, and very little respect for themselves. This root cause must be addressed as the Church seeks to develop pastoral programs to counter the cults. Lack of faith is also the root cause, in my estimation, of other Church problems, such as the vocation shortage, the lack of commitment in more than 50% of marriages today; and the continued acceptance of such positions against church teaching as abortion, woman's ordination, artificial birth control, and, most recently, euthanasia.

Before proposing a pastoral plan of action to deal with the cult problem, let me cite two personal examples.

Some years ago, we were faced with the problem in the parish of losing more than 70% of the students in our CCD program after Confirmation. One year we added a retreat day to the program, and noticed great improvement and interest as we spent an entire day together. But, the year after Confirmation, the same drop in attendance occurred in the CCD program.

As a result, in the summer of 1977, the CCD staff decided to reorganize the Confirmation program in a radical manner.

With the pastor's approval we revised the format of the Confirmation program, and removed the program from the weekly CCD program. We instituted five retreat days devoted to preparation for the sacrament, one of which was to be a weekend experience. There was great objection from some parents at first, but the plan prevailed, primarily, I think, because the students were intrigued by it.

On the weekend retreat, in the midst of a New York winter snowstorm, we managed to get everyone to the retreat house as the snowfall abated long enough for us to travel, and then came down in a fury that left 14 inches on the ground. We introduced the retreatants to the idea of an all-night prayer vigil before the Blessed Sacrament, four people each hour. We put out a sign-up sheet and everyone signed up excitedly, the wee hours of the morning going first. At the end of the retreat, when we asked everyone their reactions to the weekend, they were 100% positive, and the part of the retreat they liked best was the all-night prayer vigil. They also asked that we have a vigil in the parish, which we did on Holy Thursday.

Furthermore, after Confirmation, 47 of the 53 returned to the ninth-grade CCD class (one had moved away, two were beyond ninth grade and the other three did not come because their parents would not permit it). During the ninth grade they expressed disappointment at the shortness of the Holy Thursday Vigil, and asked for an all-night vigil, which was held in conjunction with a special program on the Feast of the Immaculate Conception, from 8 p.m. until 4 p.m. the following afternoon. Almost everyone took part, and several took multiple hours because a snowstorm prevented some from coming to their assigned turn the next day. Those present did not want to terminate the program early.

While we have lost track of many over the years, most of them I do know well, and both boys and girls are regular church-goers to this day.

The second example stems from my present assignment as chaplain to the Hudson River Psychiatric Center. It was advantageous to develop a volunteer program to make the pastoral service more adequately available to the residents. Several boys, unable to serve Mass in their local parish, volunteered to serve at the Pyschiatric Center Chapel.

Eventually these same boys began to visit the wards, interacting with the residents. Their service program was again built around the centrality of the Eucharist in their lives and the lives of the patients. Weekly instruction sessions in Christian Doctrine were held over a period of three years, and each Holy Thursday, the boys would spend time in adoration at the chapel, learning that Jesus is the center of their lives, as He is also central in the work that they do. Their activity attracted some of their friends, so that as the first group moved onto other things, others took their place.

The boys would accompany the deacon and me to the ward Communion services each week. In this way they came to see what the Eucharist means to the people served. Some have now become experienced enough to lead the services, and are anxious to reach the age when they can actually be Eucharistic Ministers and bring Holy Communion to the patients.

It is, of course, not possible to assess the long range effects of these examples, but the enthusiasm and interest sustained in the programs by the participants is significant in itself.

The question remains. What kind of plan can be implemented to counter the cults?

To counter the cult phenomenon, a basic program must be developed that will educate our people about the dangers of the cults, and the deceptive nature of their methods. Together with that, a program is needed that will excite our young people in their faith; a program that will integrate the necessary doctrinal and moral education needed to live as a Catholic and to rejoice in that fact. The program must bring knowledge of the Bible and an appreciation of biblical heritage to individuals of all ages. In addition there is a need to stress basics: commitment, pride of ownership, honesty, and devotion, to name just a few.

The long-range plan will require the efforts of many people, departments and agencies, coupled with a high level of prayer. The basic plan that is envisioned here is not new, and has been stated in other sources. It is, however, the foundation upon which can be built specific cult-countering plans discussed later in this book. It is a plan which conforms to the ideas of the Vatican Document of May 4, 1986 (see Appendix IX) as seen in Section 3.2 and 3.3:

> This ongoing program should be both informative, with information about our own Catholic tradition . . . and formative, with guidance in personal and communal faith, a deeper sense of the transcendent, of the eschatological, of religious commitment, of community spirit, etc. . . .
>
> People must be helped to know themselves as unique, loved by a personal God, and with a person-

al history from birth through death to resurrection.

The elements for the implementation of this plan have been available for many years. They are the documents of the Second Vatican Council and the various instructions and decrees that have come out in the intervening years. The theme of the plan is education and the active involvement of all age-levels in the life of the Church. Existing programs mandated by Vatican II need to be fine tuned a bit, taking into account along the way some of the things we have learned from the cults addressed. Perhaps in a way: we also have to take a lesson from the success of the cults to be a bit aggressive in our approach and strongly determined in the pursuit of our goal.

The plan is intended to bring together many elements and show how they can aid in countering the cults. The fine tuning of an already existing program is not intended as a criticism, but rather as an adaptation/adjustment to the basic program. Certain practices and procedures that have been used for years (centuries?) by the Church may have to be altered slightly to bring success. This is, of course, nothing new, as the Church has done this frequently.

As a final preliminary, note that it is not doctrine or errors in cult groups that is considered here (a later chapter will deal with that). The concern here is education, procedures and practices.

A successful foundation program to counter the cult phenomenon needs to bring to our children, at the earliest opportunity, a love of the Eucharist and the Mass. It must restore the idea of the importance of the family, and the important part parents have in the education and formation of their children. Parents who are unwilling to review their role as first educators of children may need additional lessons at the time of pre-Baptismal instructions. We need also to reinforce the role of parents and the family in pre-matrimonial programs. It will be important to include, in both instructions some information on the methods of the cults and their danger to young and old alike. In both marriage and baptismal instructions, sections on fundamentalism and its errors should be included.

The Vatican document suggests that parish structure might need revision (3.1). A rethinking of the classic Saturday evening/Sunday morning liturgical pattern (3.5) is also suggested. The Directory For Masses With Children and the Instructions on Masses with small groups already provides for this in worship, and it should be required for use in all religious educational programs, both in parochial schools and CCD programs. The various elements of the Constitution of the Liturgy should also be followed carefully, particularly in the involvement of people in the planning and execution of good liturgy. Different liturgies can appeal to different people, and parishes should accommodate the various needs, without dividing the parish.

As our young people enter school, each grade should be concerned with Christ-like service to others, with personal prayer, and with liturgical worship. No child should be admitted to the sacraments of First Eucharist or Confirmation if he or she is not a regular participant in the parish life of worship, prayer and service. (This is not meant to be a prohibition, but rather an acknowledgement of the necessity of these elements before the reception of the sacraments.) If these elements become a regular part of a young person's life, in addition to the many other youth activities, Confirmation programs demanding these activities will not seem so unusual and burdensome.

Another element in this foundation program is difficult but necessary to state. Pastors, teachers, and youth leaders must be givers of good example in their own lives. Those who are known to flaunt the teachings of the Church must not be put in positions of influencing children, regardless of their high qualifications in a particular field. Those responsible for the education of youth must be sensitive to this.

Programs in initial education and formation of young people need to stress the values of virtues (good habits), particularly honesty, fidelity, and dependibility. Children will make mistakes, and they need to be corrected with patience and love. But children need also to know that even though the corrector dislikes the incorrect action, he or she still loves the child.

Throughout the educational life of our children, we need to explain and encourage the use of our Catholic religious signs and sacraments. Young men and women today almost always wear something around the neck, and often earrings as well. Educational efforts have been lacking or have failed when a child will not wear a medal or scapular, or a cross, but will display a pagan or even satanic symbol, often not even knowing what it is or why it is worn.

For adults, a feeling of being wanted and of being valuable to the parish is very important. Many people who have drifted away to fundamentalist churches are almost unanimous in feeling unwanted or of not being known by their parish staff. They claim this is the primary reason for going to the fundamentalist church, once someone invited them. Education in the documents of Vatican II is especially important, particularly with respect to ecumenical activity, explaining what is permitted and what is not.

It will be important too, to explain the work of the Holy Spirit in our lives. The Catholic Charismatic movement has done much in this regard, but recently (as will be seen in a later chapter) a discovery was made that some aspects, notably the Covenant Communities, are actually leading people away from the Church instead of aiding their spirituality.

Finally, for young and old alike, a restatement of the reality of the devil and his power is of extreme importance. Unless our people understand the mission of satan, and that as a fallen angel he has great spiritual power, many will be attracted by the materialistic influences of today's society that invite honor, worship, and glory to the prince of darkness, rather than to the God of goodness.

The foundation then, of a successful pastoral program to counter the cults and to stem the tide of young people who are enticed into them, is the development of a love of the Eucharist in our people. Added to this is the reestablishment of the primary theological virtues of faith, hope, and charity in the lives of our (young) people. Formation programs for all age groups must correlate education about the danger of the cults, with the curative effects of their own particular curriculum.

When this foundation has been established, then in high school, college, and adult programs, complete mandatory education courses on the nature, methods, and dangers of the cults will be better understood as they are presented.

All of this presupposes the proper education of clergy, religious and other educators in the dangers of the cult phenomenon. How this is to be done is the subject of a later chapter.

III

The Religious Aspects of Cults, Sects and New Religions

From what has been said thus far, one might easily wonder why cults are generally labeled religious. Little has been said about their religious beliefs, and in what ways their practices are similar to some secular groups. Are we in fact disturbed with the cult phenomenon because they affect people religiously, . . . or psychologically? Are we dealing with a religious problem, or a mental crisis?

Of the more than 2,500 groups that have been identified as cults in the United States so far, the majority of them claim to be religious. Some seek to mimic Catholic practices and procedures. Others use a "born again" expression coupled with a charismatic experience. There are also some that seek to draw

Jewish people into a hybrid group that claims to be both Christian and Jewish, and which in fact is neither. Others pervert legitimate teachings of eastern religions and mysticism and draw unsuspecting recruits into a counterfeit religious practice that is in reality a cult.

Our high regard for freedom of worship, both as Americans and as Catholics, allows us to recognize fundamental religious freedom. If one wishes to worship the sun, one may do so. If one wants to call a particular person (guru) his master or his god, that too, is his privilege. It is objectionable, however, when an individual or a group coerces a person without his knowledge or consent.

Since cults often stress their religious nature, and often hide behind the protection of the First Amendment by calling themselves a religion, it is important to know the basic doctrines of a particular group, and how they differ from Catholic teaching (if the group purports to be Christian) or what relationship the group has to reality.

It is important to distinguish here that some groups really believe their doctrines. They cause no harm, use no deceptive or destructive techniques. These groups do not concern us. Those who seek power over individuals under the cover of religious persuasion are our concern.

The groups listed here have been documented in various media as particularly dangerous because of their mixture of deceptive practices and religious doctrines.

I. Pseudo-Christian groups

Children of God: One-time Baptist minister David Berg, now known as David Moses Berg, began this group after being expelled from his church for unbecoming conduct. Founded in 1970, it grew rapidly with thousands of members in many countries. In 1978, the name was changed to the Family of Love, but in recent years the original name crops up frequently.

Recent activity has been recorded in South America, where, among their activities is a familiar method of recruitment called "flirty fishing," in which women members act as "hookers for Jesus" on the street.

Children of God purport to use the Bible as their sacred book, but more important are the "MO" letters. These are Berg's directions to his membership, and are long, rambling, and often sexually oriented.

Berg denies the doctrine of the Trinity, as well as the divinity of Christ. He misinterprets the doctrine of the sacred nature of marriage. He encourages promiscuity among members, thereby being in opposition to the biblical teaching on sex in marriage.

New members sign a "Revolutionary Contract" through which they turn over all possessions to the Children of God (COG). Contacts with past friends are ended abruptly. Negative comments are forbidden, no member is ever left alone, and any hour not otherwise occupied will be used for "litnessing," a COG word indicating evangelizing by means of literature distribution.

Church of the Living Word (also called The Walk): The leader is John Robert Stevens, who considers himself God's chief intercessor. The source of his teachings is current revelations.

Church Universal and Triumphant (CUT): Under the leadership of Elizabeth Clare Prophet, this group puts forth a mixture of eastern religion, theosophy, Christianity and many other elements of thought. Her husband Mark was the founder, and both are recognized as the two witnesses referred to in Revelation 11:3. Elizabeth Clare Prophet claims to be the reincarnation of the biblical Martha, and the medieval Compte du Ste. Germain, a somewhat mysterious figure who is said to have only disappeared, not died, and who returns in different bodies in different ages. She teaches that she is the only present day conduit of truth of the Ascended Masters. This group is part of the New Age Movement.

A key belief of CUT is reincarnation. Denial of the divinity of Christ is obvious as well, Clare Prophet contends that Jesus was a mere human who became a christ, to serve as an example of how we can ascend by finding the christ-presence within us.

The Holy Order of MANS: was founded in San Francisco in 1968 by Earl Blighton, a former engineer who is known as Father Paul. He proclaims that his idea for a co-ed religious order was given by divine revelation. The language, activities, and the clothing of the Order of MANS is a deliberate imitation and mimicry of the Catholic Church. (The name itself is an acronym: Misterua, Agape, Nous, Sophia — Mystery, Love, Soul, Wisdom.) However, they claim to be non-denominational. Their ultimate goal is "to find a spiritual place in the new society," and to prepare oneself to have a constructive vocation. Their true goal is to "create from the individual who seeks this, a happy, joyful, smiling Christian who has attained the true Light and enjoys life" (p. 13 — booklet, "Uniting all Faiths," 1973 edition).

Some teachings that are at variance with the Catholic Faith are:

Jesus is a great teacher, but only man.

Life is continuous, uninterrupted, and ever evolving at the point of Being (reincarnation).

The basic law of the Triangle — God, Man- Woman, do things equally and together.

Scientology: The creation of L. Ron Hubbard (who died in 1985), a former science-fiction writer, it was founded as a religion in 1954. Scientology claimed more than three million adherents in 1980. It has had several encounters with the government, including proven cases of record stealing. Members are forced to divulge their innermost thoughts, including secrets, which are often used against them.

Some of the teachings of Scientology include:

The mind has two parts, analytic and reactive.

Each person's real "you" is a fallen immortal god (Thetan).

Each Thetan has been reincarnated over trillions of years.

Engrams are sensory impressions of past shock events, and can be passed on over successive reincarnations.

Scientology can remove the engrams.

Unification Church: With the imposing official title, "The Holy Spirit Association for the Unification of World Christianity," this group was founded in 1954 by Sun Myung Moon, a Korean who claims that Jesus appeared to him at the age of 16 and gave him his mission. Moon was originally a Presbyterian who took his church first to Japan, and in 1972 to the United States. He is perhaps most widely known for his large-scale weddings in which at a single ceremony he joins thousands in wedlock. While this group continues to recruit members in the usual manner, it also has a large program of conferences and front organizations.

One such program, known as CAUSA, (the Confederation of Associations for the Unity of Societies of America, operates on local, national and international levels. CAUSA-Brazil, for example, has "seventeen regional centres in the country which organize political seminars, and it claims to have 300,000 supporters in addition to 40,000 church members. CAUSA has launched an 'anti-communist manifesto' for which it plans to collect eight million signatures, a figure Mr. Moon set as his target in Brazil" (The "Independent," London, October 8, 1986).

This goal was achieved as the seventeen centers ran seminars, raised funds, and trained workers to put pressure on speakers at opposition rallies to support the manifesto. (cf. "Our Sunday Visitor," Huntington, Indiana, January 4, 1987, page 24 in the article "Are Millions of Brazilians leaving the Church?")

"Our Sunday Visitor" also reported in the same article that "a handful of conservative Catholic prelates, worried at the possibility of a communist takeover, still distrust the new democracy and covertly supported Moonie-backed groups in the campaign."

In the United States, CAUSA-USA specializes, among other things, in workshops for clergy, again stressing the anti-communist nature of their efforts.

Some basic teachings found in the *Divine Principle* (the principal source book) include:

Jesus is not the Son of God.

The death of Jesus did not effect redemption.

The sufferings of the Jewish people in the Holocaust was an indemnity for their rejection of Christ.

The Lord of the Second Advent is the messiah born in Korea approximately 2000 years after Christ. He will effect physical salvation, because Jesus only saved man spiritually.

The Way International: Victor Paul Wierwille founded this organization in New Knoxville, Ohio in 1957, teaching his first followers that God first spoke to him about his work in 1942. The WAY promotes exclusive biblical interpretations. A former minister of the Evangelical and Reformed Church, Wierwille was dismissed in 1958. The organization is formatted on the symbolic figure of a tree, with local Twig Fellowships joining into Branches. The Leaves are individual members, the Limb is the state organization, and the Trunk is the sum of the national organizations. The Roots are the international headquarters. Principal source of training is "Power for Abundant Living," a course consisting of 13 videotapes. Members become WOW Ambassadors (Word over the World) and spend a year or more in recruiting efforts and teaching first time courses. Wierwille died in 1985 but had previously turned over leadership of the group to Craig Martindale.

Some basic teachings (from a document nailed to the door of a United Church of Christ in 1977) include:

Jesus Christ is not God, never was, and never will be.

Jesus was not a Jew.

There is no Trinity.

The holocaust is a myth.

The principal teaching tool is Wierwille's version of the Bible.

World-Wide Church of God: began in the early 1930s when its founder, Herbert W. Armstrong, left the Church of God (Stanberry, Missouri) in which he had been ordained a minister in 1931. The reason for departure was the church's refusal to accept his doctrine of British Israelism. (The British are Isaac's Sons -S-c s-n -Sacsons -Saxons; vowels are not used in Hebrew.) Armstrong used the power of the media to build his following, capitalizing on the influence of the printed word and the growing power of radio (and later television). In 1947, he moved his operations to Pasadena, California, and founded Ambassador College. In a 1971 report of the church, the combination of local churches and media programs had produced a membership-following reported as high as 70,000. In later years Armstrong married and, after changing the rules of his church, was divorced in 1984. He died in 1985.

World-Wide Church of God teachings include:

The only true church is the World-Wide Church of God.

The only acceptable day of worship is the Seventh day (Sabbath or Saturday).

There is no Holy Trinity.

The soul is not immortal.

There will be three resurrections — of the faithful who will reign with God for 100 years; of those who did not believe; and then that of the wicked who will be judged and sent to destruction.

Eternal punishment is destined only for satan and his angels.

Baptism by immersion is the only valid baptism.

The principal teaching tool is "Plain Truth Magazine," supplemented by the weekly television and radio broadcasts.

II. Eastern Mysticism derivatives

There are many cult groups based on Eastern mysticism

that interest young people from Christian and Jewish families. Their attraction seems to stem from a search for something better than what is already in their possession. Some ex-members have indicated they were led into these groups unsuspectingly because of certain clergy and religious who quoted from Eastern mystics/gurus frequently, and having taken courses themselves, praised what they had learned, not from an academic point of view, but as valuable tools that helped them spiritually.

Divine Light Mission (DLM): was founded in India in 1960 by Shri Hans Ji Maharaj. He decreed that his youngest son, Guru Maharaj Ji, would succeed to the leadership upon his death. Born in Hardwar, India in 1957, "Goom Rodgie" as he is called by his followers, uses a form of mind control through the practice of meditation.

Some of DLM teachings include:

God is a form of energy, a cosmic vibration.

The ultimate goal is the merging of man's soul with the Infinite Absolute.

This realization of the merging with god can only be accomplished with the aid of a guru who leads one forward on the path of enlightenment.

A devotee who wants to attain this perfect knowledge must surrender his mental capacities. The process involved here transforms the disciples into robot-like slaves who immediately obey the Guru's bidding at once. A four-fold procedure is involved: a blinding light (called seeing with the third eye), hearing celestial music, tasting a sweet substance called nectar, and sensing a very special vibration.

Hare Krishna: His Divine Grace, A.C. Bhaktivedanta Swami Prabhupada founded the International Society for Krishna Consciousness (ISKON) in 1966. Members chant incessantly to get into the proper state of consciousness. They practice a lifestyle of devotion to Krishna and renounce both the body and the mind in surrender to Krishna. The movement is militant, inflexible, and very harsh.

There is no alcohol, drugs, coffee, meat or fish in the diet of devotees. Personal possessions are disposed of, and contact with the outside world is frowned upon. Men shave their heads, leaving only a small bit of hair (a sikha) by which Krishna can pull them up to heaven if he so desires.

Bob Larson's *Book of Cults* has an extensive chapter on this movement and should be consulted for more information.

Sri Chinmoy: Another guru, born in East Bengal, India in 1931, came to the United States in 1964. He has made an impression on the United Nations at their New York Headquarters, and has been allowed free access to their meditation chapel, where he has held public sessions. Unfortunately he takes liberties with the UN logo and has caused confusion among peoples who misunderstand his (lack of) connection with the UN. His way to God is typical of most gurus. It calls for devotion and surrender. The Hindu practice (doctrine) of yoga is at the heart of Chinmoy's systems. He calls for vegetarianism, meditation, and "siksha," surrendering of one's life to his teacher.

III. Human Potential Movements

There are additional groups that have little to do with religion, that concentrate instead on the inherent desire of people to improve themselves. They come under the cult umbrella because they use the same techniques to propagate their system, and eventually treat members as any cult does.

What is dangerous about these groups is their theological concept that they can make the individual a god; they teach that each individual can have complete control over the mind, will, and the spirit, not only of oneself, but also of others.

Some of the well known groups in this category are:

Eckankar: a group founded in 1965 by Paul Twitchell, a former staff member of Scientology, who dabbled in the occult and in mystical practices. It is often referred to as the "Ancient Science of Soul Travel."

An advertisement in a large city newspaper in 1979 stated:

> Eckankar is a way of life. It is the most ancient religion known to man, and through it the universal questions are seen in their deepest meaning and answered by the direct experience of God. The student of ECK (Spirit) lives a responsible, involved existence, paying his own way, serving a useful function in society, and fulfilling his commitments to himself, his family and his employer.

There are many who would disagree with the last part of that statement, particularly a young lady who found herself in the midst of criminal charges of grand larceny because of the undue influence of an Eckist. By manipulating her mind to a high decree, this Eckist was able to convince her that he could read her mind no matter where she was. Coupled with a fear of beatings and humiliations, she was forced to do his bidding as he sought to collect on bank loans and credit card usage.

This group promotes soul travel, mind reading, and reincarnation.

The present leader is SRI Darwin Gross.

The Forum: Originally founded in 1971 by Warner Erhard, it was known as EST (Latin for "it is"), an acronym for Erhard Seminars Training. At the age of twenty-four, Erhard moved to California from Philadelphia, Pennsylvania, where he was introduced to many religious groups. He had a conversion one day, with a flash of insight: What is, is, and what was, was, and what isn't, isn't. EST seminars have claimed over 200,000 graduates, including several prominent people in the entertainment industry.

Some basic teachings include:

The world has no meaning or purpose.

You can become your own god.

An item of concern in The Forum is an associated program known as the "Mastery Workshop," in which the targeted audience is clergy. It is nothing more than EST.

Silva Mind Control: This was the brainchild of Jose Silva, a Texan who was born in 1914. Appalled at the inept use of the mind by professional people, Jose set out to learn all about the mind and put it to its best use. According to *The Silva Mind Control Method* (Pocket Books, 1977) he found what to many appeared to be a paradox. He found that the brain was more energetic when it was less active. At lower frequencies the brain received and stored more information (p. 24). Silva Mind Control techniques attempt to sharpen the powers of the mind. However they cross over into paranormal activity, highlighting extrasensory perception (ESP) and clairvoyance, dabbling into occult sciences, leading one to conclude that one has complete control over his or her mind.

The problem of the Silva Mind Control program lies in the extent of the control that is achieved. The method brings people into deep, altered states of consciousness which can leave a person almost defenseless against the powers of evil spirits. According to Sid Roth, a former member who later became a Christian, some of the verifiable results of Silva Mind Control can only be explained through the power of demonic spirits. Roth also said that Silva Mind Control practices "open the doors for paranoia and other psychotic disorders" (Newsletter of the National Communications Office of the Catholic Charismatic Renewal, June, 1980, p.2).

According to Silva, our positive perceptions have the ability to alter reality, which is another way of saying we are all gods. He also teaches astral projection, and out of body experiences. "You can use dimes and pennies for silver and copper, a ring for gold, a small magnet for iron. You should all examine these objects carefully, then go to your level, and imagine one object at a time — picturing it several feet in front of you, above eye level. Imagine the object expanding until it is almost the size of the room, then enter it and perform the various tests" (SMC, p. 104).

Transcendental Meditation: TM was founded by Maharishi Mahesh Yogi in 1959. He was born in India in 1918 and became a guru follower in 1940. After a period of isolation in the Himalayan mountains, he brought his system of meditation for the common person to the world. In 1959 he brought his meditation system to California and presented it not as a religious but as a humanistic technique. In 1977 the group claimed about one million followers. It is sometimes taught in public schools, and has been used in prisons and other institutions with some success in calming the residents.

Some basic teachings of Transcendental Meditation include:
God is a personal Creative Intelligence.
People go through an endless cycle of reincarnation.
Happiness is attained by bringing out our own creative intelligence, ridding ourselves of ignorance. In effect it says that we are our own god.
(Consult Appendix III for the Pastoral Statement of Jaime Cardinal Sin, Archbishop of Manila, issued in 1984 when TM attempted to overrun the Philippine Islands.)

There are countless additional groups that might have been listed here. However, for brevity's sake, we have included only a few. For more information, the reader is referred to (Bob) Larson's *Book of Cults* (Tyndale House Publishers, Wheaton, Ill. 1982, eighth printing, 1985), which lists over 200 of the groups with brief, but informative, descriptions of each.

As a final note to this chapter, it is well to note the common theme that runs throughout the cult groups. This is the claim that the individual can achieve the characteristics of God Himself. This is especially noticeable among the human potential movements described earlier in this chapter. It is true too, of the New Age Movement, to be treated later. Claims of this kind reveal their true source in the identical offer Satan made to Eve (Genesis 3:5), "You shall be as God."

IV

Fundamentalism
Is it a Cult Too?

One of the most striking religious phenomena on the scene today is that of Fundamentalism. Father John Catoir, Director of the Christophers, reports in "America Magazine," ("Fundamentalism on the Move," September 27, 1986, p. 143), that "the movement away from mainline churches to Fundamentalism has been going on for nearly two decades. Many Hispanic Catholics have become Fundamentalists. Some not only leave Catholicism, they become bitter enemies of the church, attacking it and working to discredit it in any way they can." Father Catoir's thoughts are supported by Karl Keating in the Preface to his book, *Catholicism and Fundamentalism* (Ignatius Press, San Francisco, 1988):

But the allure of fundamentalism SHOULD BE taken seriously, if for no other reason than that hundreds of thousands of Catholics have taken it so seriously in the last few years that they have joined "Bible-believing" churches. Many of them have become not just non-Catholics, but anti-Catholics, because such an attitude is the natural result of the logic of their position. They perceive a duty to bring into "real Christianity" the family and friends they left at Mass.

One Assembly of God minister stated in a newspaper interview that 74% of the church's membership is made up of former Catholics. In a series of pamphlets another minister openly invites Cathoics to come over to the only true Christianity. Does this changeover also happen in other Christian denominations? Are fundamentalists to be considered part of the cult phenomenon, or a separate but equally serious problem?

The answer, in essence, is both. Chapter IX will consider the cultic manifestation of fundamentalism, often called the Shepherding/Discipleship movement. Here our concern will be basic fundamentalism. Though at times it may exhibit certain of the cult criteria, it is basically an overly enthusiastic effort to bring people to a life in Christ through the Bible. Therefore fundamentalism is not to be considered a cult.

Webster's Dictionary defines "fundamentalism" as:

> 1. Orthodox religious beliefs based on a literal interpretation of the Bible (e.g., complete acceptance of the story of creation as given in Genesis and rejection of the theory of evolution) and regarded as fundamental to the Christian faith.
> 2. Among some American Protestants, the movement based on this belief: opposed to modernism.

However, this is not the usual definition applied to this movement at the present time. For example, in their book, *Holy Terror*, authors Flo Conway and Jim Siegelman indicate how this definition has been scrapped and a new one introduced:

> As it turns out, this knot in the line of Christianity has little to do with religion and much to do with modern society. Fundamentalism began as a reaction to the material, educational and social demands of an increasingly technological world, and it continues to thrive on the conflict. In principle, the reaction was conceived as a revolt against "modernism" in Christian theology, but in fact,

then as today, it was largely a recoding of social and political disputes in religious terms. Jerry Falwell is more or less in agreement on this point. In his 1981 book, *The Fundamentalist Phenomenon*, edited by Falwell, but written by two faculty members of his Liberty Baptist College, the authors select earlier definitions of fundamentalism as a movement distinguished by its militant opposition of liberalism — viewed here in large part as modernist "accommodation to cultural change." With his own movement in mind, however, Falwell unflinchingly recasts fundamentalism as "reactionary evangelicalism," as he describes it, a revolt against the spread of "rationalism" and "secularism" on modern society (p. 199, 1982 edition).

It is important to define the subject of any examination carefully. As the two definitions above indicate, to set the limits of fundamentalism is difficult. It is further complicated by the merging of traditional meanings and philosophies. In *God's Bullies*, author Perry Deane Young notes the difficulties, but gives a good summary for our purposes:

A fundamentalist is generally defined as one who believes in adult baptism (that one should have a choice in the matter and be old enough to know what he is doing), in a literal interpretation of the Bible, and in being "reborn" or "born again" through a personal experience in accepting Jesus Christ as one's personal Savior (p. 59).

Fundamentalism is basically Christianity. It sees the Bible as the sole authority and rule of life. Its doctrine acknowledges that Jesus is true God and true man, the second Person of the Trinity (Father, Son and Holy Ghost). Jesus died for our sins, thereby effecting redemption. He promised salvation to all men, and therefore, everyone must profess faith in Jesus and commit his or her life to Christ. Some require baptism; others want baptism in the spirit. What is important in the tenets of this group is that anything, be it good or bad, or neither, is to be avoided if it cannot be proven by a biblical text.

Fundamentalism is found in all sizes and shapes. Its basic level is the local church, usually undenominational in allegiance and often called Church of Christ, Word of God Bible Church, or similar title. It is governed by a board of elders, but the minister (preacher, pastor) is actually the supreme leader, giving direction to the life of his parishioners through pulpit preaching. More established fundamentalist church organizations include the Assemblies of God, the Christian and Missionary Alliance Church, and the Seventh Day Adventists. The most far reaching fundamentalist organizations, however, are the television evangelists, and in particular the Christian Broadcasting Network, Trinity Broadcasting Network, and other similar endeavors. Through the power of the electronic media, and modern satellite technology, these networks have reached into almost every corner of the nation and into many parts of the world as well.

What is it that draws so many people to this way of life? Is it the fellowship, the preaching, the independence from authority? Or, is it the teachings? In interviews with many disaffected Catholics who have been attending fundamentalist churches, the predominant response is rarely the latter. It is almost always the friendliness of the people, the hearty welcome they receive each time they attend, and the notice taken of them when they first came to the church. Many also mention the lack of detailed commitment that is asked of them.

All of this underscores a great lack of understanding of the Catholic Faith. If one were only to search a bit, he or she would find that the Catholic Church is a fundamentalist church, but in a different manner from the others. All Catholic teachings are the teachings of Jesus. The Bible was put together in its final form more than three centuries after the Church began. The Bible contains the basic elements of the Faith because it contains the teachings of Jesus. Over the centuries, the Church, through its scholars, has amplified and clarified many of the teachings. The Catholic Church does believe Jesus is Lord, and has redeemed, or saved us. But the Catholic Church differs from the fundamentalists in a major point that is best seen in the Letter of James:

> My brothers, what good is it to profess faith without practicing it? Such faith has no power to save one, has it? If a brother or sister has nothing to wear and no food for the day, and you say to them, "Goodbye and good luck! Keep warm and well fed," but do not meet their bodily needs, what good is that? So it is with the faith that does nothing in practice. It is thoroughly lifeless. . . . You must perceive that a

50

person is justified by his works and not by faith
alone. . . . Be assured then, that faith without works
is dead as a body without breath (James 2:14-17, 24,
26).

Each person must put his own efforts into salvation. It is not
automatic.

Fundamentalism is not a religion of itself. It is a philosophy
of a religious way of life that has been assumed by preachers of
many denominations, including Catholics. Southern Baptists
have always had this philosophy and last year's elections for
their president saw a fundamentalist candidate running
against a moderate candidate, and for the second time the
more fundamentalist candidate was elected.

* * *

In a discussion of fundamentalism we need to include the
subject of evangelism and the evangelical style of church.

An evangelical is a person who sees as his mandate through
baptism a necessity to go forth personally to bring the Good
News of Jesus to as many people as possible. They preach the
Word of God (the Bible) and the love of Jesus Christ. They demand of any recruit a public commitment to the Lord. In addition, many groups offer study groups and companionship to assist members in fulfilling their mandate. This is basically a
good concept, used by many Christians. However, when help
and companionship go beyond normal bounds and coercion is
involved, we have the shepherding problem, which will be discussed in Chapter IX.

Evangelicalism is actually quite confusing when one tries to
study its tenets. For while it demands literal interpretation of
the Bible, it decides what is literal and what is not. While it demands we follow the Bible exactly, it decides which tracts are
to be so followed.

Evangelical churches are rarely involved in any ecumenical
activity. They do join together in groups such as the National
Association of Evangelicals (NAE) and the National Association of Religious Broadcasters (NARB), but they are rarely
found in Councils of Churches, Interfaith Councils, or similar
groups. Even the most independent fundamentalist church
sees the modern media as a prime source of recruitment and a
means of spreading the Word of God. Their budgets for the purchase of air time are quite large in comparison to their total
budget, and they do put Catholic, Protestant, and Jewish

groups to shame in this regard. Some groups will broadcast their service live, on radio or television and then repeat it one or more times during the same Sunday or during the week.

Evangelical fundamentalist churches make great demands on their people. The service on Sunday is long — usually two hours or more. They also require weekday attendance at Bible study and services, and they expect every member to be a constant missionary, speaking of the Lord in their daily activity. In addition, most if not all evangelical churches are hostile to Catholic teachings. At times, this will be subtle and indirect, such as lack of devotion to the saints and the Blessed Mother. Only when questioned about a particular practice (or lack of it) by ex-Catholics attending the service or Bible study, will the anti-Catholic attitude surface, as the preacher or teacher lashes out to condemn Catholics as guilty of idolatry for honoring the saints and the Mother of God. Some evangelists are quite anti-Catholic. Prominent televangelist Jimmy Swaggart, before his dismissal from the Assemblies of God in early 1988 for sexual indiscretions and refusal to accept reprimand and censure, was seen by hundreds of thousands on television every week. In 1983 he published a "Letter to my Catholic Friends," in which he took principal Catholic beliefs and tried to show how false they were. Moreover, he turned the letter into a series of television programs, highlighting Mother Teresa at one point in this fashion, as reported in the September 23, 1984 issue of "Our Sunday Visitor":

> Swaggart also described Mother Teresa's activities and said, "None of those things that Mother Teresa does will add one thing toward her salvation."
>
> In a July 29 broadcast, Swaggart accused the press of libel, saying he had never said that Mother Teresa would go to hell if she were not born again. But, he said, "I didn't say it, but I'll say it now. There is no soul under heaven — I don't care where they live or where they work — that's going to walk through that gate of pearl unless they are born again under the blood of Jesus Christ."

Here is a sample of his "explanation" of Catholic teachings:

> Catholic tradition states that during the Mass the bread actually becomes the physical flesh of the Lord Jesus Christ and the wine actually becomes His physical blood (transubstantiation). Catholic

tradition further states that priests can forgive sins. Also, tradition decrees that priests must remain celibate.

Jesus said in one of His most biting indictments of the errors of the "true church" that they were "making the word of God of no effect through your tradition. . ." (Mark 7:13a). I maintain that the bulk of the "traditions of the Catholic Church" are anti-Bible and anti-God. It was not long ago that the Catholic Church burned people at the stake — by the tens of thousands — for reading the Bible! Only a generation ago Catholics were forbidden to read the Bible, the position being that if there was anything important in there the priest would tell the common people about it. Unfortunately even the priests don't read their Bibles that much, being supplied instead with a much shorter, edited version known as The Breviary ("The Evangelist" Magazine, January, 1983, p. 8).

To a Catholic, the errors of this section should be only too apparent. The Church teaches that during the Mass the bread and wine become the true Body and Blood of Jesus under the appearance of bread and wine — a total change of substance. Persons were not burned at the stake for reading the Bible. Catholics were never forbidden to read the Bible. Priests often explained the texts because there were few Bibles available before printing was invented. Furthermore, there were few people who could read well. Finally, the Breviary is not an edited version of the Bible. It is the prayer book of the clergy, containing prayers, psalms and readings, both scriptural and non-scriptural.

Equally against the Church is the group called "Mission to Catholics International," whose avowed purpose is (to quote from one of their brochures) "to expose the deceptive teaching and practice of Roman Catholicism in the light of Scripture, to discourage conversions to Roman Catholicism, and to bring Catholics into Biblical Christianity." It was founded by an ex-priest, Bartholomew F. Brewer.

One brochure, entitled "The Church of Rome in Perspective," opens with these words: "Pope Paul VI, archpriest of Satan, a deceiver, and an antichrist, has, like Judas, gone to his own place." The author is Bob Jones and it appeared originally in the October, 1978 issue of "Faith for the Family" Magazine. One might rightly wonder why fundamentalism is so hostile to Catholics. One possible explanation is that Catholicism has such a strong doctrinal system (creed) that it is easy to criticize. In addition, because it makes demands on the faithful, the Church has always its share of those who rebel. What is different today is that conservative objectors are now insisting that they are right, and their mandate comes from God Himself.

Fundamentalists have developed the notion that they, and they alone, have the only way to eternal salvation. They have also developed a keen sense of evangelizing, more properly called proselytizing. They prey upon a person's lack of immediate knowledge of the faith, their doubt as to whether they have "received Jesus into their hearts as a personal savior." It is no wonder that many people are overwhelmed by their approach. They also know where to find the best prospects for their attention.

College campuses are ripe fields for cults, and fundamentalist evangelizers recruit openly on the campuses. Campus Crusade for Christ, the Navigators, Inter-Varsity Fellowship, Maranatha, and others feel a divinely inspired duty and right to proselytize among college students. And when you add Jews for Jesus and similar groups, the college campus is indeed a dangerous place for the student who has not been well trained in his own religious heritage before coming to the campus.

There are vast differences among the local fundamentalist Bible churches, the television evangelist, and the college envangelical groups. Each one needs to be examined in detail to learn how to identify them, how to deal with them, and how to avoid their pitfalls.

* * *

The Local Churches

Fundamentalist churches are found everywhere. They are accountable only to themselves, most of them existing as independent branches of an earlier fundamentalist church, from which they broke away due to membership size, difference in interpretation of biblical doctrine, or sometimes, simply for not liking the preacher.

The popularity of the pastor (preacher, minister) seems to be a very important factor in the success of any fundamentalist group. Sometimes the local groups select the pastor, and replace him freely whenever they do not like his sermons. Other times, it is the pastor himself who is the strong force, and he holds great power over his flock, so much so that those who do not agree are asked to leave.

Generally speaking, these churches do not join local interfaith and ecumenical organizations and activities, preferring instead to gather with those churches which share the same views. In Dutchess County of New York, for example, there is a very active Interfaith Council, which has brought together more than 90 congregations to work together for the spiritual and physical betterment of their membership and the populace at large. And yet, of the more than 63 fundamentalist, evangelical churches in the county, not one is a member, and not one has ever shown interest in the Dutchess Interfaith Council's activities.

Interest in the concerns of individual church members are not important either. A Catholic pastor reported that a marriage was to take place in which one of the parties was a fundamentalist. The marriage was in the Catholic Church, and the minister of the fundamentalist member would not even attend the wedding ceremony, much less take part in it, according to the ecumenical directives, for he would have been criticized by his congregation if they learned he was not only present at a Catholic Church, BUT ALSO took part in a ceremony.

The fundamentalist churches attempt to stress traditional spiritual values and practices in their teachings. However, in most cases, they neglect the basic principles of freedom of religion. They are not willing to worship as they desire and allow others to worship as they choose. While many believers, including Catholics, often have a strong desire to bring others to their faith, it is done with reason and conversion. Fundamentalists, however, have a strong compulsion to force everyone to their way of thinking, often through a fear of hell. This often creates dissension and alienation in a family or a community, similar to what happens in a cult.

Every fundamentalist church leader feels that he has been uniquely called to the mission of the church to bring people to (his version of) the true way of living the life of Christ. He is also unwilling to allow anyone else the same privilege, an attitude moderate Christians find difficult to reconcile with the words of Jesus, "Love one another as I have loved you."

As fundamentalists preach their literal interpretation of the Bible, they find no problem mixing religion into politics. Like the television evangelists, their mission is to ensure that EV-

ERYONE follows the plan (that is to say — Jesus's plan, but their version). To involve the government intimately in their plan by influencing laws and regulations, is perfectly acceptable for them. Sincere fundamentalists seek to live their faith and put their beliefs into practice by influencing the marketplace as any good person can and should do. By entering many professions and occupations, they seek to uplift society. Unfortunately, at times, some will exempt themselves and their programs from civil laws that do not fit into their plan. Some examples follow:

> Christian Schools in Nebraska do not want certification of teachers by the state, and local authorities have had to close some schools for noncompliance.
>
> Persons not willing to subscribe to fundamentalism are dismissed from their teaching positions. In one case a woman in a Christian School became pregnant and was ordered to quit work to begin her family. She refused because she wanted to work a few weeks longer. She was fired.
>
> A prominent instructor at a New England college converted to the Catholic Faith in 1985. He was advised soon afterward that his views and that of the school were not compatible. He resigned before he was fired.

Problems exist in the public sector when fundamentalists have too much influence. For example, in the State of Florida, all state prison chaplains until recently, were Protestant. Some are Southern Baptists, and others independent Baptists. Many of them are fundamentalists. In a few instances, the chaplain succeeded in making every prisoner subscribe to his belief system in order to obtain privileges. (Such actions actually border on that of a cult.) Also in Florida, prisoners of the Hebrew Christian Sect — a fundamentalist group, recently won the right to have their own chaplains at the prisons, while Catholics on death row were denied the visit of a priest.

Fortunately things have changed. The oppressive tactics were stopped by the Department of Corrections. At least one Catholic chaplain has now been hired by the State of Florida, and people of other religious faiths are allowed to have the benefits of religious ministry through the services of visiting ministers.

There have been problems in the public school system, too.

Some fundamentalist churches have their Sunday School program so well tuned that their young people go forth to proselytize their classmates in public schools. Some teachers have also been known to recruit new members among their students.

The big question that remains at the conclusion of this consideration is: WHY DO CATHOLIC PEOPLE FALL FOR THIS? We will defer the answer until we consider the other two elements.

* * *

The Media Evangelists (Evangelicals)

The advent of radio and television has been a boon to the evangelical fundamentalists. They quickly understood the possibility of success through the media and budgeted funds accordingly. Because television and radio time can be expensive, they often invest huge sums of money in order to obtain the needed money, and in some cases they do overextend themselves only to find themselves in financial difficulty when the donations fade. For the most part, however, they are eminently successful. They are able to get their message heard and seen by many people and, with the development of satellite transmission, low-power stations, and continuing improvement of equipment, the audience can now be counted in the hundreds of millions, including international viewers.

There are three prominent television networks involved in this venture. Christian Broadcasting Network (CBN) was founded in 1968 by Pat Robertson, the Trinity Broadcasting Network begun by Paul Crouch in 1970, and the Praise the Lord Network (PTL), until recently owned by Jim Bakker. Robertson is headquartered in Virginia and operates a number of UHF stations, but depends on carriage by cable systems for his vast audience. CBN seeks to affect the whole person, and as such does not limit its programming to religion, but provides reruns of family-type programs, and older movies as well. The most popular program seen, not only on his own stations and cable hook-ups but on many commercial stations as well, is the "700 CLUB," a Christian talk show modeled after the popular commercial ventures. PTL has its headquarters in Charlotte, North Carolina, with a similar network of owned stations and cable affiliates.

Paul Crouch on the other hand, feels that 24-hour, Christian television is needed and wanted by people. He has many of the other TV evangelists on his stations, and hosts a three-hour "Praise The Lord" show each night, which is repeated immediately afterwards, and again the next day. Generally his wife, Jan, participates in the program, and whenever they are away, the substitute host always has his wife with him on the program. Trinity Broadcasting Network (TBN) is headquartered in Santa Ana, California, and also has several UHF stations throughout the country, with a wide range of cable carriage as well. Both CBN and TBN are utilizing the new low-power repeater transmitters in parts of this country and in the Middle East. What must be noted here is the fact that 23% or more of both CBN and TBN donors (according to their own statistics) can be identified as Catholics.

There are many TV preachers who have their own weekly program, usually a church service taped for later use, who attract millions of viewers. Robert Schuller, and his glass cathedral and Jerry Falwell of the Liberty Baptist Church are two of the more prominent personalities, but we must not overlook Jimmy Robison, or Bill Kennedy. Another personality, who more properly belongs in the cultic category, instead of the fundamentalists, is Herbert W. Armstrong (who died in 1985) and his World Wide Church of God.

In examining these media programs, several things can be noted. Theatrics play a big part in the production. The music is lively, and there is much raising of hands and extemporaneous praising the Lord. The preacher often prances about the stage or sanctuary. There is frequent quoting of Sacred Scripture, much of it out of context, but some quite accurate. Most preachers seem preoccupied with the end times and feel we will witness the end soon. There is little personal contact between evangelist and follower, although most have telephone help available. The doctrine ranges from strict fundamentalism to an "easy-success if you are good" philosophy. The program has little doctrinal substance.

Many of the TV evangelists have little or no programs for education, for aiding the needy, or consoling the sick. All three networks do have some assistance programs and enlist the assistance of viewers, and frequently feature the people they have helped on their programs. The others, however, want you to send money so that they can continue on the air. It is reported also that some televangelists have asked for funds to aid the poor, the needy, or starving children. Perry Deane Young, in his book, *God's Bullies*, (Holt, Rinehart & Winston, N.Y., 1982) gives an example of this action:

In early 1980, Falwell launched the "Liberty Missionary Society" with an appeal for funds to help "thousands upon thousands of small children (who) are dying from starvation and malnutrition in refugee camps throughout the world. . . ." The first project of this society was to aid the Cambodian refugees in Thailand. As usual, Falwell covered himself by saying this was only "one of" the projects he needed money for. But when he published the projected two million dollar budget for these new "missions," $450,000 was earmarked for construction projects at Liberty College and another $450,000 was to go for training missionaries. Not one penny had been designated for food, although the appeal connected with this projected budget carried the message from Falwell, "In order to minister to starving people, we must first feed them."

Unfortunately, there seems to be no qualms of conscience over misrepresentations like this. The danger to those who put their trust and confidence only in a TV preacher is that in time of personal need, there will be no person on the local scene to assist.

* * *

Evangelical Groups on College Campuses

These are an especially dangerous form of fundamentalism. Such activity on campus possesses most of the qualities mentioned in the previous two groupings, but has an added incentive. The college student is in a time of transition, is often confused about religion, and is looking for someone or something to challenge him or her.

Dangers of these evangelical groups include their unwillingness to allow others the free exercise of religion. Their programs often have a hidden agenda. They prey upon the insecurity of young people, many of whom are new to the college scene. They take advantage of the lower level of religious education of college students today, and confuse them with an overkill of knowledge and activity as they seek to gain new members.

Catholic and secular colleges alike are prone to invasion by these groups. With the relaxed attitudes toward freedom of speech and religion, almost any group with a purposeful identity can qualify as a campus group.

Evangelical and cultic groups alike have used this means to gain entry to the college campus. With a simple act of registration, the group is given permission to post signs, meet on campus, and recruit members. Cultic groups often have difficulty gaining credibility, but the evangelical groups have a Christian umbrella and therefore are given almost instant recognition. Some of the campus groups are merely over-enthusiastic, but others are definitely cultic in nature. A few of the more prominent groups are given here with a brief history.

CAMPUS CRUSADE FOR CHRIST was founded by Dr. Bill Bright in 1951 at the UCLA Campus in Los Angeles. It is an aggressive evangelizing group whose leaders seek to recruit college students, who would be dedicated, energetic people, to be fruitful in their witness for Christ. Conway and Siegelman, in the work cited earlier, *Holy Terror*, find similarities to cultic groups in the Campus Crusade:

> We had our share of run-ins with members of this group. During our earlier research on *SNAPPING*, we had been alarmed by Crusade tactics that displayed disturbing similarities to cults we had studied: their aggressive recruiting style, their use of subtle forms of deception, Bill Bright's command — nearly identical to the cults — calling for the surrender of the intellect, the emotions and the will — the total person (p.150).

Associated with Campus Crusade is The Great Commission Army, an extremely conservative fundamentalist tactical unit which is said to have (cf. *Holy Terror*, p. 136) 6000 staff members and hundreds of thousands of volunteers in 131 countries. Their stated purpose: "to share the gospel with every person on earth."

Bill Bright is not an ordained minister. He is a business man, and as a business man he has applied marketing techniques and other business practices to Campus Crusade and is now reaping the (successful) results of this effort.

MARANATHA CHRISTIAN MINISTRIES (MCM) was formed in 1972 by Bob Weiner from Chicago, who was leading an evangelistic crusade in a Methodist Church in Paducah, Kentucky. It was ostensibily a licensed, drug prevention center and functioned as a place for fellowship and teaching. Sensing a need to bring the word of Jesus to college campuses, MARANATHA spread rapidly. The leadership is aggressive in their approach and not totally honest in their promises and demands. Early training sessions were conducted by leaders of the Christian Growth Ministries (cf. Shepherding/Discipleship chapter). The basic teachings of MARANATHA corresponds to the fundamentalist methodology. However, what disturbed many over the years was not so much the doctrine, but the methods. Coercive persuasion to an excessive degree, separation from friends and relatives, disassociation from former churches, and anti-Catholic attitudes caused many problems, so much so that in 1982 a committee of evangelicals felt compelled to confront the leadership and seek changes. MARANATHA did not abide with the agreement which had resulted in the evangelicals giving MARANATHA a conditional stamp of approval. Therefore in 1984 the same group issued a statement which included the following:

> Until we have clearer understanding of the changes which MARANATHA claims are being implemented, and until we see more discernible evidence of a change in the lives of people being impacted by MCM, we would not recommend this organization to anyone.

THE NAVIGATORS are a world-wide, missionary organization based in Colorado Springs, Colorado. It was developed in the U.S. military and after the Second World War was over it spread rapidly to the college campuses.

The TOPICAL MEMORY SYSTEM, a very disciplined training program for discipleship, was developed by the Navigators. It utilizes rote memorization, "subconscious" meditation, and heavy aggressive proselytizing tactics.

* * *

We have examined several aspects of fundamentalism. What becomes obvious to the reader, we hope, is the exclusivity of belief and the lack of opportunity for discussion and dialogue, even among members of the same group. Among different fundamentalist churches there is little agreement on belief and practice, except to unite against the non-fundamentalists.

What then, makes this so attractive to Catholics? As we mentioned earlier, many are disappointed at the lack of personal attention they received in the Catholic Church. Others are disturbed by a doctrine or practice of the Church that does not allow them to follow a certain lifestyle (divorce and remarriage for example).

It is my contention, however, that all these reasons merely scratch the surface of the problem. The basic reason for the success of the fundamentalists in this arena is that many Catholics today are not convinced believers in the Church. They might be more properly described as "cultural Catholics" or perhaps "from a Catholic heritage." Such people have not denied any doctrines, or actually left the Church. They seek a freedom of spirit and an ability to reject the restrictions, real or imagined, of the Church of their birth.

Such Catholics today do not have a basic knowledge of the faith. The relationship of the Church and the Bible is not understood. And, with so many entities of society proclaiming freedom and a do as you please philosophy, sincere churchgoers, unhappy with the faith of their fathers, seek something else.

How we solve this problem has been seen already in Chapter II. Further ideas will be found in Chapters VIII and XII.

The Bishops of the United States have begun to take steps to counter this problem. In a pastoral statement in 1987, an ad hoc committee chaired by Archbishop John Whealon of Hartford noted the lack of education of Catholic people in the Bible as a prime factor for the attraction of the fundamentalist churches. The pastoral presents some ideas for action, including a rather innovative suggestion to have people actually bring a Bible to Mass so that they can become familiar with the various passages.

In 1988, the hispanic bishops of California issued a statement examining the aggressive proselytism of some groups. They too, offered some helps to people. (The complete texts of these two documents can be found in Appendix XI.)

V

Helping the Ex-Cultist

By Rev. Wm. Kent Burtner, O.P.

As many as three to ten million people are, or may be, in need of our help — a large number by any reckoning. By the best estimates available, that is the number of people in the United States *currently* affiliated with groups referred to as destructive cults by clergy and mental health professionals familiar with the phenomenon. As cults have some "turnover," some more than others, in the next few years it is very likely that many pastoral workers will find they need to assist these people in their readjustment to society.

Ex-cultists need helpers equipped with special insights about their particular problem. The groups with which they have been affiliated have special dynamics which need to be understood. Without this understanding, helping professionals may mistakenly assume that the difficulties their clients experience are problems that originate in the personality of their clients rather than in the dynamics of the groups to which they belonged. Ex-cultists are the victims of an enforced dependency and the processes of that dependency need to be understood.

Because of the unique nature of the cult problem no one comes to an understanding easily. I am indebted to Daphne Greene, Margaret Singer and Jean Merritt, with whom I have been privileged to collaborate over the last several years and who have been an invaluable source of inspiration and insight. Daphne Greene and Neil Maxwell were my first mentors as I learned to find my way in this field. To many ex-cultists who have shared their experiences, I also owe my gratitude.

Consider the case of Carolyn S. She had become involved with a small, self-help group started by a woman who herself had been a cultist and who left that group to start her own program.

Carolyn was a student working toward her B.A. at a northeastern university, supporting herself as a part-time model. One afternoon, just after she had broken up with her boyfriend, she met Debbie. Debbie took an interest in her — she told Carolyn that she had just gone through a similar "down time" in her life — and invited her to a meeting where there would be other people who had experienced similar sorts of things in their lives and who would be a support to her.

So Carolyn went. The group made her feel welcome and special. They seemed genuinely caring. They listened, made her laugh, and talked about how the energy of a positive group made their lives better. Carolyn liked them.

That evening was the beginning of a year-long odyssey that included being called out of bed at midnight for "special important meetings" which lasted well into the next day, "clearing sessions" to root out imperfections in group members — with Debbie as the final arbiter of who had what imperfections, emergency trips to "check out" places that might have suspicious persons (enemies of the group), "dressing up to kill" to go to restaurants near "Debbie's place" to recruit others to join, surrendering her car and checking account to the group, and finally having four members of the group live in her apartment with her.

Carolyn felt totally boxed in, and out of control, but completely unable to assert herself against Debbie or her fellow cultists, who controlled her daily schedule and made virtually every life decision for her.

Carolyn says that she would have stayed in that situation indefinitely except that her father came to visit while en route to the South and she had a sudden impulse to jump in the car and make the trip with him. She knew something was wrong when she found herself looking around the roadside restaurants for signs of Debbie's followers who might have picked up her trail, and when she needed to barricade the doors of the motel rooms along the way.

So Carolyn checked herself into a clinic before she even got to her father's destination. The staff examined her and decided that while they couldn't find a particular symptom, it seemed best to send her into their drug addiction unit. Carolyn found some help there — she was dealing with a kind of addiction, to be sure — and eventually left the program feeling better.

A year later she married. Six months later the "trouble" began. Making decisions became excruciatingly painful. If her husband asked where she wanted to go out for dinner she became fearful. And if he asked her to do anything, even to pass the newspaper, she would react with enormous rage, throwing dishes and glasses at him. She found herself desperately afraid of any attempt to "manipulate" her by anyone. Once again, she needed help.

Carolyn's situation is not unlike many ex-cultists those of us in the field have seen. The problem is not that they received help from people who weren't generally competent, but these ex-members didn't get help directly related to their problem.

Profile of Cults and Recruiting

Typically cult recruits are above average intelligence, well adjusted, adaptable, from middle and upper-middle class homes, idealistic, and in relatively few cases is there any history of pre-existing psychopathology. According to studies released by researchers at the University of Oregon, Catholics and Jews are involved in cults in larger proportions than in the general population.

Why so many Catholics and Jews? My explanation for this is threefold. 1) Catholics and Jews, in different ways, to be sure, are comfortable with the notion of authority, i.e. in the Jewish home, in the Catholic church hierarchy. 2) Both Catholic and Jewish theology spend much time and energy with the notion of community, yet often enough the respective communities deliver little existential experience of community. 3) Jews and Catholics both have the benefit and the vulnerability of a rich tradition of symbolic expression of their religion, in visual imagery and in language patterns. The benefit is the ability to use them to bring about healing (consider Jung's notion of archetypes) and the vulnerability is that they are easily mimicked, making recruits "feel at home" in a situation they might otherwise consider unsafe.

So what happened? How did these folks "get into a group like that?" And what is the "special help" that is needed to get them functioning well once they get out of a cult?

Only a few cultists this writer has helped were searching for a group experience when they became attached to a cult. In most cases, they were going through normal "down" times, from which they would have recovered naturally. Instead, the group found them. Recruiters from these groups don't approach people who give off strong negative signals. They're experienced at finding someone who is open and willing to be polite despite their intrusion. They spark conversation and find something in the life of the new recruit that corresponds to their group — or invent such a correspondence, if need be. The come-on is friendly, non-threatening. As an inducement to come to the group's programs they offer some good thing, something that might appeal to anyone.

Some groups offer seminars or other inducements to go to their programs. These seminars aren't directed at the emotional need of the moment at all, but are simply some good thing that a person might want to acquire. Attending the program leads to a gradual induction done with a subtlety and finesse designed to precipitate a crisis, which the group will then "resolve."

Once in the program, the beginner is offered affection, compliments, kindness, favors, and attention. This initial warm-up leads the candidate to something far greater than he or she bargained for. There is a hidden agenda. Carefully orchestrated steps take the candidates from their normal frames of reference to those imposed by the group. A strong pressure to merge one's identity with that of the group comes as a result of emotional behavior cues, peer pressure, overwhelming affection, lack of privacy, strong emphasis on things wrong with the lives of new recruits, and outright lying about the group itself.

The group will seek to guide and control the time a person spends — not simply their time in recreation, work, school, etc., but the time they spend "between their ears." The process is dependent on the quality of time spent and getting the recruit to continue to practice the group's mental gymnastics, chants, mantras, etc., during the course of his or her day, rather than simply keeping the person on the physical premises of the group's center.

Group Behavioral Elements Open To Criticism

Three very critical elements of the control system of cults' need to be considered here:

1 — The deception they practice;
2 — The suspension of a candidate's analytical faculties;
3 — The assumption of control over the candidate's guilt and fear, which terminates in the repression of those thoughts and emotions which the group perceives as inimical.

For most cults the deception is wholesale. This is not the case of a "new born" recruit getting excited about the experience he has had, and pushing it hard, as a used-car dealer might an automobile. Rather, we see here a kind of *systemic* deception — something that is essential to the program, without which few would ever join because of what they saw at the outset. Each further step in the program implies something far beyond what is evident to the candidate.

Deception is rationalized by understanding that the group has all the essential truth *and* the rest of the world has none, or only minor parts of it. Therefore, the outside world is considered evil, "un-clear," satanic, demonic, and is filled with enemies ("yamadutas" as perceived by the Hare Krishnas, "systemites" if one is in the Children of God, "satanic figures" if a follower of Sun Myung Moon, "supressive persons" if a Scientologist, etc.). Scientology's founder, L. Ron Hubbard, was quoted to me by an ex-member as having said "S.P.'s have an incredible ability to appear *normal*." So it would be "unfair" to a potential new member to tell them the secrets of the elect, which in their unspiritual state they might reject. For a cult mind-set, far better to bring them to the truth slowly, so that "as their hearts become bonded" to the group they may be "spiritually open to the truth."

Getting candidates to surrender willfully their analytical faculties would seem a gigantic task to Americans, who are accustomed to the idea that the mind is the most invulnerable part of a personality. However, *cultists* know that the invulnerability of the mind is nothing more than a myth. One needs only to study the success of various advertising media in the national marketplace to understand just a little of what is part and parcel of the daily life of the cultist.

Logical fallacies are common. Great leaps of carefully displayed logic are followed by enormous gaps and missing "middle terms." Bold, unfounded assertions are mixed with logically reasoned ones. One *gets the impression* of something very logical, but doesn't get to test it out for himself. Tautologies are common, too. One of the better ones: "Life is so precious, for without it we'd be dead" (Guru Mahara Ji, founder of the Divine Light Mission).

In the face of some "wonderful, new" data, the candidates are led to believe their own life experiences insufficient to judge the content of the program presented to them. Prior to giving a lecture about the cult phenomenon, I was presented with a package of literature from one such group. In a cover letter, its "legal affairs officer" informed me that if I didn't base my presentation solely on the enclosed materials, I would be giving clear evidence of "speaking in a defamatory manor" (sic) and he would be forced to "take the appropriate legal action." (I assured my audience that I did not live in a "defamatory manor!")

Mystification is a common theme in cults. The common things in life are made out to be great mysteries and the real mysteries are reduced to simple formulae. People are told that normal physiological responses to stressful situations generated in the group, for instance the euphoric feeling common to activities that produce hyperventilation, are the result of divine activity. Group "highs" that are the normal response of individuals in group situations are also understood as divine intervention. Using meditation, people are "set up" to prove to themselves that the doctrine of the group is true beyond question.

The control a group exerts over one's guilt leads to a wholesale conditioning of the candidate's emotional life. The process depends on getting the candidate to believe that some part, or all, of his emotional life is intrinsically evil. It boils down to getting him to believe that "Your feelings are moral actions, for which you are reponsible."

While certain, or all, of a candidate's emotional repertory is targeted, those same emotions are being subtly stimulated. The resultant emotion is guilt, in overwhelming doses.

Of course, no one wants to feel guilty for long, and so the group is there offering various ways to cope with the guilt. All of the programs, however, are designed to do two things: to make sure that the group's control over one's guilt is increased and enhanced, and to bring the candidate into greater submission to group authority figures and "middle level management" people. One of the by-products of this kind of program is the spontaneous repression of those thoughts and feelings that have been targeted by the group as evil. It is almost as if a layer of pavement has been put over the cultist's emotional life. Only those thoughts and feelings approved by the group are allowed to filter through, the rest remaining present in the unconscious, but for the most part not experienced by the cultist consciously.

Given the paranoia that is part of the group mentality, fear becomes the next predominant emotion. The world is full of evils of every sort that will bring harm to the candidate. As a result, his sense of the world as threatening and harmful becomes exaggerated.

It is at this level that we find remarkable parallels between the practices of cults and the legitimate practices of behavior-modification therapy programs. Interestingly, the techniques of behavior-modification employed surreptitiously in many cults have been ruled unconstitutional or are legislated against under present statutes when used on prison inmates, mental patients who are confined under court order, and psychological research subjects, *without their written permission*.

If the group's program is successful, the result of the program is an individual totally unable to assert himself against the group, even if there are great moments of doubt and anxiety over whether the group is "true," and whether it's right or not to follow its practices.

Helping Someone Who Has Left

Competent counseling of ex-cultists following their departure from a group includes the following: access to information about the group and its activities that the client may not have had access to while in the group; a study of the rudiments of the control processes at work in cults; and most importantly, a therapy aimed at helping them overcome the automatic repression that follows upon the intense guilt they have experienced in the group.

Depending on the kind of help the clients have had, if any, when coming to a decision to leave the group, these elements may or may not have been dealt with. But it is clear that they must be dealt with thoroughly and competently or these clients will find themselves coping with large amounts of undifferentiated guilt, doubts about whether they should have left the group at all, and emotional difficulties such as Carolyn S. suffered. In many such cases the clients have returned to the group. If these issues haven't been resolved, arranging for that help is crucial. Had Carolyn S. had this help, a good deal of grief could have been avoided in her life.

But assuming that the clients have had this basic counsel, there are some very important symptoms to deal with, much as "post war stress syndrome" in America was found in soldiers long after they returned from Southeast Asia. Emotionally and spiritually, former cultists report feeling "spent" or "raped." They wonder how they will ever get themselves free of the experience and how they will recover any spirituality at all. Oftentimes the last thing they want to deal with is any kind of spiritual experience.

Consider that in joining a destructive cult, individuals have taken all their "old" values and in a large series of small steps discarded them in favor of the "new" values presented by the group. And now, in more or less one act of the will, they have discarded those values. Now what?

On top of that, the cult provided a kind of security. After all, no significant choices had to be made by one's self: vocational choices, sexual lifestyle, friends or marriage partners, daily routine, including what and when to eat, how to dress, etc., had all been made for the membership. Now a great deal of attention has to be paid to these things until basic decision making becomes a matter of habit again. Ex-cultists face a hard, uncertain world, full of stresses and anxieties, and, in large measure, they have forgotten how to deal with it.

From "First Aid" To Therapy

Thus, there are a host of particular considerations as we begin to look at therapy for ex-members. The broad spectrum of these is laid out in an important article by Dr. Margaret T. Singer of the University of California, "Coming Out of the Cults" ("Psychology Today," January, 1979), which is "required reading" for helping ex-members. Another useful article is by William and Lorna Goldberg, "Group Work With Former Cultists," in "Social Work: Journal of the National Association of Social Workers," Spring, 1982, helpful for those who will find themselves dealing with more than a few ex-members. The pastoral worker's job will range from "first-aid" for intense crisis moments to long-term therapy, sharing reflections and helping clients in the task of rediscovering their ability to choose everything from vocation to spirituality.

"First-aid" tasks will often deal with attacks of anxiety experienced by recently returned cultists. They come from programs which demanded that every single minute be totally full of physical and mental activity. Moving into an environment that says, "It's okay to take time to think, make decisions, and reflect on what you ought to do," will be a challenge. You can expect that when any anxiety-producing event occurs, they will be very afraid, dependent, depressed, dissociated, or all of the above. They will need your help to accept the anxiety and your listening as they talk it out and get a firm handle on reality again.

The onset of these incidents will be frequent at first, diminishing later in both frequency and intensity if the client is getting adequate help. The client will need to have someone immediately available at first. Over time, the client will become less dependent.

The on-going tasks of reintegration are the ones pastoral workers will be most likely called upon to help. Most significant of these is the recovering of internal and external communication, accepting and warmly welcoming their own thoughts and feelings. Clients need to relearn that none of their emotions and thoughts will cause them to be overtaken by any extrinsic influence. Rather, they present opportunities to think and reflect about what they want for their lives. This will be a major influence in reducing anxiety in these clients. They may need particular assurances about some of the targeted ideas that were part of the group's program.

The counselor will also have to learn from the client and from collaborative sources something of the group's ideological structure and how it worked, together with the guilt-specific practices of the group. I speak of collaborative sources because ex-cultists will often be unable to clearly identify distinct aspects of the ideology that justified certain behaviors of the group. A word of caution: a recently departed member should not be encouraged to recite very much of the group's ideology in one sitting. That activity will often stimulate the thought patterns associated with the group, and can frequently induce dissociation.

Depression is a typical experience of ex-cultists. For instance, they will inevitably have a sense that they have lost much time to the group. I find that there is some value that they can recover from the experience. Many will have learned how to deal with the public for the first time. Others have learned how to accept rejection (by outsiders). For certain, they will all have learned to spot a con artist coming at twenty yards.

An individual's sense of self worth comes under attack in the same way. The ex-cultists will ask themselves, "How could I have been so stupid as to have been taken in?" A recent case in point: a woman of twenty-seven heard about a program for good health and nutrition in central California operated by "Christian people." Having a weight problem (she tipped the scales at 267), she sent for literature, consulted with her parents, and paid the $1000 per month fee. She was literally rescued a year later by her sister: she weighed 107 pounds, had lost her hair, and had to be carried off of the airplane when she returned home. Five months later she still required physical therapy and ongoing counseling.

Not only this woman, but her parents as well, have strong guilt feelings about having allowed this situation to happen. My response to them is: There is nothing in most people's world view to tell them that there could possibly be a mind-controlling cult that would starve them into a few weeks of the end of their life in the name of good health, nutrition, and Jesus!

A sense of loneliness is often linked with depression. Making friendships, learning to trust again, and sharing the cult experience with others all present unique difficulties.

Sharing the cult experience with others is hard. Often people look at ex-cultists suddenly through new, and not too compassionate, eyes. "What ever was the matter with you?" is an often thought, but less often spoken, question.

Cults will invariably distort in one way or another a person's sexual values. Some groups tend to become quite repressive, with sex totally eschewed, or limited strictly to reproduction. Other groups encourage casual liaisons in the name of "love," "community," or "the Holy Spirit." For the ex-cultist, finding a sense of his own values becomes a difficult matter.

The above items suggest the need for good help in learning to make decisions. New, stressful situations that call for decisions may precipitate dissociative episodes that need immediate assistance. One ex-member was terror stricken when I asked her to choose between going to an ice cream parlor or a museum. Another one dissociated on being asked to choose one of four bottles of salad dressing. Ex-members recently out of their groups will need considerable shelter from these mundane choices at first, but with assistance will find that they can make decisions effectively. The process may take from several weeks to several months or longer.

Additional Needs of Ex-members

Every young person who becomes involved in a cult still has "unfinished business" with regard to the process of becoming an adult. These normal developmental tasks, which were underway in varying degrees before cult affiliation, ceased to be important to the cultist. Emotional conflicts were suppressed completely. These will surface once again after the person is out of the group. Daphne Greene, a pioneer researcher and parent counselor, labeled this the "Ice Box Effect," suggesting that it is as though these tasks were "frozen" while the person was in the cult and now they begin to "thaw out" and demand the client's attention once again.

The cult will most likely have told its members that they had these conflicts or unfinished growth and maturation because of some evil principle in their being. So when ex-members suddenly find these things at work, they are often fearful and anxious. Reassurance needs to be given often about the normality of the details of growing toward normal maturity.

Margaret Singer, in "Coming Out of the Cults," points out that oftentimes ex-members, like Carolyn S., will experience a fear of the group. Like Carolyn's experience, sometimes these are quite irrational. However, many ex-members genuinely have cause to fear. Two ex-members of an Indian-based cult reported being followed for several weeks by a pair of agents from the group. A court order stopped their activity. Others have had their residences broken into, their telephones tapped, and had their lives threatened in telephone calls they received. Three months after leaving her group one woman came home to find the group's emblem traced in blood on her front door and a dead cat nailed to the door jamb! Some fears should be taken seriously and some careful discernment made. Counseling can proceed accordingly.

Learning to cope with the normal, everyday manipulation to which we are all subjected can be a monumental task for ex-cultists. Carolyn S. found herself responding automatically to even the slightest suggestions from her employer and her husband. Then she began to react against them. It was hard for her to learn to accept others' requests as just that, and that she still had the right to say yes or no to them.

Making one's way financially after a cult experience can be a difficult thing, especially if the ex-cultist was a successful fund raiser. In her two years of fund raising, Barbara Underwood reported that she earned more than her father, a prominent attorney. She worked as a public affairs producer with a San Francisco radio station, but in that capacity did not make the same money she did for her cult. Getting a job, especially with a large gap in one's resume, can be equally difficult. Increasingly, employers, as well as admissions directors of colleges and universities, are understanding of the situation. Some ex-members have listed some of their cult job assignments on their resumes as assets. And some of them held significant posts in their groups. However, letters of recommendations from the groups are not likely to be forthcoming.

Relearning to do abstract thinking after a cult experience is a frustrating event for ex-members. They will often find that their vocabulary is narrowed, and the capacity to do "high level" mental functioning is diminished. One former member worked as a delivery van driver for nearly a year after leaving the group, though he had been a special education teacher before his cult experience. It helps to encourage clients to take their time as they work back to their former level in stages. The brain may be likened to a muscle that, having become weak with disuse, can be rehabilitated by using it.

Regaining a True Spirituality

Recovering one's spirituality after a cult experience presents the utmost difficulty for ex-members. It should be clear at this point that most cultists do not become affiliated due to a particular spiritual need, but oftentimes they do have "spiritual experiences" in the group. For many, those experiences are simply the result of group orchestration. For others, the experiences were authentic. It was, for some, the first seemingly credible group that gave them permission to have a spiritual experience. Most often those experiences came very early on and were not repeated, but the memory of them is often invoked to continue the involvement of the cultist in the group. (It might be noted that there are some who come away from the cult experience indicating no particular need for spiritual counsel, though these are usually people from groups that had a non-religious motiff.)

The emotions of wonder and awe, transcendence and mystery, are a deep part of each person (Carl Sagan notwithstanding). While in most of us those feelings are directed toward God, creation and the discovery of the "really real," like any other emotion, they are subject to manipulation. Ex-cultists have experienced these manipulations profoundly and the memory of them remains vivid. If they have not rejected those feelings totally as a result of their "heavenly sting," they question whether they can find that sense of transcendence anywhere other than in the cult.

The cult has told them that no other path exists beyond that of the group. In essence cultists have never really made a choice for the group, but rather have experienced a program that causes them to progressively close the doors of other alternatives. The only "choice" that remains to them is the group itself. The lingering question of where to experience that sense of transcendence needs to be addressed.

Going into a group, the cultist's values are one-at-a-time replaced with the values of the group. Old friendships are dropped, family ties are usually lessened, former mentors no longer seen in a favorable light. In leaving such a totalistic group, the ex-member finds himself or herself in an enormous vacuum. Barbara Underwood wrote eloquently of this in an account of her cult odyssey, *Hostage to Heaven* (Clarkson N. Potter, 1980):

> Suddenly, I'm confronted by the responsibility of relationships of my own making: with God and myself, my parents, friends, love. I face a cosmorama of sudden considerations: spiritual community, morality, my own long-supressed sexuality, pain and suffering, sensuality, individualism, political commitment, authority, eros, freedom, law, obligation, belief, fidelity, God's love and requirements, prayer, Christ's life, marriage, aging, money, honesty, my own brothers, sin, forgiveness, indemnity, career, school, mind control, trust, loyalty, children, integrity, sacrifice, understanding, joy, property, eternity, mortality, hope, judgment, messiah, confidence, choice, maturity, change, absolutism, relativism, truth.
>
> Once more, I join Everyman. Questions of purpose and existence hit me square in the face. . . (p. 255).

Her theological language can't be missed. Before proceeding, there are two important *caveats* to be observed here.

First, we must observe that cults, at least the ones that take a religious motif, co-opt conventional theological language. Saying "messiah" to a person recently departed from a group modeled after Christianity can set off a chain of thought that terminates in the "inescapable" conclusion that the leader is in fact the messiah that either did not come with Jesus of Nazareth or that the leader *is* the Christ or some other messianic figure. Thus, all theological language that is used by the counselor should be carefully defined as the counseling proceeds. The same principle applies to the client using theological (or other) cult jargon words: He needs to clearly define what he means in non-cult vocabulary. The cult related words tend to bring along by association other concepts that neither client nor counselor may intend. (A fine example of Freud's "secondary process thinking.") Here it is good to consult: Robert J. Lifton's *Thought Reform and the Psychology of Totalism* (W. W. Norton Company, Inc. 1961, p. 429, "Loading the Language"). The concept here is akin to Orwellian "Newspeak" — one limits the breadth and scope of thought by limiting the language in specific ways.

Secondly, the theological task is not usually the one taken up immediately after departure from a cult. Counselees often will need to learn to handle more mundane, less abstract emotions first, before learning to cope with larger abstractions. The clients themselves will generally tell you when these can be dealt with. The counselor needs only give him permission to do so.

Some counselors do not feel comfortable doing this because they fear setting off dissociative episodes (Is the client ready to pursue this area?), due to a lack of confidence in dealing with the area in general (referral to competent religious professionals is in order), or the questions are un-resolved for the counselors themselves. But for the foregoing reasons, it should be evident that there is some risk in *not* proceeding when the client is able to handle the discussion. If the only alternative is the cult, the client may choose the cult over society because he sees no choice, even having become aware of the manipulation and control of the group.

The process takes courage for these clients, who have experienced a "rape" of the emotions, including their spirituality. Will God let them get "ripped off" again? Yet the questions "Where do I fit in the cosmos?" and "Will I find that energy again?" and "What will I share with a spouse and pass on to my children?" linger and demand attention.

Two tasks are significant at this juncture. The first is to have the clients evaluate the ideology of the group, its philosophy and world view, with an eye toward defining terms clearly in non-cult language (as above — note that this can be hard: one very large international group has its own dictionary several hundred pages long, redefining thousands of words).

Secondly, they will usually find it valuable to go back and research the tradition in which they were raised. The value is that the clients know what is "safe" in their own tradition and what is "off base." This process will then give them a basis of comparison and enable them to open the doors that were systematically closed in the cult.

It should go without saying that this is no time for a counselor to proselytize for his own perspective. There have been a number of such cases. While it appears that someone has made a positive faith commitment, usually it is little more than the replacement of one dependency with another. The client is left with a deep-seated doubt about the validity of the new experience which will tend to manifest itself much later, resulting in the same doubt and confusion that followed departure from the cult originally.

God and The Ex-member

Several observations commonly made by former cultists may be of help to the newly returned individual. The first is that God is bigger than the limitations imposed by the group. For most cults, God is anything other than the fullness of being. Father, God is manipulable, and is quite dependent on the cult, or at least its leader. Any ultimate good to be done for the world is done entirely by the group, and the individual member must perform to enormous expectations. A theology of "grace" is totally inoperative in cult theology. There are no theological "freebies" here. The "production ethic" and the polarization of the world between inside and outside keeps the cultists always "one down" in the way experienced by mine workers and the "company store" earlier in this century.

Ex-members have observed some interesting dichotomies. These include "mystery vs. mystification," where infinity and continuing discovery is confused with circular logic, thought terminating clichés, and obedience for its own sake. Another is "reflective thinking vs. circular thinking" or "non-thinking." Particular prayer forms are used to the exclusion of reflection. In some groups, the brain is seen as an enemy, and thus the rational functioning of the mind is limited in scope.

Describing a "community of freedom" vs. "a community of coercion," is often helpful. Is affiliation obtained at some cost? What cost? What is given in return? Is there adequate information available to make a decision? Does the group see itself as providing resources for understanding and meaning or is it simply interested in converting people to its ideology? Does it emphasize its traditions in a broad context, or is it concerned more with "trappings" that merely mimic authentic traditions?

Another observation made by ex-members is that in an age where transcendence can function to make one's "place in the cosmos" clear, cults instead deliver deception and coercion. They simply can't deliver on their promises to make the world better, life more meaningful, or people happier.

One final point: ex-cultists as clients need a fairly large dose of specialized attention following their group experience and, as we can see, there are many "details" to cope with. The therapist should never presume that because we have said things once to an ex-cultist that these things have registered and are therefore useable. When the client can show signs of integrating those insights, then the therapist can rest a little easier.

As a class, ex-cultists have experienced tragic abuse. As with any suffering person, with the appropriate help they can be healed and can grow in significant ways, as can their families. Given love, the support of their families or friends, and an able counselor, these people can become whole again. After the healing process is over, they are often more compassionate than before the experience. Through their commitment to their ideals (which helped get them into cults in the first place) they can find channels of growth and fulfillment. As Paul the Apostle says, "Where sin is, there grace abounds all the more" (Romans 5:20).

VI

A Victim

Growing up in the late 1960s was not easy. Vatican II was just over and the Church was "emerging." There was a war in Vietnam and it was not going well. A "new" morality was coming on the scene as well, and for a student of these times, it was difficult to know which way to go.

Gary Scharff was one such student. Born in Hartford, Connecticut, in 1951, he went to Saint Barnabas and Saint Pius X Schools in Louisville and Saint Xavier High School. When it came time for college, he was accepted at Princeton where he majored in religion. He had been moderately interested in his church during earlier years, and even took part in week-long visits to a couple of seminaries because he had had thoughts of becoming a priest.

It was after his third year at Princeton that he met up with members of a pseudo-religious cult. In June, 1972, deciding to take a year off from studies, Gary went back to Louisville and obtained a job in a tool factory. He was on the campus of the

University of Louisville, taking a course in Shakespeare in his spare time, when he met a person who was on a bus team just passing through, trying to get recruits for the cult. Within a year, Gary entered into rigorous training in the Unification Church.

Gary's training period — a period of exhaustion and poor diet leading to virtual mind control — was about two months in length and he was one of the top graduates of the program. Out of the 50 or so graduates, Moon took the top 20 and sent them out to take charge of states. He was sent to Pennsylvania and placed in charge of the Philadelphia center for about five months. He opened a center in Pittsburgh but through a complicated letter-writing process to Moon initiated by his father, Gary was able to return to school at Princeton. Gary himself felt ashamed, and as though he had failed in his leadership position.

In an effort — perhaps — to reassure Gary that he was still in good graces, Moon appointed him National Director of the Collegiate Association for the Research of Principle, which is the student youth movement. He had this position for the '73-'74 school year while he completed his bachelor's degree at Princeton. During the first semester he spent all of his weekends (Friday through Sunday) at the Philadelphia center, lecturing at the workshops, and in mid-December all members were directed by Neil Salonen, U.S. President of the Unification Church, to go to Washington, D.C., to give vocal support to former President Nixon at the annual Christmas tree lighting ceremony at the White House.

He was put on a *Horse team*, trained by Neil Salonen himself, in which they were to give the impression at this rally of enormous support for Nixon. The Horse team was to rush up to the President, hoist him to their shoulders and carry him through the streets of Washington.

When Nixon came across the White House lawn toward the crowd, utter bedlam broke loose. As the Moonies rushed toward the president, the Secret Service was alert and ready. Gary remembers:

> "There were just two of us from the Horse team that I can remember that were running like mad, just ripping our way across, standing on shoulders, flinging Moonies right and left so that we could get to Nixon and accomplish our task.
> "And I rushed into the phalanx of Secret Service

agents protecting him with all their might, and when I got up to the line, I shrewdly tried to find a point to get through his cauldron of agents around him, and I darted under this enormous man's arm and he caught me by the back of the neck, and just threw me back into the crowd. . . .

"Later we were told by Moon himself that the reason Nixon was driven from office was that we had not lifted him that day on our shoulders. Had we done this, the American people would have loved him, accepted him, realized the errors of their ways and recognized him as a great president. It was my understanding that Moon spoke this way because he had been developing, over a period of years, a relationship with Nixon through his contacts in Washington, and he really believed that for him to bail out Nixon in his moment of agony would bring him (Moon) political reward. There is no question in my mind that this was Moon's objective."

Gary graduated from Princeton and he eventually returned to the Unification Church training center in Belvedere (Tarrytown, N.Y.).

From that time until March of 1975, he lectured to a couple of thousand people in the New York area, members and new recruits. He was then appointed Assistant Director of Planning and Development at the Barrytown seminary and also a lecturer, writer and editor for the Unification Thought Research Institute. In August of 1975 he was a public relations representative for the movement, and he became a student and teaching assistant when the seminary opened in September, 1975. At the same time he was co-editor and senior writer for the "New World" magazine, a nationally circulated propaganda magazine for the church which analyzed American history from the Moonie point of view.

People leave the cult in one of three ways. A few become disillusioned with the movement and run away — or in some cases leave voluntarily. Usually these individuals have never really been convinced by the indoctrination and have not given over their minds and wills to the cult leader. Others take another way out. Jeffrey William Daley was one such person. One day in 1975 he left the Barrytown training session and walked down to the railroad tracks that run between the property and the Hudson River. He stripped off all his clothes, lay down on the tracks as he heard the train coming, and was decapitated.

For most, however, the method of leaving the cult is not determined by themselves. It is usually their parents or friends who arrange a session of reality-inducing therapy — commonly called deprogramming.

And this is what happened to Gary Scharff in May of 1976. His father was extremely concerned about his welfare. He was not convinced that all was well, even though Moon had allowed Gary to finish Princeton and get his degree. Gary's father decided to secure outside help and found a deprogrammer.

A "deprogramming" is usually done by a team, and almost always in the presence of the parents of the cult victim. Former cult members are usually part of this team, and working together in a carefully planned, but free-style manner, the cult victim is given a tremendous amount of information about the tactics and practices of the cult. The cult member is challenged by the deprogrammers to think for himself. Charges against the particular cult are substantiated by newspaper and magazine articles, books, and sometimes personal testimonies. There is a real attention to the truth and honesty as the team explains that the cult, as an organization, has violated its own teachings, or shows ways the cult has distorted verses of the Bible, in order to draw biblical authority for something that is not biblical.

To the cult member, and especially the leaders, the very word "deprogramming" or "deprogrammer" strikes terror in their hearts. Members are told from the very beginning to run from any attempt made to have them meet with a deprogrammer. The Unification Church and others, sometimes under the guise of organizations at the time such as APRL (the Alliance for the Preservation of Religious Liberty — a curious mixture of cults with opposing theologies and philosophies) will prevail upon recently returned cult members (those whose deprogramming had been unsuccessful) to institute lawsuits against their own parents, their deprogrammers, and anyone else they can associate with them.

Much has been said in the media about deprogramming. Sensational stories have been related of psychological and sometimes physical assaults on the young people involved. The cults are the base of this characterization, and often are supported by such organizations as the American Civil Liberties Union. In my opinion, such stories are groundless.

Mind control techniques are dependent on the emotions and so is deprogramming. After a person is freed from the control of the cult, many things can trigger an emergence of emotion of attachment to the group. It is extremely important to give the "rescued" cult members support and direction through rehabilitation.

Gary Scharff, the one-time, first-rate instructor of Unification Church recruits and members, was "deprogrammed." He became the Administrative Director of the Freedom Ranch, a center for ex-cult members, operated by the Freedom of Thought Foundation, where he devoted his time and efforts toward restoring to the young people in residence there the same self-confidence, determination and indpendent thinking he worked so hard to destroy while he was in the movement.

EDITORIAL NOTE:

The above article was originally written in 1978. Since then, Gary has moved on to other things. Following his work at the Freedom Ranch, he spent several years on a voluntary basis as an exit-counselor, assisting people out of various cultic groups.

Today, he no longer does this type of work and is now an attorney. Gary has married and is raising two children. He and his wife, also an ex-cultist, have become active in their local parish.

Both regard the cult experience as a devastating time in their lives, but also realize that it taught them many things about the human mind. The experience has enabled them to look at things much differently today, and to sense implications and possible difficulties in various situations where others may be unware of the danger.

VII

A Look Inside
Ourselves

Any examination or criticism of the cult phenomenon inevitably brings an accusatory thrust such as "Why don't you look at the problems in your own church first before casting criticism on others?" Or, a variation is hurled, "Well, the group you are discussing acts no differently than the Catholic Church." Then at one time or other, someone will quote the Bible and you will hear, "Let him who is without sin cast the first stone" (cf. John 8:7).

It is appropriate now to consider this aspect of the cult phenomenon. Are there "Catholic" cults? Are there practices in the Catholic Church that can be compared to the cults? Are there groups operating with church approval that use the same techniques, the same methods of operation that may confuse people? Unfortunately, each of the above questions can be answered affirmatively, with the possible exception of the first.

In the strictest sense, there are no Catholic cults, because of our system of accountability and responsibility. Should a person or group go astray, the competent authority, be it local (the pastor), regional (the bishop), or international (the Vatican, or the Holy Father himself), after due investigation, corrects them, or excludes them from the Church.

Refining the first mentioned question above will, therefore, give us an opportunity for investigation. Are there groups within the Catholic Church which have turned into cults? Has the competent authority dealt with them properly?

The Unification Church, for example, is very fond of comparing itself to a religious order (community) in the Catholic Church, thereby hoping to gain respectability. I have often been asked by them to elaborate on this matter. For example, in 1982 in the Federal Court trial of Unification Church, Anthony Colombrito, et al., vs. Galen Kelly, I was asked to give expert testimony about the cult phenomenon and this group. Amidst the questioning the following dialogue ensued:

> Q. Let's take a look at other criteria of the isolation. Aren't monasteries and convents isolated communities?
> A. Years ago, but today they are not.
>
> Q. How many years ago?
> A. Prior to Vatican II, which began in 1962.
>
> Q. When a nun takes her vows and dedicates her life to service of the Church, doesn't she give up her worldly possessions and devote her life to one of sacrifice to the Church?
> A. She does. But she does so voluntarily and willingly, and the things she gives up don't go to the Church. It goes to her family, which I think is a very important distinction.

At other times I have been asked about the novitiates, and the fact that candidates were sent away from family and friends for a number of years. I have been asked to comment on the fact that members of the religious communities take vows of obedience, (as well as poverty and chastity). It is pointed out by the questioner that this is, in fact, what happens in the Unification Church as it prepares its membership.

The response to such allegations is simple, but the questioner rarely grasps the meaning, although (in a public forum) the audience certainly does.

A candidate for a religious community is already a member of the Catholic Church. He or she seeks to find a better way to know, love, and serve God. In most cases the family of the recruit is closely involved in the decision, and is welcomed by the community several times for visits before the young person enters. (There are instances, of course, where a person enters the religious community over the objections of parents, but the person is still already a Catholic who has spent a long time determining this course of action.) There is also some visitation during the novitiate period. Further, the vow of poverty that is taken does not require the applicant to give over everything to the community, but possessions can be disposed of in any manner. The candidate spends some time as a postulant, learning the spirit and rule of the community, and then, having accepted the way of life, moves on to the novitiate where the rule will be practiced and the spirit of the founder will be lived. At any time the candidate may withdraw, and at times a novice will be asked to leave. A director of novices in effect seeks to find the reasons why the candidate cannot stay, while the candidate is doing everything possible to be accepted.

This is vastly different from the procedures of the Unification Church and other groups. To begin with, the recruit is not already a member. Secondly, there is extreme isolation and a steady diet of new material without time for reflection. Finally the Unification Church insists that all possessions be turned over to them.

This is just one instance of how cultic groups try to confuse the issue.

However, there are some situations that do give rise to legitimate questions within the Catholic Church. Four groups which have drifted into this category, and have been condemned by the competent authority are the Fatima Crusaders of Coeur d'Alene, Idaho, under the leadership of Francis Schuckardt until 1984; the Bayside Movement of Veronica Leuken; the Apostolic Formation Center (formerly of Somers, Connecticut,) now in Heath, Massachusetts; and the Integrated Humanities Program in Lawrence, Kansas. Though technically not under

Church control, this last program used Catholic practices and facilities for a number of years, causing harm to many students of the University of Kansas.

Some movements within the Church have been accused of cult-like activity by Catholics and non-Catholics alike. The legitimate operation of these movements are not cultic in any fashion, but extremes in local situations might give rise to such allegations. Two such groups will be considered in this chapter.

A brief historical sketch of each group is in order first, to be followed by an assessment of where each group went wrong, and how the Church handled the problem. We also need to determine if the problem still exists.

* * *

THE FATIMA CRUSADERS are also known as the Tridentine Latin Rite Church (TLRC). However, it cannot be called a legitimate expression of the Roman Catholic Faith because, for one thing, it denies the legitimacy of the last four popes.

The "Inland Register," newspaper of the Diocese of Spokane, Washington, published an extensive, in-depth look at the group in 1980, from which we have extracted much of our information here. The group has about 800 followers in the local area, and about 5,000 nationwide (figures from Bishop Schuckardt). (An October, 1988 article by Thomas W. Case in "Fidelity Magazine" entitled "The Fatima Crusaders: Anatomy of a Schism," indicates that presently there are only 2,000 members.)

According to the newspaper article the name Fatima Crusaders actually describes only a part of the TLRC, not the Church itself. Schuckardt indicated that the TLRC is also known as the "Mary, Immaculate Queen of the Universe Community." It is incorporated in the State of Idaho as "Christ the King Priory." In Washington, it is incorporated under the title of the "Tridentine Latin Rite Catholic Church of St. Joseph."

The primary problem with this group is that it rejects all the progress that the Catholic Church has made since the Second Vatican Council. Schuckardt broke away from the Church in 1968 with seven followers. He and his members are skilled in citing pre-Vatican II documents to point out what they believe are glaring contradictions to church statements after Vatican II.

The "Fidelity Magazine" article quoted above gives a good summary of the belief system of this group:

"We declare that the New 'Mass' is invalid. . . . We declare that the introduction of this New 'Mass' also signals the promulgation of a new humanistic religion in which Almighty God is no longer worshipped as He desires to be worshipped. . . . Those who have accepted this New 'Mass' have, in reality and without taking notice of it, apostasized from the true Faith; they have separated themselves from the true Church and are in danger of losing their souls, because outside the Church founded by Jesus Christ no one can be saved. For this reason we invite the faithful to return to their faith from which they have strayed" (ibid.).

According to the "Inland Register," many ex-members of the TLRC consider it to be a cult in the fullest sense. Bishop Schuckardt's legitimacy as a bishop is called into question as well, for his credentials are certainly not in conformity with the Catholic Church.

In 1984, Schuckhardt was forced to flee the Church under a cloud of scandal. The Crusaders sought leadership from men consecrated by the Vietnamese schismatic, Archbishop Ngo-Dinh-Thuc.

Without going into the details of Thuc's justification for his position (for it does not concern us here), let let it be said that he welcomed the overtures of Fatima Crusaders. George Musey was consecrated by a Thuc protege in 1982, as was Robert McKenna, O.P. by another Thuc bishop. Because both bishops are not in residence, the current actual leader seems to be Father Denis (Robert Chicione), who was responsible for the ouster of Schuckardt.

The statement of Bishop Lawrence Welsh of Spokane on this subject can be found in Appendix V.

THE BAYSIDE MOVEMENT, also known as "Our Lady of the Roses," was founded by Veronica Leuken. The basic history of the movement can be best seen in the "Background Story" printed regularly in the issues of "Roses," the Movement's periodic newsletter:

Veronica Leuken, the seer of Bayside, is a wife and mother of five children. She is in her early sixties and lives on Long Island, New York. The story of her heavenly visitations goes back to the year 1968 when St. Theresa started appearing to her and giving her poems and sacred writings by dictation. Prior to this Veronica had not received any manifestations from Heaven.

Our Lady Herself appeared to Veronica in her home on April 1970, informing her that She would appear on the grounds of the old St. Robert Bellarmine Church in Bayside on June 18, 1970; that vigils of prayer be held there (now temporarily held at the Vatican Pavilion site in Flushing), and that full directions be given to the clergy of the parish for Our Lady's first visit there. Our Lady also requested that a Shrine and Basilica be erected on this Her chosen Sacred Site, which is to be named "Our Lady of the Roses, Mary Help of Mothers." She promised to come on the eve of the great feast days of the Church, which dates would be given to Veronica beforehand. The Blessed Mother also instructed Veronica to disseminate the messages given to her throughout the whole world.

Our Lady has requested that the Rosary be recited aloud by the crowd during the whole of the vigil. All are requested to kneel in the presence of Jesus. The Message is repeated word for word by Veronica. Veronica also describes what she sees. All is recorded by tape (taken from the newsletter of June 6, 1987).

(NOTE: Capitalization and punctuation is as given in the newsletter.)

Because Veronica also stressed the older traditions of the Church, she attracted a large following, so that now, twenty years later, there are centers in many parts of the United States, and in other parts of the world as well. The followers of Veronica are militant, aggressive and very intolerant of others, particularly those who object to their tactics and methods.

Another problem that casts a shadow of doubt over the Bayside Movement is the content of the messages. In the "Roses" newsletter we find many statements which contradict church teaching and the present discipline of the Church. Two examples will suffice:

In the June 18, 1986 edition we find this statement: "My children; but I as your Mother, must treat you at this time as adults, being able to reason with the god given reasoning that Heaven gave unto

you when you were conceived by the Holy
Ghost.". . .

Here is a direct contradiction to church teaching. Only Jesus
was conceived by the Holy Ghost. Humans are conceived in the
natural way God intended.

The second example comes from August 21, 1985.

Jesus is speaking and says: "My child and My
children, be it known now that We have looked into
the churches about the world, and We are much confused and perhaps cannot understand the nature of
humans who can in such little time do so much to
destroy My Church, My House upon earth. You
must restore My houses to their original condition.
We ask that you return the statues to My churches,
that you restore the main altar, that you re-place
(sic), the gating so that others may kneel in adoration to their God.". . .

There are several problems. First of all, since God (Father,
Son and Holy Spirit) is all knowing, why would Jesus say He
was confused? Why would He say He doesn't understand the
nature of humans — a nature which He created?

Furthermore, here is an instance of the directives of the Second Vatican Council being called into question, and, in fact,
being repealed.

It is highly unlikely that Our Lady would be giving messages
contrary to the teachings of the Church or the legitimate laws
of the Church. It is inconceivable that Jesus Himself would re-
voke the authority of His Vicar (the Holy Father) over the
matters of the Church.

Thus, we must conclude that the messages are not valid.

Finally, in all the verified apparitions of Our Lady, the seers
have always been remarkably humble, obedient and charitable. Their messages have always been kindly, even when re-
buking was necessary. Such is not the case with the Bayside
activity. Veronica herself has repeatedly been unwilling to
submit herself to the authority of the bishop of the Diocese of
Brooklyn, where she lives. An investigation was made of the
alleged apparitions in the early 1970s and the conculsion made
was negative. In 1986 Bishop Mugavero of Brooklyn issued a
letter warning the faithful against Bayside: "No credibility
could be given to the so-called apparitions." (Complete Text of
the letter is in Appendix IV.)

It wasn't long before Veronica's group reacted to the bishop's letter. Frank Albas, listing himself as director of the group sent a letter to the membership on March 19, 1987. "This new declaration mandates no change in policy vis-a-vis the promotion and dissemination of the Bayside Message throughout the world," he said. Once again the leadership refuses to obey legitimate authority.

The bizarre messages, the confused theology and the refusal to submit to legitimate ecclesiastical authority should make it obvious that the Bayside Movement is to be avoided. Whatever Veronica is doing, she is not leading a Marian apostolate. She is using deceit and who knows what else to attract well-meaning people who want to be good Catholics. In this sense it is very cult-like.

THE APOSTOLIC FORMATION CENTER was the brainchild of L. Roy Legere, a prominant lay retreat leader of the early 1960s. He wrote several books which had wide circulation. As he found his popularity growing, he established a retreat center and began to feel responsible for the spiritual formation of people who were "so lost in the modern world." He was commended for his work by Pope Paul VI, and eventually convinced a number of people to join with him in living a communal lifestyle. At the same time he began his retreat center, Sister Marie Bertrand, a cloistered Dominican nun entered the picture and began to advise people, including some clergy.

When L. Roy Legere died suddenly in 1978, his son, Paul, assumed leadership of the group. However, discord and division erupted after a time, and in 1983 Charles Shattuck became President of the Center. In 1984 he changed the name of the organization to Mary, Queen of the Apostles Formation Center. According to one source, there were 36 chapters with a membership of 2,500 people in the Northeast at one point, all subscribing to Legere's belief in the second coming of Christ which would occur in Somers. Some families even moved from great distances to be close to Legere.

As the group grew stronger and more closely knit, a particular expression of practice developed. Called "divine intimacy," it was, in reality, homosexual activity practiced during the retreats given at the facility.

Reporter Dan Barry of the "Journal Inquirer," Manchester, Connecticut, has followed the activities of this group extensively. Writing in the August 31, 1985 edition, he said:

Emboldened by the spiritual support of Sister Louise (Bertrand), Legere began espousing his interpretation of Catholic doctrine, which gradually became centered around himself.

The most startling example of this was a practice that came to be known as the Divine Intimacy of the Holy Seed, in which Legere and certain members of an elite core of followers known as "emissaries" participated in ritualized homosexuality, even though such acts are forbidden by Catholic doctrine. The "Divine Intimacy" was based on the belief that Legere was the "twin" of Christ, and had been directed by God to spread Christ's seed (p. 4).

The usual mind manipulations, controls and fears were used by the leadership to cover up and prevent disclosure. However, former members eventually did disclose this and other practices of the group, and Bishop Daniel Reilly of Norwich issued a condemnation of the group and expelled them from the diocese in 1985.

In a letter to his membership dated February 26, 1986, Charles Shattuck wrote:

Yes, I have heard many stories circulating around of how much I am being disobedient to the bishop. How can one make a judgement without knowing the facts. I would like to quote a paragraph of a letter I wrote last fall to the Bishops and to the President of the Pontifical Council of the Laity in Rome. "As President, to avoid any further bitterness, and being in complete obedience to the Church authorities, I humbly submit to you the actions which I am taking at this time. I am dissolving the entire apostolate along with all thirty-eight chapters, and all assets will be distributed to Mother Teresa's religious order."

However, they did not disband. According to a front-page article in the Greenfield, Massachusetts, paper "The Recorder," dated July 5, 1986, they moved to Health, Massachusetts, where they have begun work anew. The Bishop of Springfield, in whose diocese the group has moved, was quick to establish the fact that they had not come at his invitation, and the group has no connection with the Catholic Church.

On the civil level, the Connecticut Attorney General's Office has been conducting an investigation to ascertain if all the assets had been distributed properly.

Unfortunately, many former members of this group have yet to understand how such things can happen.

Bishop Daniel Reilly's Pastoral Letter on this subject can be found in Appendix VI.

THE INTEGRATED HUMANITIES PROGRAM was a beautiful idea conceived by three Catholic professors at the University of Kansas. It was their thinking that students could live in the environment of a medieval university where subjects were not separated. In this way they would be able to appreciate the academic success of the methods used in the Middle Ages. Since the milieu was thoroughly Catholic at that time, they taught the doctrines of Catholicism within the humanities, and even sent their students to a monastery in France to live the experience.

Unfortunately, not all the students were Catholic, and those who were not Catholic were required to study the Faith and receive Baptism. Furthermore, the professors declared that their milieu was pre-Trent, and thus anything that happened in the Church since that Council of Trent (1545-1563) was not applicable to them. They contacted a Traditionalist priest to baptize the candidates, and to celebrate the Tridentine Mass. The Monastery of Notre Dame de Fontgombault in France was under the control of a Traditionalist Abbot as well, so while the students thought they were going to a monastery just for a visit, they ended up by staying for nine months or more, and many were ready to join the Benedictine Community there, influenced in no small way by the control tactics used by the leaders.

As one might easily discern, as non-Catholic and even Jewish students were required to join the Church to participate in the course, this caused distress among families, and they complained. Because the program was not under the control of the Church — it was a State University — it took quite a while to convince church and university authorities that unethical and sometimes evil things were going on. Eventually, the program was denied further funding, and was put under the direct control of the department chairman. Without the freedom to work, the professors resigned and the problem disappeared, but not without leaving scars on many young people (and their families).

* * *

Other programs very popular in the Catholic Church today are occasionally criticized and even denounced by cult opponents. However, while much of the problem comes from the questioners' lack of understanding of the many forms of spirituality in the Church, the groups themselves aggravate the situation because they do not perceive any danger in the consequences of certain practices and procedures.

THE CATHOLIC CHARISMATIC RENEWAL MOVEMENT is one group that has frequently been accused of cult-like activity by Catholic and non-Catholic alike. Because the legitimate operation of this movement is not cultic in any fashion, but extremes in local situations might give rise to such allegations, the matter needs clarification.

This movement began in 1967 at Duquesne University in Pittsburgh. It grew into a very popular movement in less than twenty years, and has had the support of two popes and countless other church authorities. The Charismatic Renewal itself will admit, however, that while there are a good number of priests active in the movement, there are many more who have adopted a hands-off policy toward the movement.

The Charismatic Renewal has evolved into two distinctive groupings: prayer groups and covenant communities. The former are usually found in parishes or schools, and have a relatively small, local membership. The covenant communities developed out of a desire to live the Christian life more fully. Often families involved quite actively in the Charismatic Renewal decided to move into the same neighborhood and place themselves under the common leadership of a single individual. Others, unable to relocate, or unwilling to do so, would travel many miles to the meetings of the community and to Sunday Mass.

The Catholic Charismatic movement has been extremely active in the renewal of the Church. It has brought back many people to the Church, and helped others to know, understand, and practice their Catholic Faith in an active manner. Through the parish prayer group, people have had the opportunity to grow closer to the Lord, to understand the Scriptures better, and to realize the power of their Faith.

The Catholic Charismatic Renewal Movement has organized nationally with a service committee for its constituents. The National Conference of Catholic Bishops has a committee with Bishop Joseph C. McKinney, Auxiliary Bishop of Grand Rapids, as chairman at the present time. There is also an international liaison committee with an office in Rome. There are also several ecumenical coordinating committees, and it is here where problems can arise. The ecumenical (sometimes called interdenominational) coordinating groups do not always understand the relationship of Catholic people to their pastor and bishop.

The Sword of the Spirit is a coordinating and unifying organization, particularly concerned with the covenant communities. This particular group has adopted the practice of SHEPHERDING/DISCIPLESHIP, which can cause severe problems in relationships (see Chapter IX).

Because of their allegiance to a leader, sometimes called a "head" or "shepherd" who is someone other than the pastor or the bishop, these covenant communities have come under some close scrutiny by Church officials in recent years.

For an explanation of the proper relationship between the covenant community members and the local bishop, see Appendix VII, a letter from Jan Cardinal Willebrands, President of the Secretariat for Promoting Christian Unity to Archbishop Peter Gerety of Newark, New Jersey on April 2, 1986.

* * *

Can religious communities fall victim to the cult phenomenon? What are the elements that would cause such a change? Is it possible that the proper superiors would not recognize what is happening? In at least one instance, it appears that this is what happened.

The Religious Sisters of Mercy of Alma, Michigan, the Franciscan Sisters of the Eucharist of Meriden, Connecticut, and the Benedictine Nuns of the Primitive Observance of Regina Laudis Abbey in Bethlehem, Connecticut have interesting histories with several common threads running through them.

Each is a spin-off of a larger, more established community. The Sisters of Mercy and the Franciscan Sisters separated from their original community, while those dissatisfied with the new look of the Benedictines departed the monastery. They all are under the spiritual direction of the same priest. Each has established an associated community of lay people.

According to the Alma, Michigan, edition of the "Morning Sun" (December 10, 1986, page 5), these three communities are closely linked through "the articles of incorporation of the Comprehensive Health Care Corporation," an organization incorporated by the Sisters of Mercy of Alma.

The manner in which these sisters operate their associated groups is quite similar to the "shepherding/discipleship" method of operation (cf. Chapter IX). Within the convents themselves, reports from former members indicate a total lack of freedom, an inability to see God's will anywhere but in total obedience to the superior and the priest in charge, far in excess of normal practice within religious life. Lay associates are not able to make decisions for themselves, and often are expected to do things that are at variance with church practices and in some cases, even with church teachings.

Let the words of Susan Cook, in the front-page article of the "Morning Sun" of December 10, 1986 provide the documentation:

> Mr. McMackin's story is similar to that of a number of sources interviewed about this series. The three orders, although sanctioned by the Roman Catholic Church, have engaged in activities that have caused some well-respected church officials to question the effect and meaning of the theology to which they (the sisters) subscribe.
>
> However, unlike many others, Mr. McMackin expressed no fear at possible reprisals from the orders for detailing the specifics of those activities. In addition, he has kept letters and other documents pertaining to his relationship with the sisters and their associated lay communities.
>
> His break with the sisters and their adjunct lay communities came after he and his wife were "challenged" by the Sisters of Mercy to give their soon-to-be-born fourth child up for adoption in December, 1980.
>
> Challenges are part of the way of life of the Sisters of Mercy of Alma, and the religious orders and lay communities with which they are associated. Challenges are issued to stimulate "growth crises" designed to foster the dedication of members to the community, Mr. McMackin said.

At various times during his approximate eleven-year association with the orders, Mr. McMackin was "challenged" to"

> — Shun his brother, who decided to marry despite the lay and religious community belief that he had a vocation as a monk.

— Put his farmhouse and land in trust for the Benedictine Abbey of Regina Laudis in Connecticut.

— Physically "beat up" another community member whose behavior warranted severe punishment, according to the community; a challenge he did not carry out.

His refusal to accept the challenge to put his land in trust and the challenge to give up his fourth child for adoption resulted in the McMackins receiving a "leave of absence" from the communities — a leave from which they have not returned.

If one were to refer to the characteristics of a cult group given in an earlier chapter, it would be apparent that they apply to these sisters. But Susan Cook elaborates further in her second article the next day on the "child adoption" challenge:

Mrs. McMackin spent the last trimester of a physically and emotionally difficult pregnancy at the Home of Mercy in Alma. Mr. McMackin remained in Connecticut with their three young children. It was an unhappy time for both, preceded by Mr. McMackin's growing disenchantment with the community life in opposition to Mrs. McMackin's still strong desire for the communal experience, he said.

About a week before their baby was due, Sister Mary Sarah, R.S.M., now deceased, told the McMackins she had received a message from the Holy Spirit, indicating that the couple should give their child up for adoption. The Religious Sisters of Mercy issued a "challenge" — a common method of precipitating decisions among the community, Mr. McMackin said.

The pregnancy has been the focal point of great stress, and the Sisters said giving the baby up would be a move toward healing a troubled marriage, Mr. McMackin said. . . .

"When they spoke of it to me, I was utterly shocked. . . . yet the pregnancy was a terrible time for me," Mrs. McMackin said. She and her husband had grown apart and she had come to feel that the community, not her husband, had been supportive, Mrs. McMackin said.

She seriously considered the challenge and what it meant to her, their marriage, and their relationship to the lay and religious communities. She talked at length with her husband, who was adamantly opposed, — in the first serious, in-depth communication they had had for many months, she said.

They decided to accept the challenge that their marriage was in a precarious state, and met it by seeking marital counseling. They did not accept the challenge to give the baby up for adoption.

These three groups of sisters have had other problems, only indirectly related to their cult-like behavior. Their expansion into Shaw Island in western Washington, in the Archdiocese of Seattle has been the source of considerable controversy.

Attracted to Shaw Island by the offer of a donation of property from Henry Ellis, a long-time devotee of the Benedictine spirituality and way of life, the Benedictine Nuns established Our Lady of the Rock Monastery. Unfortunately (for local residents) the other two groups arrived on the scene as well. The Sisters of Mercy ignored local laws and violated several building code statutes in the process of constructing their center. They have disturbed the entire community on the island by their secretive actions and attempts to change the rural nature of Shaw Island. A November, 1988 court decision has required them to remove certain parts of a building they had altered without approval of the zoning board.

The Benedictine Nuns are also embroiled in legal disputes. When Henry Ellis donated fifty percent of his property to them, he indicated that the remainder would come later. When he decided not to give them the remainder of the property, because of their "un-Benedictine" behavior, they went to court over the matter. The initial court decision was favorable to the Abbey, but the decision is under appeal at the time of this writing. The nuns are seeking to have the court force Mr. Ellis to make the donation to them (instead of to some other organization).

The Franciscan Sisters are on the Island too. At last report they are running the ferry system, and the general store.

This dispute is another indication of the manner in which these sisters operate.

The complaints of many people, coupled with the unfavorable publicity these communities have received, have resulted in a church inquiry into their operations. Because they appear to adhere to traditional values and practices in religious life some people, including church leaders tend to support these sisters. Others who look at the aberrations can see, dangers.

* * *

It should be obvious by now that the dangers of the cults, sects, and new religions abound both inside and outside the Church. What makes a difference is the fact that when a person or a group (a religious community, for example) goes astray, there is a proper mechanism for remedying the situation, although it may take some time.

The examination of the groups in this chapter has indicated, to be sure, that cultic behavior is possible at any time in any place. It has also been demonstrated that some legitimate actions of Catholic Church groups can be carried to excess, so that the cult label is applied. What has not been discussed here is the fact that some legitimate actions of Catholic Church groups can be misunderstood so that the cult label is applied without justification. Sometimes a fine line separates the two. Church leaders must be vigilant to make sure that cultic practices do not creep into otherwise legitimate groups.

VIII

Education Efforts & Plans

By Rev. James E. McGuire, S.T.D.

If a person were to look for the one element that has caused so many people to be duped by the cults, sects, and new religions, it would have to be a "lack of education" in this matter. The constant refrain in speaking to ex-cultists is always: "If I had only known. . . ." It is the one element that can be utilized by everyone, and can have great results. The Vatican Document of May, 1986 on the subject (Appendix IX) recommends that "it is necessary to inform the faithful, especially the young, to put them on their guard, and even to enlist professional help for counseling, legal protection," and other similar matters.

Unfortunately, there has been little concerted effort on the part of the Church to educate in the area of cults. A few individual dioceses have sponsored special programs on the subject for young people and adults. The Archdioceses of Philadelphia and New York have pioneered in this field by providing clergy, on a limited basis, to study this problem and provide educational programs. The Diocese of Cleveland dedicated a lay employee of the Youth Ministry Office to this problem for a time. The Western Province of the Dominicans has released one of its priests to do this work in Oregon. However, there is no coordinated church effort to combat the influence of the cults, sects, and new religions at the present time.

As a priest of the Philadelphia Archdiocese, my involvement and participation in several pastoral and educational programs were done with the approval and direction of His Eminence John Cardinal Krol, then Archbishop of Philadelphia. The Cardinal and his priest delegates were all very much involved in the planning, implementation, and facilitating of the Philadelphia programs.

It should be mentioned that whenever I was personally coordinating or participating in these programs, the opportunity for discussing the specific vision of Roman Catholicism was always present. Evangelization and catechesis became necessary in all these situations because a definite Catholic apologetic served to draw distinction from many of the cults, sects, and new religious movements which claimed a doctrinal, structural or procedural affinity with Catholicism.

All these efforts were made possible primarily by the fact that I was then assigned to the Office of Catholic Education as Director of Teacher Services in Religion, during the same time the cults and sects were gaining influence. The ability to integrate resources and gain the cooperation of the various offices of the archdiocese were the keys to the success of these pastoral and educational programs.

I. Educational Conferences

In the Archdiocese of Philadelphia, as early as 1981, there were programs at St. Charles Seminary for 400 high school, college and university students, and their teachers.

The first conference was intended to be informational in nature, i.e. designed for the consciousness-raising of all participants. The conference brochure set the purpose of the conference: "Many young men and women are being lured into some type of pseudo-religious cult. These individuals are misled and often manipulated in some way or other. Their personal freedom, spiritual well-being and individuality are taken from them. . . . It is our hope that as a result of today's workshops you will be empowered to counter personally, and in organized ways, the deleterious effects cults are having (on families)."

PROGRAM 1

The Dangers of Pseudo-Religious Cults

Schedule of Events

1. Registration of Participants
2. Welcome address
3. Keynote Address — Flo Conway and Jim Siegelman, authors of *Snapping*
4. Panel — What was it like to Live in a Cult? Joseph Flanagan (Former Scientologist) Barbara Dole (Former Unification member) David Clark (Former Walk Member-Bible Cult)

These former cult members were all in the 18-21-year-old range and in a college/university when recruited. One was from a Roman Catholic family, and two were Protestants. All were deceptively recruited and vulnerable at the time.

5. Questions/observations (from the participants)
6. Afternoon Session: Young People and Personal Maturation

Attention to the social and political implications of the cult phenomenon. State Representative Joseph Lashinger, Pennsylvania House of Representatives, was the presenter.

7. Questions/observations (from the participants)

Conclusions reached:

1. The concept of a Conference on Cults proved very successful. Teachers and students were given a chance to dialogue with "experts" and one another.
2. The most persuasive, interesting and effective speakers were the former cult members. Their vivid and shocking experiences had a powerful impact on the participants.
3. Church and state were able to work together at this conference by addressing their common concerns and sharing specific areas of competency.
4. The inclusion of both theoretical information and actual, lived experiences enhanced the interest and participation of those attending the conference.

5. An annual conference should be seriously considered.

The following year another conference on Pseudo-Religious Destructive Cults was held on March 18, 1982 at St. Charles Seminary, again for teachers and students. His Eminence, Cardinal Krol, suggested that the specific differences between genuine charismatic renewal and pseudo-religious practices be explored, so we invited participants with this information. We sought to respond to these topics:

> Many Christian educators continued to express deep concern about the numbers of young people, truly searching for guidance in the Bible who are being led astray by "wolves in sheep's clothing," that is to say, "false teachers."
>
> The possible involvement of Catholic students in groups such as Campus Crusade for Christ, and the Fellowship of Christian Athletes, which can de-emphasize Catholic nuances in the common interest of "Christian teachings" needs to be studied as more Catholic graduates enter state universities and sectarian colleges not Catholic.

PROGRAM 2

Challenges to Biblical Doctrine and Personality Development

A Christian Perspective

FOCUS: Bible groups which distort traditional Christian teachings and biblical interpretations. Also, human potential groups such as EST and Lifespring.

Cult groups — Moonies, Scientology, Hare Krishna, etc. which continue to recruit members and expand their operations, especially in urban areas and collegiate environments.

Schedule of Events

I. Panel — Challenges to Biblical Authenticity and Personal Development

1. TELEVISION EVANGELISM — Msgr. Charles Mynaugh (Archdiocesan Communications Director)

2. BORN AGAIN CHRISTIANS — Karen Praetzel (former member)

3. COVENANT CHRISTIAN COMMUNITIES — Connie Aigeldinger (former member)

4. HUMAN POTENTIAL GROUPS — Mary Grace Haenn (former member)

5. THE WAY INTERNATIONAL (Bible cult) — Charlie & Ken Grush (father and son)

6. Questions/discussions

II. Catholic Teaching on Charismatic Renewal and Biblical Authority

Msgr. Vincent Walsh, J.C.D. (liaison for Charismatic Renewal)

Questions/discussions

III. Documentary Film on the Unification Church

IV. Cult Impact — the Member, the Family

Panelists: Joseph Flanagan (former Scientologist), Patricia Flanagan (his mother), Arthur Dole, Ph. D. (father of former Moonie)

Conclusions reached:

> 1. As in the previous year, the testimony of former members proved the most informative and powerful.
> 2. The comparisons between the new religious movements, sects, and cults and the genuine Catholic Charismatic groups were highly illustrative of how subtly powerful human spiritual and emotional experiences can be manipulated without proper official guidance and direction.

It was not only the Archdiocese of Philadelphia that saw the dangers of the cults and acted. In their joint statement of pastoral concern for parents and youth, the Pennsylvania Conference on Interchurch Cooperation, a statewide ecumenical agency composed of representatives from the Pennsylvania Council of Churches and the Pennsylvania Catholic Conference, made the following observation:

> The process of mind-control involves the dramatic alienation from family, traumatic destruction of

one's sense of personal identity, often which includes change of name, elimination of all significant human relationships outside the cult, extremely strong peer pressure, purposeful diet manipulation to starve the brain, and the arduous and fatigue-producing daily discipline.

There were others, too, apart from the religious community, who saw the dangers of the cults. Concern for the psychological and emotional well-being of present and former cult members and their families prompted the seventeenth Annual Arthur P. Noyes Memorial Conference at Norristown State Hospital to discuss the topic, "Cults: Clinical Significance." I attended this conference of distinguished psychiatrists, including John G. Clark, Jr. M.D., Assistant Clinical Professor of Psychiatry, Harvard Medical School, and Stanley H. Cath, M.D., Associate Clinical Professor of Psychiatry, Tufts University School of Medicine.

Their conference brochure asked these questions: "Are cults an unmitigated evil in today's society?" "Why do people enter cults?" "What is life really like there?" "What are the ramifications of rescuing people from cults?" "Do people emerging from cults need treatment?" "If so, what kinds of treatment work?" "What should be the stance of mental health professionals and others vis-a-vis the cults?"

I mention this conference especially, because many former cult members, their parents and family members, as well as many ecumenical writers on this subject, believe that the most severe threat of the cults can be to the entire consortium of a person's mental, physical, emotional and spiritual wholeness. Hence the psychological description of cults as "destructive," a term used generally by most American commentators.

Many times the central theme of a person's involvement in these groups is more a matter of psychological dependency than religious persuasion or conviction. The agencies of the Church and state need clear and decisive guidelines of inter-cooperation especially in dealing with the "rescued," former members now deprogrammed, and hopefully, in rehabilitation programs.

In 1982, the Archdiocese of New York joined with several other religious groups to form the Interfaith Coalition of Concern about Cults (ICCC). For the first time, Protestant, Catholics, and Jewish leaders joined forces to address this problem.

The stated purpose for the existence of the Interfaith Coalition is an active concern that each and every person have the freedom of choice that is so vital to living a full life.

His Eminence, Terence Cardinal Cooke, approved participation in the coalition, seeing it as an important step in developing an awareness of the problem. His successor, John Cardinal O'Connor, has continued the approval. Several officials of the archdiocese participate, including the Vice-Chancellor, Father Ferdinando Berardi, who served as co-chairman for several years, as did his predecessor.

One of the coalition programs, a one-day seminar entitled "Cults and the Media," was presented on May 28, 1985 at the Graduate Center of the City University of New York.

PROGRAM 3

Cults and the Media

1. Morning Session:

Overview of the problem.

TV Reporter recounts his experience in cult investigations.

"Inside Cult Public Relations": an eye-witness account from an ex-cultist

2. Afternoon Session:

Media Roundtable: Representatives from major newspapers and television networks respond to questions from a panel of cult experts as well as from conference participants.

The Conference had as its stated goals:

1. What can the cult educational network (i.e. organizations who are united in the battle against destructive cultism) do to assist journalists and media professionals in their effort to present a balanced and informed view of the cult phenomenon?

2. What are the limitations of the media with regard to cult coverage and investigation?

3. How can the relationship be strengthened between the media and the cult educational network?

4. What resources are available to the media on the cult issue?

Those who attended from the media had all experienced the cults through their work, and all were anxious to learn more about them. Many were perplexed by what they found. All had many reservations about cult practices, and wanted to portray an accurate picture of the group(s). This conference also established a good working relationship between ICCC members and members of the press, radio and television media.

These three examples of one-day conferences present a wide spectrum of biblical, theological, clinical, and sociological considerations in a decidedly pastoral, educational and ecumenical context. Because they included both studied experts and people with direct experience in the sects, cults, and new religious movements under consideration, their impact was immediate, intellectually satisfying and pastorally applicable. Such one-day meetings can be a convenient and thorough attempt to inform the faithful, the teachers, the clergy and the religious. A program of this kind is especially useful for the young people not only of the Catholic Church but of the larger community as well.

* * *

II. Formal Religious Education of Youth

The Vatican Report in Section Three, "Pastoral Challenges and Approaches," has certainly put the finger on the restless pulse of today's world when it mentions "industrialization, urbanization, migration, rapid development of communication systems, all rational technocratic systems, etc." as leaving many individuals "confused, uprooted, insecure and therefore vulnerable," to the allurements and ideologies of the sects, cults and some new religious movements. This restless seeking for "new truths," a sense of belonging, and a feeling of meaningful participation is especially acute among the youth of the world, particularly in the United States. Why else would five thousand American teenagers a year successfully commit suicide, while another three million a year attempt, but fail such self-annihilation?

The Catholic school remains the most solid foundation for building and forming a living, active, and conscious faith. The Congregation for Catholic Education called attention to this when it stated: "The Catholic school has as its specific duty the complete Christian formation of its pupils, and this task is of special significance today because of the inadequacy of the family and society" (*The Catholic School*, 1977).

The Archdiocese of Philadelphia is presently blessed with the ninth largest school system in the United States, public or parochial. Begun by St. John Neumann, fourth bishop, the commitment to formal Catholic education begun in the nineteenth century has continued and prospered under Cardinal Krol's direction and encouragement. It has succeeded too, because the faithful of the archdiocese continue to make incredibly generous sacrifices to maintain more than two hundred parish schools and twenty-eight high schools.

Teacher guidelines for presenting the reality and the challenge of cults and sects were developed not only for these Catholic school teachers, but also for the teachers of Christian Doctrine in CCD programs. These guidelines developed as a result of my teaching a course on this problem at St. Charles Seminary which was open not only to the seminarians and diocesan priests, but to the religious priests, brothers, and sisters, as well as the lay catechists. These guidelines, coupled with this kind of course, can be one of the most important and far reaching educational efforts a diocese can undertake.

The lesson plan for parochial school and CCD programs consisted of four sessions which covered the sociology of cults, their ideologies, their methods, and their ability to induce excessive guilt and fear into people, particularly the new recruits. (The complete lesson plan can be found in Appendix II.)

What is presented in class at the seminary is much more detailed than the lesson plan for the schools, and understandably so, for the students of the seminary course will more than likely be the teachers of the classes in local parish schools and CCD programs. In addition to the basic cult education, this course also treated the legal aspects of the problem, and the doctrinal relationship between the cults and the Church. Most importantly, it gave a pastoral emphasis to this topic.

This course contained the following elements:

Lecture I — General Introduction — THE EXISTENTIAL PROBLEMATIC.

What is the Church and contemporary mankind facing in the challenge of the cults, sects, and new religious movements?

Lecture II — SOCIOLOGICAL BACKGROUND.

Emphasis is placed on the U.S.A., 1963-1986. What events and sociological factors account for the proliferation and spread of these groups during the past three decades?

Lecture III — CHARACTERISTICS OF A CULT OR SECT.

Various definitions and descriptions of a cult or sect, especially from American writers and commentators, are presented and discussed so that some clear analysis of these groups may result.

Lectures IV through VII — PHILOSOPHY AND PHENOMENOLOGY OF CULTS & SECTS.

This is a study of the main types of cults and sects, their ideologies and charcteristics, their leaders, their goals and objectives, historical roots and present activities, including: The Unification Church, Church of Scientology, Hare Krishna, Children of God, The Way International (Bible cult), Divine Light Mission.

As was done in the conferences, former members are invited into the classroom to sensitize the class members to the implications of daily "living" in these groups. These speakers not only enrich the lectures but are essential to a full understanding and appreciation of the theological, ecumenical, and family-living challenges they present.

Lecture VIII — HUMAN POTENTIAL GROUPS.

The rise of self-discovery and self-help human potential movements, primarily in the American experience is examined. While these groups do not possess ALL the characteristics of a cult, they have many things in common. Their real threat to the integrity of the Christian faith is their implied (and at times even overt) secular humanism which sees human potential and development possible and apart from the mention or inclusion of the transcendent, sacred mystery, revealed doctrine and structural authority.

Groups considered here include EST (Erhard Seminar Training) now called the Forum, Lifespring, Transcendental Meditation (TM) and Direct Centering. Here also, the testimony of former members is valuable and enriching.

Lecture IX — LEGAL PROBLEMS OF CULTS & SECTS.

The American Constitution in the First Amendment guarantees a citizen "freedom of religion." The possible misinterpretations and resulting confusion that occur are discussed. The legal difficulties in defining "brainwashing" or "mind control," as well as properly understanding "deprogramming," are analyzed. (In all instances a civil lawyer is included in the presentation.)

Lecture X — PASTORAL RESPONSES.

Among the topics discussed are:

— Parish CCD and elementary school programs

— Adult education programs: formal religious education for parents

— Preaching by parish clergy

— Youth retreats: opportunities for articulating the challenge of the cults/sects

— Spiritual renewal programs of the parish. These programs are always well attended. A high degree of lay interest and concern emerges. This is also an excellent forum to discover if the particular neighborhood is being influenced by the cult/sect recruiters.

Lecture XI — ROMAN CATHOLIC DOCTRINAL AND SOCIAL RESPONSE.

Here we prepare people to handle the situations in which Catholics, especially young people, are approached to join these groups. Role playing is very effective in these efforts.

Also treated here is the need to prepare high school and college/university students to answer apologetically, the polemics of very skilled and studied cult/sect recruiters. Increasingly in the United States, evangelical recruiters have become more active on college and university campuses.

Lecture XII — CULT, GUILT, FEAR, and EMOTIONAL ADDICTION.

The powerful inducement of guilt, fear and emotional addiction occurs when the following abuses are present:

— abuse of authority,

— abuse of intimacy,

— abuse of time,

— abuse of money,

— abuse of discipline.

Lecture XIII — THE RISE OF CHRISTIAN BIBLE GROUPS AND SEPARATED COMMUNITIES.

Specific differences are examined among genuine, approved Bible study groups/movements and "individual" shepherds, or gnostic leaders.

It is essential for teachers to be attuned to the various groups that work in the same field. For example, in 1985, the American Family Foundation convened a meeting of mainline denominations and Evangelical representatives to discuss the probems of proselytizing on college campuses. As a result of this meeting, the American Family Foundation devoted an entire issue of their "Cultic Studies Journal" (Fall, 1985) to the subject of "Cults, Evangelicals, and the Ethics of Social Influence," in which both Father LeBar of New York and myself contributed articles. In addition, Inter-Varsity Fellowship and other organizations are working on a code of ethics for religious groups to be observed in recruiting on campuses. A three-year follow-up on this initial effort is presently underway.

The use of television programs and film documentaries is also an important and necessary element of any course or conference. Media of this kind give the participants an opportunity to see and hear the cults in action.

My personal reaction in teaching this course for ten years is that an interdisciplinary educational approach is the most successful and enduring kind of preparation for the advances of the cult/sect recruiters. It is this kind of approach that fulfills the intention of the catechetical document "Sharing The Light of Faith," in which the American bishops wrote about the relationship of growth in faith to human development. In articulating the role of the behavioral sciences, the document states, "The Church encourages the use of the biological, social and psychological sciences in pastoral care" (No. 174 & 175).

* * *

III. Political and Legal Dimension

American jurisprudence rightfully protects the guaranteed religious freedoms enshrined in the United States Constitution. Citizens cherish these rights including their freedoms as found in the First Amendment. Cults, sects, and some new religious movements claim that their First Amendment rights are being usurped when agencies of the state or federal government, or mainstream American churches, question their beliefs or activities. Needless to say, the burden of proof is on the critics of these new groups to demonstrate that there is a violation of either the spirit or the letter of the First Amendment.

Other critics, legal and ecclesiastical, cite hundreds, even thousands of instances of violations of the 13th and 14th Amendment because of the excessive hours of fund raising under "false pretenses," with much of the funds collected going to the leader personally.

On May 31, 1979, I was invited to testify before the Pennsylvania House of Representatives which was considering a resolution to investigate the activities of these cults/sects in the Commonwealth. I accepted and was permitted to testify to these points:

> 1. A young person searching for God and self-identity in a normal, loving, and inquiring environment, is potentially capable of free assent and personal commitment. Genuine faith invites a person's free and informed acceptance. Genuine faith never imposes or commands blindly. Genuine faith liberates; it does not tyrannize the inquiring and searching young believer.
>
> 2. The Catholic Church's officially stated position on guaranteeing basic human rights is found in the Second Vatican Council's *Declaration on Religious Liberty* together with the United Nations *Declaration on Human Rights* (1948). There is common agreement that religious liberty and immunity from coercion in religious matters of civil society is an inviolable human right. The same Declaration, however, also states that it is the right of society "to defend itself against possible abuses committed on the pretext of freedom of religion" (No. 7).

Here was an excellent opportunity for a Catholic viewpoint to be expressed and entered into the official proceedings of a state government committee. (Father LeBar had a similar experience on the federal level in February, 1979, when he testified as one of many expert witnesses called in the aftermath of the Jonestown tragedy by the United States Senate.)

Through this testimony I met the Speaker of the Pennsylvania House of Representatives, who agreed to visit my class at St. Charles Seminary. He spoke to my students about the difficulty of writing laws in Pennsylvania to investigate these new religious groups without violating the First Amendment rights claimed by such groups. The advantages of this kind of contact between Church and state are important in the ongoing dialogue about the cults, sects, and new religious movements.

IV. Clergy Conference

Several years ago, John Cardinal Krol recognized the necessity of having a clergy fully informed about, and sensitive to, the philosophical and ideological teachings, as well as the pastoral challenges of the cults, sects and new religious movements. On September 8-10, 1981, Kevin Flanagan, father of Joseph, a former member of Scientology, and I spoke to the bishops and priests of the Archdiocese of Philadelphia at St. Charles Seminary.

On these occasions, I cited four main reasons why a clergy conference was a timely idea:

> 1. While public consciousness about cults and sects has certainly been heightened after the events of Jonestown, evidence indicates that recruiting continues in groups such as the Unification Church (or Moonies), Hare Krishna, Scientology, the Way International, the Church of Bible Understanding, and countless other groups.
>
> 2. Our priests increasingly report the presence of cult groups in their parishes. Parishioners have become involved in human potential groups such as EST (now the FORUM), and LIFESPRING, and several pseudo-evangelical gnostic communities with definite anti-Catholic overtones.
>
> 3. Information supplied by elementary and secondary school principals, parents, teachers, and students all confirm that cult/sect recruiters are no longer restricting their activities only to college or university age students. The Bible cults, especially the Way International and the Church of Bible Understanding are actively seeking out high school students.
>
> 4. The integrity of Catholic doctrine, especially Christology, Church authority, and discipline, are all being assaulted by the teachings and the practices of these cults and sects.

The phenomenon and challenge of pseudo-religious, destructive cults, sects, and cult-like, spin-off groups, are primarily directed at the evangelical and catechetical visions of the Christian Churches and seek to undermine, ever so subtly, traditional Judaeo-Christian anthropology.

While genuine ecumenical dialogue and interdenominational

113

cooperation are both highly desirable Vatican II directives, to-day's cults, sects and new religious movements must not be confused with churches and religious traditions, which, unlike many of these new groups, do respect the freedom of conscience, a person's family, and the social network of relationships. The Vatican Document of May, 1986 (found in Appendix IX) warns of this in Section 4.

A clergy conference is an excellent forum for discussing the many theological, philosophical, sociological and psychological distinctions that must be made between "traditional, conventional" religious movements and today's new "non-traditional, non-conventional" cults and sects.

Mr. Flanagan, at the 1981 Philadelphia archdiocesan clergy conference, encouraged priests to become fully informed about these new religious movements so that they, like the Apostles, could warn their parishioners about the "wolves in sheep's clothing," the false teachers. In his address Mr. Flanagan stated:

> Pseudo-religious, quasi-scientific cults and self-awareness groups, seemingly attacking a godless vacuum in our society, have proliferated. These groups have undermined the very foundation of our society: the family. Their purposes are diabolical; their methods are fraudulent; their effect is incalculable.

These words are strong and direct. Mr. Flanagan wanted priests to hear first-hand how devastated his own family was for four years as they searched from Pennsylvania to California for their son. Their lives were constantly disrupted and their family financial resources almost destroyed by their determined efforts to rescue their son, have him deprogrammed, and finally rehabilitated. A fine Catholic family came face to face with mind-control, kidnapping, private detectives and phone tappings by the cult group.

The priests were both stunned and fascinated by Mr. Flanagan's story. He appealed to the priests to become knowledgeable about the cults, and to preach to their parishioners and to teach them, especially the youth, about the dangers posed by these groups:

> As Catholics we recognize what we choose to call legitimate religions, and since Vatican II, we have tried to engender an ecumenical dialogue with

them. If we are to have the unity that Christ so desires, this is surely the first step toward that end. But I would hasten to point out that fundamentalist groups are also attacking the tenets of our faith by challenging the Catholic interpretation of the Scriptures and distorting our viewpoints. I'm afraid that these fundamentalist groups are the anti-Catholic cults of the future.

As an example of what should be covered in a clergy conference, here are the points I covered in my address to the clergy of the Archdiocese:

1. Sociological Background — The rise of cults/sects in the United States during the past twenty years.

2. Spiritual and Mental Health Considerations — The major threat represented by the new groups is to the spiritual and mental well being of the individual.

3. The "so-called" Theologies and Philosophies of the Cults/Sects — Totalitarian ideologies are the common penchant of these groups for ideological eclecticism and syncretistic maneuverability.

4. The Cults' Legal Challenges to American Jurisprudence and Democracy — The freedom to believe according to one's conscience is one reality; the freedom to act on those beliefs is quite another.

5. Political Dilemmas — The authorities of Church and state need clear guidelines for dealing with the cults, sects, and new religions. The consequences of the absence of such guidelines means that families like the Flanagans are left abandoned and almost bankrupt as they seek to combat these well organized, well financed groups.

There must be strong, effective, and appropriate pastoral response if the clergy of the Church are to be prepared for the challenges of today's new religious movements. I suggest these initiatives to priests as effective counter measures on their part:

1. Read *Snapping*, Flo Conway and Jim Siegelman's book on sudden personality change. In addition, Robert J. Lifton's book, *Thought Reform And The Psychology of Totalism* is a

must, especially Chapter 22. Priest-educators should have a bibliography for themselves and their students and direct them to reading and research projects. Such bibliographies are in libraries (see also Appendix XII).

2. Study seriously the sociology, theology, spiritual and mental health, legal and political dimensions of cultic groups and include this information whenever appropriate in homilies and teachings.

3. School assemblies, church youth groups, PTA meetings, and home and school associations should collect information about cults and hear from former cult members and their families.

4. Interdenominational and interdisciplinary study groups should be set up and mobilized since the cult threat cuts across denominational and ethnic lines. The opportunities for ecumenical cooperation are manifold.

5. Religious communities must study the reasons why growing numbers of their members drift toward human potential groups such as EST (now the FORUM) and Lifespring.

6. A thorough restudying of our Catholic biblical roots and dogmatic developments must be undertaken by preachers and teachers. The dangers of large numbers of Catholic youth possessing an abiblical, adogmatic, and ahistorical sense of their specific Roman Catholic identity can be the fertile soil for later cult enticements.

7. The doctrinal writings of Pope John Paul II, especially *Redemptor Hominis*, should become an integral part of our personal spirituality as well as our preaching and teaching. These writings represent a brilliant compendium and synthesis of our Catholic doctrine.

8. All parish ministry team members need to address, in a pastoral manner, the serious personal and family problems of tension, ambiguities, and frustrations that afflict so many of our people. They need to affirm our people lovingly and to remind them of our fundamentally optimistic Catholic theology of God's grace and mankind's response in faith to give them a sense of belonging to us, their spiritual fathers, and to one another.

9. All of us must carefully screen all potential participants in Cursillo, Marriage Encounter, Charismatic, Search and other life enrichment experiences. The heavy emotional trip and resultant mind and soul expanding experience may in the long run be detrimental to some people who do not belong to these groups.

The professional and academic credentials of those leading and directing these groups must also be carefully scrutinized. There must be Christian accountability concerning the conduct of all such close encounter experiences.

* * *

V. Ecumenical Activity

American priests actively engaged in pastoral and educational work concerning new religious movements, cults and sects, find numerous opportunities for ecumenical and interreligious dialogue. These opportunities range from church and school to media cooperative programs. Many times rabbis, ministers and priests sit side by side on panels in church and community sponsored workshops. The same is true in radio and television production. I can recount many situations in which I participated with rabbis and ministers in discussing the philosophies and strategies of cults and sects. Additionally informed and interested clergy are actively sought out to be part of interdisciplinary panels and workshops alongside psychiatrists, psychologists, family counselors, law enforcement personnel, and former cult members and their parents. In each case the Church — through the individual parish priest — has a marvelous opportunity for both evangelization and catechesis.

Cults and sects are especially fond of drawing comparisons between Roman Catholic formation programs in seminaries and novitiates, as was discussed in an earlier chapter. Charges of cult indoctrination and confinement of members by established mainline denominational church personnel usually draw immediate comparisons with the seminary or novitiate. A priest then has an excellent opening to point out that the integrity of an individual's free will and freedom of choice is not interfered with in a religious formation program. Media interviewers also like to dwell on this subject. It is vitally important that priests be available to respond to these dilemmas.

The Cult Awareness Network and the American Family

foundation both have priest members. Such valuable interdenominational and ecumenical enterprises are building valuable links within contemporary American religious experience.

A less public but nevertheless extremely important area of ecumenical activity has been the counseling of families over the telephone. Priests with whom I have contact in this apostolate have indicated to me that they have collectively spoken to thousands of people by phone during the past ten years, people whose families have been in crisis with cults, and have no one else to whom to turn. Many of these people never actually meet the priests, but have been assisted by the power of the telephone in communication.

Like these priests, I have also spoken by phone, and in person in the office, with hundreds of families of all religious denominations regarding their sons or daughters who are involved in cults and sects. The Church is truly apostolic and catholic in these situations.

The central point is this: where the legal and social agencies of the local, state, and federal governments were unable to assist these families directly, the Church ministered to them through the priesthood. Thousands of dollars spent for the services of private detectives, counselors and deprogrammers because their children were robotized by these new religious movements, cults and sects, definitely justifies the long hours and personal commitment of our presently involved clergy to the educational and pastoral apostolates of the Church.

In closing this chapter it is important to keep in mind that while some of the cults and sects may disappear, many well financed and organized groups, e.g. Unification Church, Hare Krishma, Scientology, the Way International, Church Universal and Triumphant, will not. They are here to stay.

The formal religious education programs of the Catholic Church must meet the changing doctrinal positions and strategies of these groups with sophisticated and informed apologetics, officially approved and sponsored. The American bishops and the Vatican Congregations seem agreed on this modus agendi. The youth of the Catholic Church need to be prepared for the advances of every new religious movement, especially in the United States. The contents of this chapter have hopefully pointed to some possible models and attitudes that will enable our clergy, catechists and teachers to meet the inquiries of our Catholic students for many years to come.

IX

Shepherding/Discipleship Movement

By Rev. Walter Debold

The words, "shepherding" and "discipleship," are used to describe what appears to be a relatively new phenomenon in the world of religion. Both words are used with affection by Christians who have always seen Jesus as the "Good Shepherd." He presented Himself in those terms, and then He invited men to follow Him as His disciples. It is not surprising that the walls of the Roman catacombs portray Jesus with the recovered lamb over His shoulders. "I know mine and mine know me" (John 10:14), He said, and He explained that He had come to recover "the lost sheep of Israel" (Matthew 10:6).

Jesus came with a message and He invited His followers to take that message to heart: "I have come to cast fire on the earth. How I wish that the blaze were ig-

nited!" (Luke 12:49). He wanted hearers who would prove to be "good ground" in which the seed would take root and bear fruit. The disciple is one who takes the word to heart.

For two thousand years the Good Shepherd has had many disciples sharing in the task of shepherding the flock. The genuine shepherd is one who conforms to the model, who is Christ. He is no mere hireling; he receives the message and hands it on to all in its integrity. The style of indoctrination is the style of the Master: appealing, inviting, straight-forward.

This chapter will assess the contemporary "shepherding/discipleship" movement. It will take the position that Jesus' time honored words have been given a meaning subtly different from their usage among Christians during the apostolic era.

The "Shepherding/Discipleship" movement is not yet a quarter of a century old. It seems to have begun in the decade of the sixties, a time of ferment and turbulence. College campuses reflected the anxieties of the time. Students were impatient with the world shaped by their elders. They were fed up with wars and violence. They may have been inspired by the nonviolent protests of Martin Luther King, Jr., in spite of the fact that their own demonstrations often became unruly. They staged protests against existing authority and leadership.

In the Catholic Church, a new leader, Pope John XXIII, came on the scene, a man with a uniquely attractive personality, open, optimistic, and looking to the future with confidence. The new pope called an ecumenical council to bring about an updating in the presentation of Catholic faith and practice.

Events such as these proved stirring to great masses of people, but they were also unsettling to many others who experienced confusion over the extent of revolutionary change in so many aspects of life.

This change was especially painful in religious matters. In addition to the many innovative formulations of faith, there were entirely new questions posed for the moralists. Since not all theologians see eye to eye in their solutions of contemporary problems, they only added to the annoyance and the insecurities of the average man who wanted to be loyal to the church of his childhood. People felt themselves caught in a "no-man's land" between the warring forces of light and darkness.

In the realm of intellect, wider horizons have opened up as a result of a knowledge explosion and the development of technology to manipulate and exploit that new knowledge. All of this is sensed as a mixed blessing: Western man is loosed from his moorings and adrift in a sea of ambiguities. With an understandable longing for security and with what has been called a "lust for certitude" it is no wonder that people search for a savior, or a system to cut through the complexities in order to reestablish "the simple verities."

In the midst of this climate of anxiety and confusion, television responds with a flood of evangelical religion, as already has been noted. Radio, too, offers many cheerful, charismatic preachers who answer the longings of simple people with an uncomplicated gospel and a gracious willingness to accept financial donations. This search for simple answers is also found within the ranks of Catholics, having, it is said, a powerful impact on both clergy and laity.

One religious movement which does not depend upon radio or television to advance itself is the "Shepherding/Discipleship" movement. It relies primarily on personal contact in small groups or communities, and when it gathers members, the meetings are usually in private homes.

The origin of the movement has been attributed to various sources, but it is likely that no single person deserves to be designated as its "inventor." Many varying personalities have contributed to its present state. What they have in common is a remarkably organized fundamentalism, and a motivation that is forceful, even if somewhat mystifying.

According to one view of the origin of the "Shepherding" movement, there was, in Argentina in 1970, a former Assembly of God pastor, Juan Carlos Ortiz, who saw the impact Cuban Marxists were having upon his people.

Ortiz' response to the challenge was to mount an effort which mirrored the Marxist technique. This involved a structure that included a pyramid of authority and a rigid discipline. In a book entitled, *A Call To Discipleship*, Ortiz designed a model community in which each member gives strict obedience to his "head" or "elder." Within two years, a Fort Lauderdale, Florida Bible teacher, Bob Mumford, brought the Ortiz methodology to the United States. By 1979 the headquarters of the effort had moved to Mobile, Alabama and came to be known as the "Christian Growth Ministries." Other personalities become identified with its history: Basham, Prince, Pilkington, Simpson, Tomczak, and many others. One media vehicle for the message of Christian Growth Ministries is the "New Wine Mazagine." These ideas seem to have answered a need, as missionaries of these shepherding groups find thousands of disciples across the country, and beyond, who are willing to surrender the direction of their lives to men whose qualifications and motivations should be first evaluated.

The current ecumenical thrust on the part of Christian churches has been a great boon to those promoting the shepherding concept. The ecumenical atmosphere fostered in society has favored a warm, friendly collaboration among Christians in a wide variety of social undertakings and in shared prayer as well. Into this situation came the charismatic clergy with a great zeal to reach out across denominational lines to foster spiritual development, especially among middle-class Americans.

One shepherding group has printed its covenant agreement in ten points, six of which are aimed directly at the control of the individual:

> 1. We agree to be faithful to our commitments to Community gatherings and to service.
>
> 2. We agree to respect and submit ourselves to the way of life established among us, especially as set forth by our coordinators.
>
> 3. We agree to contribute regularly and faithfully to the financial support of the Community.
>
> 4. We agree to receive gratefully the pastoral care of those in the Community who have authority over us as individuals and groups.
>
> 5. We agree to recognize and honor the special headship of the Coordinators over our whole life together.
>
> 6. We agree to be held to the Covenant and these Agreements and to hold one another to them.

In all of these groups there is nothing so important as submission to the leaders.

It should be noted that to date there has never been a shepherding group which selected its leaders in a democratic manner. Some faceless authority invariably designates the elders or coordinators, and, sometimes for the process of selection, a divine inspiration is claimed. The leaders, once put in place are required to give an accounting to no one beneath them in the chain of command. Blind obedience is expected of members. In most cases these same members never seem to be aware that during their period of training for acceptance in the group they were schooled to this docility. The men are won over to the idea of obedience so thoroughly that they demand the same obedience from their wives and children. Once indoctrinated, the member's speech and thought patterns mimic those of the group. This is so disturbingly obvious to the outsider that he suspects that the disciple is trying to be amusing. (On the contrary, the disciple is bemused.)

* * *

Bruce Barron, in his book, *If You Really Want To Follow Jesus* (Partners Press, Kenmore, N.Y., 1981, p. 26), has written of his recruitment to the community, which took place in September, 1978, when he was a freshman at Michigan State University. His indoctrination assured him that "all that the Lord offers comes with membership in this covenant community."

> After returning home from this exhilarating weekend, having learned that community is the answer to society's woes, that community is the most practical way to live as a "body of Christ," and that community enables "right relationships of brotherly love" — and, most powerfully, having been showered with love by the community members, the candidate is free to decide whether he wishes to join the work of Christ! (p. 26)

It is just this type of enthusiasm that is both enticing and blinding. It urges the candidate to continue on to find the love of Jesus (as any good movement might do), but it also puts the person into a frame of mind that is not ready to take an objective look at future developments.

The shepherding/discipleship movement is pernicious because it aims to dominate the individual. Susceptible victims do not grasp the fact that they are giving away more of themselves than they have a right to surrender. Their manipulators adopt a personal vocabulary, emphasizing familiar words such as "mother," "father," "brother," "sister," "family," "body," "community," among others. Then like all the cults, they exploit their own specialized jargon. The elders or coordinators are, in actuality, the official interpreters of reality. (They and they only, are the receivers of the message from on high.) Thus, "submission" is made THE great virtue!

It is difficult to identify shepherding/discipleship groups. As we have noted, on the surface they appear to be dedicated Christians (and Catholics) seeking a greater union with God coupled with a desire to follow Jesus closely as a disciple. It is from their practices and procedures, more so than from their beliefs, that we discover their involvement with the shepherding concept.

Two examples will suffice for the Christian groups: GREATER GRACE WORLD OUTREACH (formerly called BIBLE SPEAKS) and the group originally known as the CROSSROADS CHURCH OF CHRIST, but now more commonly known as the CHURCH OF CHRIST (with a community name appended to the title, e.g. Boston Church of Christ).

BIBLE SPEAKS was founded by Carl H. Stevens, Jr., who began to work as a minister at the age of 31, after serving for a time as a lay preacher in North Paris, Maine. According to *The Bible Speaks Book of Miracles*, published by the group, God called Carl Stevens to the ministry and he was promised an "anointing" on his pronouncements. In 1962, he became a preacher at a Baptist church in Montsweag, Maine. After some difficulties there, he started his own church in South Berwick, Maine. One of his main teachings was that of "delegated authority" which proclaimed that in every generation, God assigns power to one select individual who is above reproach. His ministry prospered and in 1976 he purchased an eighty-six acre campus in Lenox, Massachusetts, which became his headquarters.

The Christian Research Institute, in a copyrighted report in 1983, had several comments on BIBLE SPEAKS. Author Elliot Miller indicates in the opening paragraph that the Institute began its study in 1979. He writes: "Early in our relationship with the Bible Speaks (TBS) we were persuaded that their membership is largely composed of genuine Christians. TBS has, up to the time of this writing, also maintained an orthodox, biblical position on those doctrines most essential to the Christian faith. Thus we do not consider TBS a non-Christian cult, but rather a Christian ministry."

Their confidence was short lived however, for soon after the initial report was made public, many complaints came in, particularly over the doctrine of "delegated authority" which Stevens had expressed a willingness to modify, but which in fact, had not.

The report goes on to explain that CRI did not give TBS a clean bill of health. The report also seems anxious to find some good in the organization, and as is the case with many of the cultic groups, some people did receive some benefits, at least for a time. However, after fifty-five pages, CRI reaches another conclusion:

> In this report we have chosen not to delve into the details of scandal and controversy that have been brought to our attention. This is because it is not our desire to destroy the organization or disgrace its leadership. However, to bring things into what we consider to be the proper perspective, we must point out that after having approached the Bible Speaks' problems in the past from a doctrinal standpoint, our conclusion is that the reason past negotiations did not reach a satisfactory conclusion is that the real issue is less doctrinal than it is one of personality.
>
> The root problem with TBS is that Carl Stevens (in spite of whatever good he has accomplished in other respects) has been guilty of serious error (in both teaching and conduct), and though he has made some effort to change, it has not been decisive enough to effectively clear the air. Instead, the theological and social situation that was established in the 1970s continues in a less pronounced form, and is subtly used to perpetuate irresponsible patterns of leadership. Thus it would be misleading for this report to imply that the entire problem with the Bible Speaks is the "delegated authority" doctrine. The ultimate problem is more an attitude in Carl Stevens, which he has passed on in varying degrees to many of his associates. That attitude has been directly responsible for abuses of power which, in turn, have contributed significantly to TBS' internal turmoil and controversial public image. What is needed now is repentence, accountability, and the structural and practical changes that these would produce" (p. 56).

The final pages of the report voice the fear that Bible Speaks might go downhill, and subsequent events have proven this to be true.

In 1987, after a long trial the Bible Speaks was ordered by

Federal Bankruptcy Court in Massachusetts to return 6.6 million dollars that Elizabeth Dovydenas had been duped into donating to the church. In his written opinion, Judge James Queenan wrote in part:

> This is a case of undue influence exerted upon a church donor which appears unsurpassed in our jurisprudence in its variations and in the sums involved. Revealed is an astonishing saga of clerical deceit, avarice and subjugation on the part of the Church's founder, Carl H. Stevens. He has abused the trust of many good and devout members of the church.

The property in Lenox was sold to pay this claim, among many others, and the group moved to Baltimore, Maryland, where it is seeking new members, having assumed a new name, Greater Grace World Outreach.

* * *

Our second example of shepherding/discipleship has caused concern in several large metropolitan areas. The Boston Church of Christ, for example holds Sunday worship services in the Boston Garden, with attendance reported to be well over the 8,000 mark. The New York City Church of Christ has grown from some twenty members in 1983 to a 1987 membership nearing one thousand. A majority of membership seems to come from the college campuses of the area. Parents began to raise objections when their children not only abandoned the faith of their family, but often abandoned the family as well, having no time for anything but evangelizing.

This group began in Gainesville, Florida as the 14th Street Church of Christ. Later, when Chuck Lucas became the minister, he changed the name to Crossroads Church of Christ, basing this on the biblical verse of Jeremiah 6:16: "Thus says the Lord, stand at the crossroads and look; ask for the ancient paths, where is the good way; then walk it, and find rest for your souls."

The group grew rapidly, fostering the discipleship image, demanding total obedience and submission to the leadership. It was brought to Boston by Kip McKean, who had been converted by Chuck Lucas while a student at Gainesville. Later, he was responsible for the New York City Church as well, although it soon became independent.

In 1985, the "Crossroads" name and association were dropped, probably because of the resignation of Chuck Lucas from the Crossroads Church of Christ. Because of the intensity of its evangelism and its plantings in many other parts of the world, the Boston Church of Christ is becoming the unofficial headquarters of this new shepherding group.

Lucas taught strict adherence to the Bible, but he put a peculiar emphasis on the concept of discipleship or "one-on-one conversion." He taught that Jesus controlled the lives of His Apostles. He taught that Jesus taught the Apostles to disciple by controlling the lives of others. Therefore Christians should imitate this process when bringing people to Christ.

The Church of Christ operates in a simple, and direct way. It often begins with a simple invitation to a bible study. Once a person accepts the invitation, the recruit finds a group of kind, loving people anxious to please. Very shortly afterwards, however, the recruit experiences another message, opposite to the first. The recruit sees that those who do not abide by the rules of the church are shunned, cut off, and ignored, and told they are going to hell.

The members of the Church of Christ are told to dedicate themselves completely and entirely to the work of evangelism. Many former members complain that they had no time for family, friends, or anything else, including school.

Members are taught that their previous baptism is invalid, especially if it was received as an infant. Doctrines and practices of the Catholic and Protestant churches are held up to ridicule in front of the members, and those weak in faith are humiliated, laughed at and made to feel worthless. Members are required to attend EVERY church service, and are made to feel guilty should they miss one for any reason.

It is not difficult to see that shepherding/discipleship concepts are hard at work in these two groups.

* * *

The most notable example of this phenomenon within the Catholic Church has been the covenant communities. Originally begun as an attempt of Charismatic people to live the life of a disciple more intensely, later developments seemed to place them at variance with Church structure and authority. In recent years, they have united in an ecumenical endeavor called "Sword of the Spirit," and operate a "Catholic branch" of this grouping.

Questions have arisen in several areas concerning the methods and ideals of Sword of the Spirit Covenant Communities. In 1984, for example, Bishop Anthony Pilla of Cleveland, Ohio, found it necessary to lay down these four directives for the Bread of Life Covenant Community, which at the time was active in his diocese:

1. Members are to attend Mass in their own parishes. (Prior to this they had been accustomed to a special, exclusive Mass for their own group.)
2. Community leaders are to receive formal, religious training.
3. The organization is to publish a document on its identity and community order.
4. The organization is to stop their recruiting and outreach programs.

According to the *Akron Beacon Journal* of November 17, 1984, these directives were the result of the findings of Auxiliary Bishop Gilbert Sheldon who said that adherence to these directives "would remove certain cultlike tendencies" attributed to the group.

In 1986, Archbishop Peter Gerety, of Newark, New Jersey, found these same tendencies when he had to deal with the inner workings of the Sword of the Spirit as one of its affiliates, the People of Hope, became involved in a public controversy. Archbishop Gerety retired later that year, but not before he held several meeting with leaders and members. His successor, Archbishop Theodore McCarrick has carried on the dialogue begun by his predecessor, seeking to provide proper spiritual care to Catholic people who are members of the People of Hope.

In that same year, the Archdiocese of Baltimore began an inquiry into the Lamb of God Fellowship, another Sword of the Spirit affiliate.

An excellent clarification of the position of ecumenical organizations within the Church, with particular reference to statements of the Sword of the Spirit, was written to Archbishop Gerety by Jan Cardinal Willebrands, President of the Secretariat for Promoting Christian Unity in April, 1986. The text of this letter can be found in Appendix VII.

In conclusion, we need to state the basic problem with shepherding/discipleship. Briefly, members are required to be too docile. They are indoctrinated to accept several key ideas which are at variance with traditional Christian attitudes:

1) There is foisted upon them a pessimistic world view that is completely at variance with Christian hope.

2) They are persuaded to accept an undervaluing of the human person, his freedom and his responsibility,

3) There is a demand for total submission of the individual to a system which is not in harmony with the Gospel, one which calls for dehumanizing blind obedience.

4) Members are subjected to a manipulative control of information and environment aimed to manage and control them.

5) They are subjected to a lifestyle which has a demeaning attitude toward women and marriage.

There is little doubt that this type of organization can also be a threat to mental health even as it now appears to be a threat to authentic religion. People who are deprived of their freedom of thought, action, and decision, can eventually crack under the strain. Sometimes they come to a decision that the group in which they are involved is indeed harmful. Unfortunately, in most cases it is someone else who sees the danger and the need for mental health assistance.

The authentic shepherd is one who lays down his life for his sheep. Too many of the contemporary claimants to the title reverse the relationship, requiring the disciple to lay down his life for the shepherd. There is no other pattern than that offered by Jesus.

X

Satanism

The next topic in this consideration of cultic phenomenon is actually the antithesis of everything else. It is the negation of everything positive and good, and the embodiment of all that is evil. It is the occult, and includes, among other things, satanism and witchcraft.

In its basic sense, the word "occult" means "hidden or secret, beyond human understanding." It refers essentially to the many things that God has hidden from human creatures, and is coupled very closely with the Bible and Christianity. A study of history and literature, particularly in the Middle Ages, reveals an active presence of both satanism and witchcraft, and various measures taken to deal with the problem.

In his book, *The Devil's Bookshelf* (Aquarian Press, Wellingborough, Northamptonshire, 1985), Christopher McIntosh gives us some insights into this subject, not all of them necessarily good. He writes:

Occasionally in the annals of occult literature we

hear of some book that has appeared at the critical time and place, played an important role and then vanished into the realms of legend. Such a book features in the remarkable story of the French alchemist Nicholas Flamel, a figure whose life is surrounded by an aura of mystery.

The outer facts of Flamel's life are briefly as follows. He was born about 1330 and died in 1417. He lived in Paris. . ., a man of simple piety who lived a quiet and retiring life. While earning his living as a bookseller, scribe and legal draftsman, he devoted his real energies to the study and practice of alchemy.

Suddenly, after years of unrewarding toil, assisted by his devoted wife, Pernelle, Flamel apparently became rich. . . . What was the source of his fortune? The answer seems to be that Flamel finally discovered the secret of transmutation, thanks to a mysterious grimoire which an unknown man brought into his shop one day. . . .

Flamel and his wife studied his book for twenty years without success. Then Flamel in desperation set out for Spain. . . . When he returned, his efforts were finally crowned with success as he himself recorded: "At last I found what I desired. It was on 17th January about midday at my house, with only Pernelle present, in the year 1382." Flamel goes on to say that on the 25th April, using the "red stone" and mercury, he succeeded with the aid of Pernelle in producing a quantity of pure gold.

The author goes on to note that Flamel's book disappeared, which quite conveniently eliminates the principal evidence in verification.

Mysterious origins, magic books, special formulas and years of searching are all part of the occult phenomenon. Everyone wanted to have gold, and if you could make it in the laboratory, you would be famous. Unfortunately, there has never been any indication that the incidents described here or elsewhere were real. No one who practiced alchemy got the gold they sought.

Another book, somewhat vicious in its disdain for religion, particularly Catholicism, is *Satanism and Witchcraft* by Jules Michelet (translated by A.R. Allinson) has been published by the Citadel Press in Secaucus, New Jersey. It speaks of our topics extensively. The promotion on the back cover states:

> Long out of print, Jules Michelet's classic study of medieval superstition has been reprinted in this edition to bring the general public's attention to one of the truly great sociological works of modern times.
>
> Michelet brilliantly recreates the Europe of the Middle Ages, the centuries of fierce religious intolerance, the Inquisition and the auto-da-fe. He depicts the feudal barons, the great manors, the fiefs and serfs ... and the witches, hobgoblins and wizards of whom the masses lived in mortal fear.
>
> Michelet draws flaming word pictures of the witch hunts, the Black Masses, the reign of Satan, and the weird rites of the damned. Here is the age of unbridled pleasure and sensuality, of luxury beyond imagination and squalor beyond endurance. Here is the time when a girl might be accused of witchcraft merely because she was young and pretty and did not survive the test of immersion in water or boiling oil. Here is the day of beatings, floggings, tortures and summary decapitations.
>
> *Encyclopedia Britannica* called this book "The most important work on medieval superstition yet written." It is indeed one of the great works of the Age of Darkness.

The theme of this book is immediately evident from the first paragraph in the book:

> Sprenger said, before 1500: "We should speak of the Heresy of the Sorceresses, not of the Sorcerers; the latter are of small account." So another writer under Louis XIII: "For one Sorcerer, then ten thousand Sorceresses."

But today's increasing popularity of both satanism and witchcraft cause concern not only because of their religious or anti-religious stance of all that both Christians and Jews call sacred. It causes concern also because innocent people are led into activities and belief systems that deprive them of freedom of choice and the power to act in a rational manner.

It is important to understand at the outset that what is popularly called satanism is not the traditional worship of the devil — the angel who fell from heaven and goes about the world seeking the ruin of souls. Also, today's witchcraft bears little resemblance to the ancient practices, which in Salem, Massachusetts, for example, caused many a person suspected of being a witch to be put to death for fear of these powers.

Some witchcraft is associated with satanism, but it is more properly a pantheism worship of nature. Witchcraft is discussed as part of the New Age Movement in Chapter XI.

To understand this problem, it is necessary to establish who the devil (satan) is, and the source and extent of his power. In the Old Testament there is little reference to satan. The Talmud does make reference to a certain "sutun," the evil one, who can practice his temptations for 364 days a year — YOM KIPPUR, being the only day he cannot act. The New Testament is filled with many references to satan, and so we turn to Christianity for the answer. In Catholic theology, satan is an angel, a fallen angel. Just as God created man and put him to the test, so God also created the angels and gave them a test. From the Book of Revelation we determine what happened to those who did not give their allegiance to God when called upon to do so:

> Then war broke out in heaven; Michael and his angels battled against the dragon. Although the dragon and his angels fought back, they were overpowered, and lost their place in heaven. The huge dragon, the ancient known as the devil or Satan, the seducer of the whole world was driven out; he was hurled down to earth and his minions with him (12:7-9).

There has always been speculation as to what caused the war. Many would suggest that it was a test for loyalty and fidelity. Catholic theology teaches that because human creatures were created with intelligence and free will, God tested them. He wanted their allegiance not because of His power and commands, but as an act of the free will He had given them. So too with the angels. However, the angels' act of the will was to be complete and single — no changes, no second chances. In response to the question of what kind of test they received, a rather prominent suggestion is that the angels were given a glimpse of the future, of how God would redeem the world. They were asked to bow down and worship the baby — the God before man. Under the leadership of Lucifer, (the dragon in

Revelation), some angels refused and they are the ones referred to in this passage.

The remainder of Chapter 12 of Revelation and the succeeding one describe in a mystical manner the activities of Satan and forms the basis for much of the satanic symbolism and actions, particularly the famous "666" (Rev. 13:15-18):

> The second wild beast was then permitted to give life to the beast's image, so that the image had the power of speech and of putting to death anyone who refused to worship it. It forced all men, small and great, rich and poor, slave and free, to accept a stamped image on their right hand or their forehead. Moreover it did not allow a man to buy or sell anything unless he was first marked with the name of the beast or the number that stood for its name. A certain wisdom is needed here; with a little ingenuity anyone can calculate the number of the beast, for it is a number that stands for a certain man. The man's number is six hundred sixty-six.

To understand this passage, it is helpful to know that the first beast represents false Messiahs, the second (mentioned here) indicates the false prophets. Christians at the time of this writing had either to worship the emperor and his image or suffer martyrdom. Also, each of the letters of the alphabet in Greek and Hebrew has a numerical value. Many possible combinations of letters will add up to a total of 666, and there have been many candidates for this infamous honor. The most likely, however, would be the emperor Caesar Nero, whose name in Hebrew letters adds up correctly.

In Catholic theology, the devil has great power. He is frequently called the Prince of Darkness, or the Prince of evil. (He is never called king — because God remains King of all creation.) As a fallen angel he suffers the pains of hell — the most serious of which is that of loss — the loss of the sight of God (usually referred to as the Beatific Vision). While satan or Lucifer and his minions never experienced that vision, they possessed, as pure spirits, a greater awareness of God and lost all rights to enjoy God's presence by their disobedience. Another pain is that of fire which devils experience to a superior degree. Satan's one ambition is to bring as many creatures of God (humans) to reject all that is good, since he cannot influence the angels who, like himself, have made their irrevocable decisions.

Diabolical Activity

The devil acts in three ways. The one most familiar to all is temptation. The suggestion, very strong at times, comes from the evil one as he goes about trying to draw souls away from God. The second activity of the devil is to annoy people. He annoys them so much that it is referred to as obsession. Other times he can even take over the operation of a person so that the person is not aware of what is happening (and not morally responsible either). This third activity is called possession. It is this last item that requires the expulsion of the devil through exorcism. An example of the latter two will suffice for a basic understanding of the terms.

Obsession

When a person strives very hard to be a good person, the devil often seeks to discourage the person to the point of despair or rejection of that way of life. Such a person is constantly meeting unexplained obstacles, having strange experiences in losing objects, or in finding things in different places. Sometimes things will shake, or rattle in the room. Occasionally, too, the person's sleep will be disturbed by mental or physical means, such as shaking the bed or being awakened by a noise (such as a picture falling off the wall).

In his biography of the Curé of Ars, St. John Vianney, Abbe Francis Trochu (Tan Books, Rockford, Ill. 1977 — orginally published in 1927 by Burns, Oates and Washbourne, London), describes this type:

> Once resolved upon upsetting M. Vianney's outward tranquillity, the devil began with some rather trivial vexations. Every night the poor Cure heard the curtains of his bedstead being rent (i.e. torn). In the beginning he imagined that he had to do only with common rodents. He placed a pitchfork near the head of his bed. Useless precaution: the more he shook the curtains in order to frighten off the rats, the louder became the sounds of rending, and in the morning, when he expected to find them in shreds, the curtains were undamaged. This game lasted for quite a while (p. 235).

Abbe Trochu goes on to elaborate on other manifestations of the devil in the Curé's life. He is also careful to document the testimony of physicians, including his personal one for seventeen years, Dr. J. B. Saunier, who stated that M. Le Curé had "a perfect regularity of all the functions of the organism" (the body). He had a "serenity of ideas, a delicacy of perception, a sureness of view and miraculous health which hardly ever failed him, notwithstanding the incessant labour that absorbed his life." (p. 236 note 2 - originally in Proces de l'Ordinaire, p. 1112)

For example, Doctor Aime Michel of Coligny (Ain) when asked for his opinion, . . . made the following statement on May 31, 1864: "All that I have seen or heard of M. Le Cure d'Ars strengthens my convictions that he was absolutely self-possessed and endowed with great soundness of judgement. Nothing could persuade me that he was the victim of delusions or hallucinations. As regards demoniacal attacks, I have heard of them, and if M. Vianney affirmed that he experienced them, I believe them to have taken place" (ibid.).

Here is a more direct annoyance of the devil to the Curé:

It was now the time of superhuman toil when M. Vianney spent the greater part of the day in the confessional. Although utterly exhausted when evening came, he would not go to bed without first reading a few pages from the Lives of the Saints. It was likewise the hour when at close intervals he inflicted on himself bodily disciplines. When that was over he stretched himself on his thin straw mattress and sought repose. Just as he was about to fall asleep, he would start up, awakened by shouts, mournful cries, and formidable blows. It seems as if the front door were being battered in with a sledge-hammer. Suddenly, without a latch having been moved, the Cure d'Ars perceived with horror that the devil was close to him. "I do not ask him to enter," he used to say, half laughing, half annoyed, "but he comes all the same."

The uproar now began. The evil spirit remained invisible, but his presence could be plainly felt. He threw over the chairs and shook the heavy furniture of the room. With a fearful voice he shouted: "Vianney, Vianney! potato-eater! Ah! Thou are not yet dead! I shall get thee all right." Or roaring like a beast, growling like a bear or snarling like a dog, he rushed at the curtains of the bed, which he shook violently. . . . On more than one occasion M. Vianney experienced a sensation as of a hand passing over his face or of rats scampering over his body.

One night he heard the buzz of a swarm of bees. He got up, lit his candle, and was about to open the window to let them out, but he saw no bees (pp. 239-240).

To be sure, the Curé d'Ars had a time with the devil. But the Curé also noted that whenever he was particularly tormented, a very great sinner would come to confession the next day. On one occasion the Curé was visiting another parish, and there was such a noise in the Curé's room that the other priests thought he was being murdered. When they opened the door to his room, they saw the Curé peacefully on his bed, which was now in the middle of the floor. "It is the grappin (Vianney's name for the devil. — ed.) who has dragged me thus far," he said with a smile, "It is he who has caused all this tumult. It is nothing, I am sorry, I forgot to warn you beforehand. However, it is a good sign: there will be a big fish tomorrow" (p. 247). The big-fish, of course, is a sinner. Obsession is certainly a force to be reckoned with at all times.

Possession

This more serious method of diabolical activity is not usually caused by the person so afflicted. In olden days it was thought to be the result of a curse, but today we know that is not true. A person becomes possessed when the devil or some of its demons actually take over the body of a person. In a documented case of possession in Earling, Iowa in 1928 (*Begone Satan!*, Tan Books, Rockford, Illinois, 1973, pp. 17-19) the following dialogue is reported during an exorcism:

Exorcist: How long have you been torturing this woman?

Devil: Since her fourteenth year.

Exorist: How dared you enter that innocent girl and torture her like that?

Devil (sneeringly): Ha, did not her own father curse us into her? . . .

Exorcist: Is then the father of the woman also present as one of the devils? Since when?

Devil: What a foolish question. He has been with us ever since he was damned.

The reason for the possession is given in the next paragraph. "Later developments disclosed the fact that he had led a frightfully coarse and brutal life, a passionately unchaste and debased life. He now admitted that he had repeatedly tried to force his own daughter to commit incest with him. But she had firmly resisted him. Therefore he had cursed her and wished inhumanly that the devils would enter into her and entice her to commit every possible sin against chastity, thereby ruining her, body and soul."

A Modern Day Example

A case of possession was witnessed by a bishop friend of mine.

He spoke of a time during the Second Vatican Council, in 1962, that he went to visit a friend in a Rome hospital. As he was walking down the hall, he heard screams of an unusual nature coming from a nearby room. Upon investigation he found two doctors in the room trying to restrain a young lady who was literally climbing up the wall. It seemed to be a psychiatric case, but the bishop sensed something more. He spoke to the girl and blessed her with his cross, invoking as well, the name of the Blessed Virgin. Immediately she went into convulsions, rose to the ceiling, and emitted a terribly foul odor. The bishop left, to attend to his original purpose. Later, he returned to the room. The girl, who had, by this time, been returned to the bed, immediately became agitated upon seeing the bishop again, and exhibited similar signs as before. This time the bishop was ready. He took out the Blessed Sacrament and invoked the name of Jesus, and that of His holy Mother, and ordered the demons out. With this effective but simple exorcism, the girl fell to the ground, completely awake now, and asked what she was doing there in the hospital, in the room, and on the floor. She remembered nothing of her activities of the previous weeks.

To summarize then, the devil is real. It is a fallen angel whose sole purpose is to roam the world and "get even with God" by tempting people to sin. C.S. Lewis in his work, *The Screwtape Letters*, highlights the work of satan in this manner:

There are two equal and opposite errors into which our race can fall about the devils. One is to disbelieve in their existence. The other is to believe, and to feel an unhealthy interest in them. They themselves are equally pleased by both errors and hail a materialist or a magician with the same delight" (preface, 1961 edition).

Our particular concern here, however, has little to do with theology. It has to do more with a phenomenon that takes elements of the theology about satan and interprets and personalizes them into a cult-like operation that capitalizes on society's active search for comfort, convenience and pleasure, without regard to propriety, lawfulness, or morality.

Satanism manifests itself today in acts of violence to property, person, and mind. It is the result of a generation of people who have not had proper education in religious matters, and therefore who are weak in faith. Traditional values and Judaeo-Christian morality are no longer even considered, much less respected. Satanic activity among youth in particular, has attracted the attention of law enforcement agencies throughout the country because much of this activity runs contrary to the law. Our consideration here will examine satanism first, and then other manifestations of the occult. Our focus will be the characteristics of cults, explained earlier, with particular attention to the unique aspects of this problem.

Satanism is a wide term that embraces four separate and distinct behavioral patterns. There is the religion of satanism, represented by the Church of Satan, founded by Anton LaVey, the Temple of Set, led by Michael Aquino, and since 1985, there is the Worldwide Church of Satan Liberator founded by Paul Valentine.

A second category of satanism concerns those who dabble in the rituals to get a thrill, or to scare a few people. Beyond them is the third group, those who have adapted satanic rituals and practices into a full fledged cult. Finally there are the occult groups, who are secretive, destructive and protective.

Dale Griffis, retired Police Captain in Tiffen, Ohio, has made a study of these groups, and calls them the four faces of satan: experimental, traditional, self-styled, and the occult. Each needs to be considered in detail to obtain a proper understanding of this aspect of the cult problem.

Satanism As A Religion

There is an increasing number of people who have decided to

"spiritualize" their hedonism and perversity. Acknowledging in deed if not in words, the existence of the devil (and consequently the existence of God), these people practice rites and rituals that are opposite to familiar and honored Catholic practices.

More than a century ago, Aleister Crowley, an acknowledged murderer and perpetrator of numerous other crimes, became the personification of modern-day satan worshipers as he saw himself as the beast (of the Book of Revelation). To demonstrate this, he had the number "666" indelibly placed on his forehead. Crowley put out two books, a *Satanic Bible* and *Satanic Rituals*, to guide those who might wish to follow him. One hundred years later a disgruntled Christian, Anton LaVey, considered himself the successor of Crowley and instituted the Church of Satan in 1967 in San Francisco, and had it registered as an official religion, thereby gaining for it the status of a religion and the protection of the First Amendment. He took Crowley's books and republished them under his own name and had them distributed through public book stores.

In the introduction to his satanic bible, Burton H. Wolfe quotes Anton LaVey, giving us an insight into his reasoning.

> "I saw the bloodiest, grimiest side of human nature," LaVey recounted in a session dealing with his past life. "People shot by nuts, knifed by their friends; little kids splattered in the gutter by hit-run drivers. It was disgusting and depressing. I asked myself, 'Where is God?' I came to detest the sanctimonious attitude of people toward violence, always saying it's God's will" (p. 13).

LaVey gives us the reason for his actions in the same introduction: "He saw the need for a church that would recapture man's mind and carnal desires as objects of celebration" (ibid.).

Documented sources indicate that LaVey practices all the rituals with his followers. They use dolls and stuffed animals to simulate the sacrifices.

In addition to the Church of Satan there is the Temple of Set, based on ancient Egyptian cults of evil. According to Dr. Joel Norris and Jerry Allen Potter in an article entitled "The Devil Made Me Do It" ("Penthouse Magazine," January 1986, pp. 48, ff.) the Temple of Set was founded in 1975 by Michael Aquino, who "holds a lieutenant colonel's rank in the United States Army" (ibid., p. 180, col. 2). Stationed for many years at the

Praesidio in San Francisco, he was sent to the National Defense University in Washington, D.C. in 1985, subsequently receiving another active duty assignment.

Paul Valentine broke away from LaVey's group and established his church to get back to the primary reason for worship of satan — the destruction of Christianity.

Dabblers in Satanism

A second category of satanists is the dabbler. Composed mostly of teenagers, the dabblers have found the Satanic Bible and the Book of Rituals and, usually in small groups, have decided to try it "a bit." They will gather in empty, secluded places, such as a cemetery, where they practice the incantations and ritualistic dances, oftentimes sacrificing an animal by burning it or cutting its throat. They will often spread the word about their activity in high schools and teenage hangouts, inviting one or two people (who show interest). Frequently their actions seem innocent. They babble in unintelligible sounds, put on long robes after completely disrobing, and dance around the animal to be sacrificed, until in a type of frenzy, they throw off their robes to dance "skyclad," and mix the blood of the animal with their own, at times even drinking it. Dabblers sometimes get so enthralled with this activity that they decide to go to satan, and they take their own life, leaving a message such as "I'm going home to satan." Dabblers will also seek to make satan known by vandalizing churches, synagogues and cemeteries, leaving messages, symbols and signs at the scene.

Satanic Cultists

Much more serious are the satanic cults. Chief among them are the Manson Cult and the Symbionese Liberation Front. What makes this category different from the one above is the definite intention these cultists have to inflict harm and to commit crimes because "they are above the law." Charles Manson has a following even today which is ready to do his bidding at a moment's notice. In the early 1970s he was responsible for a rather bizzare cult that was involved with the murder of Sharon Tate and others.

At the trial Manson showed no remorse or sorrow, and indicated a willingness to continue making things right as soon as he got the chance. Patti Hearst, daughter of millionaire publisher William Randolph Hearst Jr., was a victim of another political-satanic cult called the Symbionese Liberation Front. Transformed into a completely different person called Tanya, Patti Hearst finally surfaced during a bank robbery and was recognized on the bank's videotape. Her trial brought out much about the movement, but it was not until years later that the true nature of her mind control, manipulation and complete change of personality was recognized for the evil it was, and she was pardoned.

Occult Satanists

This last group of satanists consists of the occult practioners who have a decidedly evil purpose in mind through the use of the rituals of satan for their own benefit. This category is quite dangerous, for according to more than one expert in the field, there have been many unexplained homocides.

In several parts of the country over the past few years, there have been investigations of child day-care centers where ritualistic sexual abuse of children have taken place. In 1985, ABC Television did a segment on this topic on the 20/20 program.

> Jarriel (voice over): . . . sexual abuse aimed at destroying faith in God. It's being described by numerous children.
>
> (Interviewing) What were the parallels with what the boys have told you and the worship of Satan?
>
> 3rd Mother: Well, first of all, the sexual abuse, the pornography, which always seems to go hand in hand. The boys talked about how these people actually said, "I hate God," and they used a very deep voice when they talked about that. . . .
>
> Jarriel (voice over): Cannibalism. It's difficult to believe, but in every case we examined, children described it.
>
> Grandmother: The hearts were cut out, and the children were made to chew pieces of these children's hearts, pieces of their flesh.
>
> Jarriel (to Ms. Gallant): Is cannibalism part of the ritual?
>
> Ms. Gallant: The children have spoken about this in almost every instance. Also human feces, or drinking the urine or drinking human blood.

Jarriel: That's part of the ritual?

Ms. Gallant: Right.

Mr. Warnke: I have an old, three-inch scar here on my wrist where my friends used to cut my arm open and bleed my blood into a cup and drink it mixed with wine and urine four times a year as a ceremony to satan.

NOTE: Ms. Gallant is a San Francisco Police Officer; Mr. Warnke is a former high priest of satanism.

In California, the most notorious case of all is still in litigation at this writing. Officials of the McMartin School were found to have engaged in these practices for several years with allegations that more than 100 children were ritualistically abused.

In a similar case, an account in the "New York Daily News" by staff writer Gene Mustain (May 24, 1987, p. 4,18) relates the testimony of a child:

The main villain of Jenny's story was her father, a part time security guard, student, and bit actor on trial for twice raping and sodomizing her — once on her fourth birthday after he gave her a pink doll and toy gun.

But her story — which she had told the same way many times before — included accusations of even greater evil.

The reporter goes on to relate the history of this case, indicating that Anna was a woman several people in the neighborhood knew, but had not seen in a while. The girl's mother was not married to the father. Although they had lived together for a while, he had eventually moved out of the apartment. One day, Jenny's mother heard noises in the night and was startled to find Jenny somewhat in a trance and standing in the middle of the living room.

The article continues:

On her fourth birthday and other times, he took her to Anna's house. There Jenny said, her father and other men and women wore black robes and masks; they had sex with each other and with Jenny and several other children. The adults forced the children to do despicable things with human waste and the blood of animals they had slain with knives.

And then Jenny said, her father "killed Anna's children."

In the Midwest, an even more difficult case to understand took place in 1984 in which a group of twenty-four parents were accused of regularly committing these ritualistic acts of sexual abuse on their own or their neighbors' children.

Since many of the children in cases such as these just mentioned have told of the murder of infants and small children, and their subsequent destruction by eating, incineration or dismembership, a natural question raised does concern the origin of these victims. No one seems to be missing in the community, and the children (except in the most recent case quoted here) did not recognize the victims. Is this the ultimate fate of the children pictured on milk cartons, subway and bus posters, and billboards?

Sandy Gallant, of the San Francisco Detective Bureau, has indicated on more than one occasion that a possible answer to the whereabouts of some of the thousands of missing children may lie in this area.

* * *

Foremost in the mind of anyone who has studied recent developments and expansion of satanism is the question of how and why it happens. Are some of the theories put forth accurate? Is there a relationship between satanism and the lack of religious training among young people? What is to be said of the influence of rock music on the present generation?

The answer is quite affirmative to all these questions. But to discover the reason why is much more difficult.

The mind is a wonderful gift from God. Scientists tell us that even after the many thousands of years that mankind has existed on the earth, we have only developed a small part of the capabilities of our mind. Some of the gurus and cult leaders have tried to utilize this information and have promised great things to their membership, but none so far have achieved their goals.

Perhaps the answer is to be found not in religion, but in science. For the past twenty years behavioral scientists have been intrigued and alarmed by the possibility of bringing messages to the mind of a person unknowingly. Subconscious, or subliminal messages have been the subject of several experiments over the past decade or so, and when you add to that the growing certitude of the correlation of satanic activity in vandalism and suicide, and some types of rock music, a very convincing theory can be developed.

In the 1950s it was discovered that messages could be introduced electronically into records and visually into movies. These messages could not be perceived by the active mind, but only by the subconscious. At first it was looked upon as a strange, unique possibility, but was soon regarded as a reality.

Here, in succinct form are some reports and results.

According to Jacob Aranza in his book, *Backward Masking Unmasked*, (Huntington House, Shreeveport, La., 1984):

> The Beatles started using backward masking on their "White Album" with the song, "Revolution Number Nine." The lyric repeatedly says, "Number nine, number nine, number nine. . ."
>
> Played backwards it became "Turn me on dead man, turn me on, dead man. . . ." Why? At this time the Beatles were trying to make the public believe that Paul McCartney was dead, merely as a publicity stunt (p. 6).
>
> Then, between the songs "I'm So Tired" and "Blackbird" there's a gibberish kind of song. Played backwards, this says, "Paul is a dead man. Miss him, miss him, miss him" (p. 7).

While this may seem harmless, and even a bit amusing, others who took up the technique were not playing games or amusing people. Anti-Christian and hateful attitudes were processed into the recordings of some rock albums. Several suggestions seek to explain this phenomenon, but most of them avoid the obvious, that it is a deliberate action designed to seduce a person to evil.

Jacob Aranza, in the book quoted above, notes several examples of early backward masking. It will suffice here to quote just one:

> The group called STYX derived its name from the legendary river that flows through hell. A song of theirs entitled "Snowblind," when played in reverse, says "Satan, move in our voices" (p.7).

If this be true, such additions to the music and songs of rock and roll now become a greater concern to us. They are no longer amusing tricks but rather propagators of a specific message that on the surface would be rejected by most people.

Several scientific studies indicate that there is reason for concern. For the mind does receive not only the conscious messages we intend, but can also receive subconscious or subliminal ones as well, even those not desirable. Dr. Lloyd Silverman's studies were highlighted in the May, 1982 issue of "Psychology Today." His method is called subliminal psychodynamic activation. It consists in flashing a picture, then a verbal message on the screen of a small box into which the client is looking intently. In this article by Virginia Adams, Silverman's activity is called a "technique for investigating the unconscious.

> In his laboratory . . . he shows subjects such messages as "Mommy and I are one," . . . and "Beating Dad is okay," presenting them subliminally, that is so briefly, that they cannot be consciously recognized. Silverman's aim is to test psychoanalytic ideas by stirring up unconscious anxieties, wishes, and fantasies, and then observing the effects on behavior.
>
> Silverman believes he has accomplished that aim. To date, he calculates, some 50 students have demonstrated that the subliminal presentation of emotionally charged messages can trigger unconscious thoughts thus alter behavior — usually for a very short time — in ways that are predictable from psychoanalytic theory (p. 24).

A sidebar story goes on to say that in 1956 there was an experiment conducted by James Vicary, a market researcher, which proved the power of subliminal advertising. His experiment consisted in flashing the words "Drink Coca Cola" on the screen for 1/24th of a second, every second (the same length of time that a single frame of a movie is on the screen). Another day he had the word "Popcorn" flashed in the same manner. On a third day, he did nothing. Sales of Coca Cola went up 18 percent, and popcorn up 59 percent when the corresponding words had been flashed on the screen during the film.

Although many colleagues did not accept these theories in 1982, other experiments have given the scientific nod to the reality of subliminally induced ideas.

Some radio stations experimented with subliminal messages, and eventually the Federal Communications Commission of the United States Government intervened, held hearings, and banned the practice without deciding on the reality of the influence. Advertisers and broadcasters agreed to. eliminate this practice because of possible dangers.

Subliminal messages seem to be possible, but what about the backward messages? Other researchers have indicated that the brain does not have to receive its information in logical order. The brain has an amazing capacity to accept the information, process it, and either store it away or to use it immediately. Consider, for example, a frequent occurrence among television viewers. Some sit down in a chair to watch TV, others may choose to lie down on a couch or on the floor. Even when a person lies on his or her side while watching TV, the brain is not sensing a TV screen 45 or 90 degrees changed from normal. The person watching TV in this position sees a normal TV screen, and can enjoy the program.

* * *

We must digress a bit further to ascertain another important factor, namely the relationship of rock, heavy metal, and similar forms of music, to the occult and to satanism.

Quotations from rock stars abound on both sides. Some openly admit the connection and their purpose, others deny it vehemently. Here is a sampling of the side that concerns us, followed by some evidence in the album covers, the lyrics (forward as well as backward), and some disastrous incidents culled from news sources.

Bob Larson, in his book, *Rock For Those Who Listen To The Words And Don't Like What They Hear* (Living Books, Tyndale House, Wheaton, Ill. 8th printing, Oct. 1986), packs a lot of information into a single page as he examines a one time popular rock song, "Hotel California":

> The Eagles are a Southern California rock group with a country-rock blend. The band was formed on the occultic teachings of author Carlos Castaneda and nurtured with the help of peyote (an Indian drug — ed.) They chose their name from a major spirit in the Indian cosmos (reported in "Time" Magazine, August 15, 1975, p. 4). The darker side of the supernatural seems to have invaded their lyrics. In "Witchy Woman," they sing of a "restless spirit" who flies through the air with sparks flying from her fingertips. "One of those Nights" has the singer

searching for the "daughter of the devil" who possesses both desires and demons.

Less explicit, but possibly just as diabolical, is their million seller "Hotel California." A man driving in the desert stops for the night. He doesn't seem to be sure where he is ("This could be heaven or . . . hell"). While hearing voices in the night, he orders wine, only to be informed "that spirit" hasn't been around "since 1969." In the end he learns in terror that he can check out but he "can never leave" (p. 40).

One of the most popular groups on the scene even today is Led Zeppelin. "Stairway to Heaven" is perhaps their best song. First glance at the title would not suggest a problem, but an examination of the lyrics indicates that "there are two ways to go, two stairways to face, one to heaven and the other to hell. Me . . . I'll take the second." Furthermore, this particular record also has some of the most obvious backward masking, stating quite plainly, that "there's no escaping it. It's my sweet satan. The one will be the path who makes me sad; whose power is satan."

Here is another example. The British group "Black Sabbath" were reported to hold black masses before some of their concerts (*Backward Masking Unmasked,* Aranze, p. 69). Their first album, "Black Sabbath," pictured a witch on the cover. Another album, "Sabbath, Bloody Sabbath," shows a nude satanic ritual with the numbers 666 across the front of the album. There appears to be little doubt as to their intent.

Investigating further, Geezer Butler of the group is quoted in "Rolling Stone" magazine on October 19, 1971 (p. 41) as claiming to be the seventh son of a seventh son, namely Lucifer, and he can see the devil. "It's a satanic world," admits Geezer, and he also believes in reincarnation (*BMU* p. 71).

Finally, consider Ozzy Osbourne, Black Sabbath's front man until 1979. He was one of the first to link an image of satanic power with the gut-wrenching kick of the music he performs. ("Circus," July 31, 1982, p. 35 — quoted in *BMU* p. 99). On one of his albums he has a song entitled "Mr. Crowley," referring to Aleister Crowley, the late satanist. Osbourne is quoted in "Hit Parader" magazine (February, 1978, p. 24) as saying "I don't know if I'm a medium for some outside force or not. Frankly, whatever it is, I hope it's not what I think it is, Satan."

Returning now to the main topic, it is no longer unusual to hear or read about vandalism with satanic signs and symbols, or about some teenager (usually) who has decided "to go to satan." In September, 1986, for example, a county prosecutor in an eastern state spoke on TV of six cases with satanic signs and symbols, in which all the perpetrators admitted to an inordinate amount of listening to rock and heavy metal music, with some even admitting they got the idea from some of the songs.

Sometime earlier in May, a teenage boy called into a morning television talk show in the Midwest. He admitted to being a satan worshiper for ten years, and was awaiting (with joy) the announcement by the high priest that he was ready to go to satan. The high priest would etch on his body the pentagram and the inverted cross, and when the scratches are just about healed, it would be time. He would then take his own life to be with satan. When questioned as to whether his parents knew his practices or intentions, he replied that they just thought he was going through a fad. He also indicated that he listened to heavy metal music for several hours a day, and found great enjoyment from it, rather than from family, friends, or anyone or anything else.

These examples are public knowledge. It should cause us to wonder how many other cases exist in our communities, just waiting for an opportunity to become known.

Satanism as we have described it here has little relationship to the classical or traditional religious satanism. Most of the perpetrators of vandalism are not seeking to worship the devil. They are seeking to imitate the rock stars. The rock stars themselves may know the full import of their actions, and then again, they may not. But certainly the quotations given here and in other places indicate not only knowledge of satanic activity but a desire to have the power gained from communication with the devil himself, if that be possible for them.

There seems to be, however, yet another element to consider in addition to the subliminal messages, the suggestive music and the propensity of young people to reject anything their elders have to say on a subject. This element might provide the answer to our problem.

Years ago, when people learned the doctrines of their religion carefully, and learned by memory the precepts of morality, they had a firm faith. They could withstand pressure, opposition and even persecution. Oftentimes a persecution would only serve to strengthen the Faith, as is true, for example in Poland today. Individuals were always on guard, lest they be deceived or compromised in any way.

This is not so today. Many people seem to have lost their faith in God, in their country, and in themselves. Examples abound in which people betray friends, exploit family members, and seek to advance themselves in a life of comfort, convenience and pleasure without regard for anyone else.

To provide one possible (and hopefully, plausible) answer for this state of affairs, consider the brain as a receptacle. In this example, the former receptacle is filled with information, knowledge, and motivation, so that when a "foreign message" seeks entrance, it is rejected. Thus the brain would reject "Satan is lord" quite readily. Today, however, without a firm belief in God and the fact that Jesus is Lord, the brain that receives the "satan" message, scans for acceptance or rejection, and not finding a reason to reject it, (i.e. no opposition is in the memory bank) it stores the information, without necessarily accepting it. Later, when other stimuli begin to bring the message "satan lives" or "satan is lord" the brain senses no opposition to these new messages because it recalls the information already received, and now begins to accept it because of the additional accumulation of similar messages.

After a while, with constant messages of a similar content received (such as through continuous listening to the immoral lyrics of certain songs), the brain will then object to that which was normal before. Thus in our example, the content of the music is the norm, and the parental objections are the cause of alienation.

Another element that seems to come into play here is the beat of the music. It annoys parents; it is defended by teens. The repetitious beat, always played loud, of course, has been called hypnotic on more than one occasion. An indication of the validity of this premise comes from Bob Larson in his book, *Rock And Roll: The Devil's Diversion*. He tells of a missionary who took back to Africa with him records of semi-classical music and acid rock. He played both to members of the local tribe. When the semi-classical was played, the people responded with smiles and nods of approval, and they were generally calm and peaceful. Without comment the missionary switched to rock. Immediately their expressions changed, they became confused and agitated. Some grabbed their spears and were ready for war.

A variation of this is told by another missionary who brought back the rock music and was playing it in his own tent. The tribal chief came up to him and inquired why he was playing music to invoke the evil spirits. It seems that the beat of the music was exactly what the tribes used for the evil spirit dance.

The proliferation of opinions on almost every subject by almost anybody, coupled with court decisions on freedom and invasions of privacy have produced a situation which promotes the opinion that there is no absolute truth, no moral standards, and therefore no reason to uphold or obey them. The groundwork for this kind of wholesale "permissiveness" was discussed in Chapter I.

XI

New Age Movement
What Is It?
Is It Really New?

By Rev. Wm. Kent Burtner, O.P.

The "New Age Movement" is not easily defined. A conflation of a variety of non-traditional religious organizations, self-help programs, modern witches, large-group awareness trainings and esoteric satanist groups, New Age expressions are poorly coordinated and differ widely from each other. Despite their differences, however, they share some common ideologies and behavioral manifestations that allow us to talk about them as a whole.

Probably the first common element lies in the type of people attracted to the "New Age." By and large, New Agers are explicitly seeking transcendent experience. Many started off as participants in traditional Christianity, who for lack of understanding, interest, or leadership from within their respective tradition, have become alienated. Following upon the descriptions of societal change found elsewhere in this book, the assertion about new forms made by "channeler" J.Z. Knight is understandable enough: "We're pulling away from congregational, fear-oriented religions" (quoted in "New York Times," 9/29/86).

While Knight mischaracterizes Christianity in general, we know that many Catholic Christians have, rightly or wrongly, perceived themselves as participants of a tradition that dispenses guilt rather than reconciliation. Our large congregations often fail to provide a sense of intimacy to members, leading to the often-heard criticisms that parishes are unfriendly or "cold." Another factor is that the sense of being "special," somehow set apart by virtue of Catholic tradition experienced by our forebearers, has evaporated as the Catholic Church has been "mainstreamed" into the general culture in the U.S. It's not surprising this alienation has produced a longing for more personal, integrated spiritual experiences.

A lack of distinction among the divergent New Age strains is all too typical of both proponents and critics of the New Age. While this writer doesn't share their perspective, there are those, like attorney-turned-New-Age-counter-evangelist Constance Cumbey, who are convinced that there is an enormous conspiracy coordinated by the forces of darkness to bring about the ruin of Western Culture and Christian religion in particular. (Cumbey's *The Hidden Dangers of the Rainbow* is a clear statement of this premise.) Nor do I hold that the New Age movement is a form of "creeping Hinduism" (my term) as would authors such as Carole Matriciana (*Gods of the New Age*). While much of the New Age Movement is impelled by curiosity about the East, there is plenty in our Western tradition to be used to validate it and not all of it is inherently evil.

The New Age: Common Ideologies and Divergent Difficulties.

While the behaviors of New Age groups continue to be of serious concern, common themes, some with dramatic implications, are found in New Age ideologies.

Most New Age groups include blends of some Eastern religious expressions and Western psychology. For instance, Bhagwan Shree Rajneesh developed a group which used Hindu religious forms and some Hindu spiritual disciplines, but blended together with that were many different forms of encounter group therapies and "Esalen" type sensitivity training. Sylva Mind Control training gives some interesting and useful Western technical information and skills at the basic level, but higher levels of training lead one to study "chakras" and other concepts derived directly from Hindu theology.

Not all the ideas found in New Age groups are intrinsically problematic. Rather they are an admixture of truisms, useful ideas, notions antithetical to Christianity (such as gnosticism and monism), and in some particular groups, ideas that could lead practitioners to pathological states of mind.

If there is such a thing as a New Age primer, Richard Bach's *Illusions: The Adventures of a Reluctant Messiah* (Laurel Books, Dell Publishing Co., Inc., 1981) would be a good selection. Professor Bach, who is most famous for *Johnathan Livingston Seagull*, is neither a leader of a destructive cult nor is he insincere. But *Illusions* gives a cursory look at ideas that are part and parcel of the New Age.

The protagonist of *Illusions* is given a book called *Messiah's Handbook and Reminders for the Advanced Soul*. From it he gleans pieces of "wisdom." A few are excerpted here for our consideration.

> You teach best what you most need to learn. . . (p. 60).

This is an example of an idea that is not at all crazy: oftentimes people do teach things that are significant in their lives, things about which they need to understand in themselves. How many counselors do we know who were motivated to enter the field by their own need for self-understanding? Many such truisms are contained both in Bach's book and in the New Age movement generally. These serve to validate the whole picture for its adherents. But it goes a step further:

> Learning is finding out what you already know. Doing is demonstrating that you know it. Teaching is reminding others that they know just as well as you. . . (p. 58).

With this we reach a new order of magnitude. This statement assumes each of us carries within ourself the totality of knowledge about everything. It's a far cry from *tabula rasa*!

But it is not enough that we know everything, we also create it:

> . . . Remember where you came from, where you're going, and why you created the mess you got yourself into in the first place. . . (p. 56).

This truism is not simply a metaphor saying your choices are meaningful and the ones you make will have their direct effects on your life. Rather it implies that whatever is happening to you is directly a result of your choosing to create it. This creation includes illnesses, traffic accidents, inheritances, random events, what you read in the paper. But there is a reason for this ability to create reality:

> . . . What is going on around you is not reality. . . The world . . . is not reality, although you can express reality there if you wish (p. 127).

The implication is simple: all of life is a form of illusion. Reality rests only in your consciousness. How you project it is the only distinguishing element. If you are sufficiently advanced, all you have to do is to change your projection, and you will no longer be limited by your environment. The idea is basically a return to infantile omnipotence and narcissism, but coated with mystic garb in a monist philosophy. Phrased in the negative this reads:

> Argue for your limitations, and sure enough, they're yours (p. 100).

This thinking has implications for relationships with others:

> Your only obligation in any lifetime is to be true to yourself. . . (p. 59).

Shakespeare said, "To thine own self be true. . ." but the dispensation from responsible living finds a new order of magnitude in New Age thinking.

> The best way to avoid responsibility is to say, 'I've got responsibilities' (p. 61).

No doubt, some may make excuses for their lives and dodge real issues on the basis of "other responsibilities," but this same sort of axiom can be used, and has been, as an excuse to avoid responsibility. To whom should you be responsible if the following is held to be true?

> If you will practice being fictional for a while, you will understand that fictional characters are sometimes more real than people with bodies and heartbeats (p. 135).

Bach also quotes from the *Messiah's Handbook* to refer to

some ground of being: "The original sin is to limit the Is. Don't." (p. 128)

But just whether this statement refers to anything outside one's own consciousness is not clear either in *Illusions* or other New Age literature.

Paradox is inherently a part of most belief systems. But the New Age viewpoint tends to become paradoxical in a very different way than one finds in Christianity. We speak of the power of God being manifested on the cross. Of course, on the face of it, the cross is a symbol of weakness and failure. Jesus becomes powerful precisely because He is able to lay His life down. Truly a paradox, yet one which can be reasoned about, discussed, and at some real level, made sense of.

What is known to the psychological community as "cognitive dissonance theory" says that one cannot hold two contradictory ideas in one's mind at the same time. Yet when a group insists on its members trying to do just this, the distinctions between the real and unreal are blurred. One modern cult, having developed a process claimed to eliminate all the adherent's personality defects, asks as part of one of its exercises, that adherents "recall an imaginary event" from their past. After much pressure, the participant in this exercise inevitably will perform this seemingly impossible act, having strained the boundary between reality and fantasy. They are now primed for a whole series of exercises that will cause them to reframe their perspective on their entire life. This last example from the *Messiah's Handbook* typifies just this sort of paradox:

> Everything in this book may be wrong (p. 181).

The social implications of New Age thinking were underscored in an article by journalist B.J. Williams:

> . . . the emphasis on the positive, on individual responsibility and on the importance of self-esteem and fulfillment long have been clichés of counseling and education. But the twist that New Agers give these concepts places them in serious conflict with traditional moralists.
>
> . . . The emphasis on the positive comes at the expense of duty, obedience, penitence and humility . . . New Agers stress the subjective nature of reality. — *Taken from "Head Trip: The Troubled Search for Enlightenment." (Portland, Oregon: The Oregonian Sunday Northwest Magazine. 8/9/87)*

Another idea consistantly found to be a part of the New Age ideology is reincarnation. This belief offers some comfort for those who believe that if they didn't get things "right" this time around, they can return and perhaps get it right the next time. Former professor of religious studies and counselor Kathleen McLaughlin observes this is a Westernized version of the Hindu concept of karma that becomes a cosmic guilt trip for some adherents (Lecture, Professional Development Seminar, Portland, Oregon, 1987).

McLaughlin points out that the Hindu notion of karma is simply that one's actions of today have specific consequences that don't necessarily show up immediately, but which nonetheless are the result of particular behaviors. New Agers oftentimes allow themselves to become riddled with guilt because of karmas from past lives or fearful of accruing bad karma that will be passed along to future lives. Conversely, they sometimes will completely exempt themselves from personal responsibility because "it's my karma." One therapist reported that a New Age believer came to her frazzled: she was working many extra hours, literally burning herself out on all the promotional activities of her group, while struggling to hold down a job, raise children, and keep her marriage together. She concluded that she had "bad karma." The fact of her overburdened schedule had not occurred to her as problematic.

Responsibility to others often falls victim to the way of karmic consciousness, too. As Williams observes:

> The charge of self-centeredness . . . has been leveled at the New Age since the 60s . . . for them, social responsibility finishes a poor second behind self-discovery (Williams, Op. cit.).

Compassion is also a victim of such thinking:

> . . . When channeler Paul Tuttle was asked what would have been an appropriate New Age response to the Nazis . . . the heart of his prepared statement was this sentence: "The energy for Hitler's growth was resident in those victimized." In so many words, Hitler was at least partly the creation of the millions who died at his hand (Ibid.).

New Age: Groups and Phenomena

A plethora of both cults and more open "movements" co-exist within the context of the New Age. Groups on both ends of the spectrum are oftentimes externally indistinguishable from one another, but some have the typical hidden agendas and "insider teachings" kept from neophytes that are characteristics of traditional cults.

The Calfornia-based "Family of Friends" and the "Fourth Way," which study the teachings of mystics Gurdjieff, an Armenian, and Ouspensky, his Russian interpreter, are typical of this genre. Seen externally, these are typical of a variety of "study groups" based around New Age teachings. The difference is the authority structure within them, making them little different from other modern cults. The authors of this book heard numerous accounts of family members being alienated from one another, parents deserting children and spouses, and persons coming under the undue influence of leaders in such groups.

But one does not have to find a New Age cult in order to have the same magnitude of consequences. Merely a group that will unbridle you from your immediate frame of reference and seemingly remove your frustrations will do as well.

Typically, New Agers find study groups gathered around one or another "teachers" or "teachings." Those who cast themselves in the role of teacher may be quite well intentioned, and not profit personally from their endeavors; others are very much concerned with maintaining a highly structured group in line with whatever they perceive should be the proper relation to the "tradition."

Most New Age teachers will appeal to the authority of an "ancient tradition" from which their teachings are derived. While such allegations may or may not be a manipulation used to convince potential believers, the fact of such an appeal is curious in light of the fact that so many adherents have fled other "traditions" they felt were stultifying.

Among the variety of teachers who pull their students "close-in" are "channelers." These individuals have learned, either spontaneously or through explicit training from others, to allow another "entity" to take possession of their bodies for limited periods of time, in order to give lectures, seminars, or personal consultations about various New Age "truths." Upon completion of the lecture, channelers are allowed to "come back" to their own bodies. The "entities" rarely have their own bank accounts: most commonly, the channeler receives compensation for the services rendered.

The "entities" are usually mystical types from human prehistory, persons who have evolved to live in "other dimensions," or occasionally who come from other solar systems. The most popular of these speak through their channelers in a language style that could be typified as New Age "newspeak" couched in the King's English. (A notable, recent exception is a young African member of Sun Myung Moon's Unification Church. He claims that the spirit of Moon's son, Heung Jin Nim, who was killed in an automobile accident in 1984 at the age of 17, has assumed his body. Moon has accepted this as authentic, and the pseudo Hueng Jin Nim goes about the world speaking to Moon disciples encouraging them to "follow center" and be faithful to Moon's program of international political influence. Cf. "Washington Post" article by Michael Isikoff, March 28, 1988.)

Channelers tend to have a larger influence over their followers than typical New Age teachers. Under the influence of J.Z. Knight's entity, Ramtha, hundreds of people have fled their homes and moved into the area surrounding Knight's commodious residence in Yelm, Washington, so as to be protected from the coming world cataclysm. When such ethereal entities suggest a divorce is in order, adherents often act without further thought of the consequences.

But one is hard pressed to wonder whether an illiterate 35,000-year-old warrior from the lost continent of Atlantis (Ramtha) is any better qualified to give advice than the clerk at the local all-night convenience store. I'd trust the clerk — at least the chances of finding a humble listener would be much better!

Psychic readers are also among the most common New Age practitioners. These folks offer advice and assistance by giving their clients "readings": obtaining self-revelatory information that can be used to better their lives. This information may be gleaned from seeking the clients "aura," a kind of bodily halo which gifted psychics can perceive; from perceiving in a mystical way a person's past lives: i.e. where the client lived in past ages, what social rank they held, whether they were romantically or otherwise involved with their present friend, lover, or relative, etc.; from doing "energy readings," i.e. picking up one's "vibrations" and so obtaining requested information. Some of the "old standbys" are also employed: palmistry, phrenology, Tarot cards, and trances. Often good sense and common advice gets "mystified" and most clients come away sufficiently satisfied to plan their next "reading."

Some New Age practitioners are concerned about their

clients' physical and mental health, which they claim can be helped by the wearing of or application of crystals to their bodies. These stones vary from simple pieces of cut colored glass to expensive mineral crystals costing hundreds of dollars. Crystals can be "tuned" to give off the proper energy for their wearers. Clients can be given treatments with crystals to align the "energy patterns" in their bodies so that they will no longer be out of balance. Some New Age adherents become quite attached to their crystals, to the point of becoming fearful if one is broken. Truly, crystals have become the talismans of the New Age movement.

Large group awareness trainings (LGATs for short) are part and parcel of the modern age. Starting two decades ago, William Penn Patrick packaged a multi-level marketing program called Holiday Magic. One of its subsidiaries was Mind Dynamics, a group that was eventually put out of business by the civil authorities of the state of California. As its name suggests, Mind Dynamics combined a number of powerful therapeutic strategies that could be mass marketed.

The key to these programs was to put individuals in a situation where they participated (unknowingly) in group hypnosis and a variety of encounter-group exercises. Individuals quickly found that they had surrendered part of their super-ego to the "trainers," who in exchange gave them a "group high" and developed a dependency coupled with notions that created a sense of omnipotence.

Typical of all LGATs is the New Age idea that "you create your own reality." The notion is often carried to such extremes that people abandon their professional training in favor of the new outlook they have been given. Literally, entire lives have been "reframed" and value hierarchies radically altered. One particularly striking example comes from a case in the Pacific Northwest. A counselor attended an LGAT, paid for by her professional agency. During one of the sessions, she told the trainer that she had been sexually abused by her older brother when she was a child. Her trainer, having laid the groundwork ahead of time, insisted that she explain how it was that she had caused that rape to happen. Having experienced the pressure of the LGAT and having come to "understand" that she "creates her own reality," she proceeded to explain that she had really wanted to have this happen to her. One shudders to think what this professionally trained person, now having shed what she learned from many valid sources about child molestation over many years, will now say to a child coming to her for professional assistance. Among Patrick's subordinates were John Hanley and Werner Erhard. Erhard went on to start "e.s.t.," or Erhard Seminars Training, later slightly modified to become known as "The Forum." Hanley subsequently began LifeSpring.

These people don't have a corner on the market for LGATs, however. Similar programs have been launched around the country by "John-Roger" (Insight Seminars), Randy Revel (Context Training), Gary Koyen (Wings), and Thomas D. Wilhite (PSI world).

One interesting byproduct of the LGATs and some of the groups more commonly perceived as "cults" is in the field of Management Training. An excerpt from the "New York Times" (9/29/86) is telling:

> Ford Motor Company, Westinghouse, and the Calvin Klein fashion house are among the scores of major companies that have sent employees for training, according to "human potential" organizations such as Transformation Technologies, Life-Spring, and Actualizations, all of which include techniques modeled to a greater or lesser extent after the techniques started by Werner Erhard, the founder of EST. "We teach new patterns of thinking" said Stewart Emery, Chairman of Actualizations.

The bottom line for these activities is clear: money — and lots of it. One "management training program" affiliated with Scientology in Portland, Oregon, grosses $240,000 per month on programs in the Pacific Northwest.

Another aspect of the New Age is the reemergence of an old favorite — witchcraft. For most of us, the term "witchcraft" conjures up images of old crones standing around a boiling cauldron, or Halloween-style witches with craggy faces and long noses flying about on broomsticks, vestiges of the Wicked Witch of the East from "The Wizard of Oz." Modern witches on the other hand, tend to be young women, many of them feminists, who are more concerned with replenishing the energy of the mother earth than fussing with eye of newt. According to research by Margot Adler and others (*Drawing Down the Moon*, Beacon Press, 1986, p. 444). Converts to witchcraft come from virtually every present day tradition, and in the same proportions as represented in the general population.

Practitioners of Wicca (the name of this tradition, "wicca," is Middle English) refer to their religious style as "the old religion" or "the Craft." The modern age is dominated by the disciples of the "Sky Father," who enjoys domination of the world at the present time. Once there was a pristine time when the disciples of the earth mother were predominant. Then the world enjoyed peace and harmony, for the ways of compassion were more important than power, and the energies and intuitions supressed by modern humanity were given more emphasis.

Modern Wicca resembles a spiritual support group more than a church. Like other aspects of New Age spirituality, Wiccans are often as not "divided by a common spirituality." A variety of "traditions" exist and the various interpreters of those traditions often disagree.

Their common thread is the concept of a "nature religion," often referred to as "neo-paganism." The cycles of nature are taken seriously, and practitioners seek to perform their rituals according to the energies and moods of the seasons. Some of them feel that they are the spiritual aspect of the ecology movement.

Wicca is a poly-theistic tradition. Like Hinduism, it accepts "all the gods," and one would be faulted for being exclusively tied to just one god. Practitioners believe they have tied into an interior power which may be worked for good purposes. (If used for evil it's called "black witchcraft.") Ultimately, one's problems and the problems of the world will be worked out ritually. Wicca has a compassionate side: working rituals and laying on of hands for healing, helping the process of world peace by its prayers, making its magic available to benefit others, and giving honor to the earth mother goddess from whom Wiccans believe they have been derived. Because of their association with nature, it is also pantheism.

Modern new-paganism would have made psychologist C. G. Jung quite happy. Jung believed that there are many "archetypes" present in the unconscious mind, images that are the product of our common life experiences and the ways in which we encounter the world. Many of these are plainly evident in the Wiccan religious system, and are dealt with according to the needs of the various practitioners. There are "traditions" against which one's work may be evaluated, but the ultimate test and responsibility rests with the individual.

Wiccans tend to organize into small groups, called "covens," several of which are sometimes grouped into "groves." Some practitioners are designated to instruct the initiates; teaching basic rituals; giving them guidance along the path of Wicca; as well as instructing them in the keeping of their individual Book of Shadows, a personal spiritual journal that includes one's subjective record of religious experience, including rituals and their effects, and which should be destroyed upon one's death or departure from "the Craft." A variety of periodicals (c.f. Adler, op. cit.) keep Wiccans in touch with each other and loosely knit associations put together occasional conferences and large-group rituals.

All of this paints a fairly benign picture of Wicca. For the great majority of practitioners, this seems to be true. However, besides the obvious theological implications some occasional problems surface.

There is an indistinct boundary between the more "mainline" Wiccan practitioners and those whose drive for power might be less than well motivated. For example, Wiccans generally profess no belief in the Christian fallen angel, satan. For them, satanism is seen as a Christian heresy. But unfortunately for the advocates of modern Wicca, much of the twentieth-century interest in Wicca is the legacy of Aleister Crowley, the late British "Luciferian," whose writings have influenced other modern day groups such as Scientology (if we are to believe accounts written by founder L. Ron Hubbard's son and others), the Process, and certain satanist and "black magic" groups. Organizations like the Ordo Templis Orientis, for whom satan is the source of power, also claim the Wiccan tradition.

There sometimes emerge patterns of manipulation within some Wiccan groups that can be cause for concern. For example, Wicca is intrinsically not organized along lines of accountability. Thus, a manipulative individual can more easily cause problems for others within this context than in some other social groups. Wiccan practitioner and writer Starhawk, in an interview with this author, cited the need for a given coven to be in communion with other groups in the Wiccan community.

Additionally, she is critical about any group that would practice ostracism, or any form of physical abuse, or other cult-like manifestations, for example not having a set length of time of apprenticeship prior to initiation. She would insist that counseling and guidance be a separate function from training in "the Craft."

Author Margot Adler (ibid., p. 509) quotes a list of fifteen concerns that form a Cult Danger Evaluation Frame for those who might wish to be involved. These roughly parallel those marks of cults found in other places in this work. Wiccan groups are not intrinsically cult-like, but as in society at large and as in any other ideology there are sociopathic and opportunistic individuals who are able and willing to exploit anyone.

Many sources are available to learn about Wicca, the use of crystals, finding your past lives, seeing and reading auras, understanding yourself, and all the tenets of the New Age.

Among the most popular of the later genre is *A Course in Miracles*. This three-volume text was written by Helen Schuckman in Marin County, California, between 1965 and 1973, Schuckman claims that the content was given to her from a "Voice" she heard within, supposedly Jesus Christ. She teaches that each person can become a Savior-Son of God through change in mental attitudes. The body of the material has much in common with transpersonal psychology and modern gnosticism.

New Age: Use and Abuse of Altered States of Consciousness.

A variety of altered state of consciousness exercises has long been available. Up to the present, the usual means of learning these has been through the training of therapists, hypnotherapists, and some religious practitioners. These exercises include relaxation techniques, behavior modification, deep meditation, visualization/imaging, as well as other related techniques. What has happened in the New Age movement is that these tools have been "mass marketed" with two very interesting effects.

The first is that many of the groups using such practices do not tell their clients that their selected techniques are part of a standard mental-health or religious collection, most of which have been around for a long time. The impression is given that these are the unique tools of the New Age movement, or that they are uniquely available in that particular group. Thus the practitioners come to believe that their group has a unique power or special insight and often will surrender autonomy to the group in order to get the special benefits of being part of the "elect."

Secondly, these tools are then used to provide certain experiences to the participants. The group will interpret the meaning of the experience in such a way as to validate the authority of the group, rather than attributing these experiences to the individual himself or herself. The "unique insight of the leadership," or some similar other agency, is then in control of the responses of the individual. LGATs commonly use techniques borrowed from hypnosis; quite easily, whole groups of people are put "under." While under the influence of hypnosis, the participants will be led through emotionally charged experiences. Afterwards, the group will disavow the fact that the participants were under such a state, and will cause them to believe that it was due to the special charism of the leader or group that such an experience was even possible. The fact is, the experience could be completely reproduced anywhere if the subject were to undergo hypnosis.

So it happens that an uninformed person under the influence of a particular group, is led to "discover" wonderful new techniques, and comes to believe the techniques to be exclusively available within that group. The person then allows the group to interpret the significance of the experiences. In this pattern lies a serious threat to the autonomy of the individual and a powerful means to attract and keep followers.

These techniques are not in themselves harmful when used by trained, experienced clinicians. But within the New Age movement, they are too often used by persons unfamiliar with the context from which they are derived. The results can sometimes be quite hazardous.

Most altered state exercises begin with relaxation, and then continue with intensified concentration. Relaxation techniques themselves are usually quite beneficial. The reduction of tension and stress can lower blood pressure and relieve headaches.

Once a state of relaxation is reached, one may then proceed to use the accompanying ability to concentrate intensely for good or ill. To be sure, whatever messages are given at that point are apt to be well remembered. Particular suggestions can have long-lasting implications.

Proposing scenes with spiritual or psychological themes in a clinical environment is referred to as "visualization" or "guided imagery." Again, experienced clinicians can use these as tools to good effect.

One can continue to use this state to cause people to have "experiences" such as reliving their birth ("rebirthing"), imaginary travels to other places ("soul travel" or "astral projection"), discovery of their "past lives," and other "inner space" events that could be either real, imaginary or a combination of both (see below).

Post-hypnotic suggestions may also be given. These may include the order that the subject will not recall certain parts of the exercises, or other things that took place during the sessions. (One particular group, PSI World, is notorious for producing participants who are unable to even recall what took place during their weekend "trainings.")

Another aspect is the induction of stress and sensory overload. Intensifying an environment with the addition of pulsating sound, heightened information input, or other sensory stimulation has the effect of breaking down one's normal means of processing incoming information. The group can then give information to their overloaded subjects who will retain it uncritically and at sub-conscious levels.

The phenomenon of "channeling" can be more easily understood in the context of altered states training. When a person is in an altered state, the boundaries in one's personality between five-sense reality, imagination and memory are lowered. It is then possible to see and experience as real, things which are only products of imagination and memory. Virtually every person I have interviewed who has experienced a recollection of past lives has done so in an altered state of consciousness.

Extending this to the phenomenon of channeling, if a person is disposed to believe in channeling and has practiced placing him or herself into an altered state of consciousness with the intention of allowing another "entity" to take over, it is rather certain that the practitioner will have that experience. This experience is in reality similar to an actor or actress "putting themselves into their character" (in a much less severe manifestation of the same phenomenon), and analagous to the development of a multiple personality in a person with dissociative psychopathology.

Legitimate altered states of consciousness exist in both Eastern and Western religious traditions. Trappist Thomas Merton found much in the East that paralleled his experience born of the Western mystical tradition. Zen masters have found in the writings of medieval Dominican mystic Meister Eckhart an example of their own understanding.

Psychologist Carl Jung (*The Collected Works of C. G. Jung, Vol. 11, Religions East and West*) observed that the Eastern meditation practice of sitting and staring at a mandala is similar to the Roman Catholic practice of Adoration of the Blessed Sacrament. Simply looking at the circular form has an unconsciously healing benefit. Persons reciting the Rosary often find themselves in a slightly altered state of consciousness that allows them to dispel the "noise" of their surroundings and concentrate on the symbols of their religion, not unlike the mental states reported by Zen meditators.

Jesuit William Johnston, in his book *Silent Music*, observes many such similarities. He points out that in a meditative state, one is still "in touch" with one's surroundings in a way that is qualitatively different from what takes place in more intense forms of altered states.

Legitimate altered states are not harmful to their practitioners. What marks the difference between these and some New Age forms is that practitioners generally know what to expect here, there is no hidden agenda with regard to what will take place, and the practices have been shown over the years to be without harm to their practitioners.

The "bottom line" in our consideration is that there is a wide variety of altered state experiences which may be used to the betterment or harm of those who participate in them. In either abusive or in well-intentioned but ignorant hands, these exercises can validate ideologies in a totally illogical manner, and the ideologies can be used to validate the experiences produced. There is no guarantee of truth, only of a circular involvement that may prevent the person involved from coming to grips with the ineluctable burden of discovering truth and may prevent them from making free, informed decisions about life.

Conclusions About the New Age Movement

Some researchers into New Age groups have suggested that the movement resembles a kind of "leaderless cult." Indeed, some of the manifestations we see are similar to the psychodynamics of cults.

One example is the way in which double messages quickly translate into guilt:

> One of the channelers predicted an earthquake last summer. "I took the pictures off the wall and set the television on the floor. And then, of course, I warned all my friends about it. When it didn't happen I felt really betrayed for a day or two."
>
> And then he felt guilty. Recognizing that thought creates reality, he felt the pressure to be careful about letting his mind wander. "If there had been an earthquake," he explains, "the energy of my thoughts would have been added to it" (B.J. Williams, Op. Cit.).

In the midst of many protests about new found freedoms and rejection of traditional authority figures, many New Agers find their way to the camps of charismatic leaders who exert great authority over their followers often in a way much stronger than traditional figures.

It is interesting to observe a striking similarity between New Agers and Fundamentalists. For instance, with regard to channeling, those who "believe" in the phenomenon claim that there really *are* entities out there coming to give us information and wisdom. The Fundamentalists typically respond by agreeing that, "yes, indeed, those really are spiritual entities doing the talking through their trance mediums. But they are evil spirits with the wisdom of the Devil!" Both extremes agree on the validity of the phenomenon while disagreeing on the righteousness of the source.

Such agreement isn't surprising. Fundamentalists and New Agers both admit to an appeal to the emotional, intuitive side of things, to a capacity for suspension of disbelief and an appeal to the heart rather than the mind.

Not everything in the New Age movement is necessarily harmful. The movement is eclectic, borrowing from any human discipline that "seems to fit," but a number of potentially threatening elements have converged in the New Age movement.

A former devotee of Ramtha made a salient comment: "The drug of the 60s was LSD and marijuana. I think the drug of the 80s might be cosmic consciousness" (Carey Klinger, quoted in "New York Times," 9/29/86).

In our times, social, political, and economic conditions seem chaotic. These conditions pressure us, make seemingly endless demands that often seem senseless. An ideology that removes one from the objectivity of this world and leaves real responsibilities to be decided on a purely subjective level has an appeal which can be understood if not accepted. The success of the New Age movement may be explained by the fact that we are creatures who seek to make meaningful the events of our world. The New Age offers ways and answers, albeit often bizarre ones.

The New Age movement poses some serious challenges for all of us. It operates on an ideological base that is quite different from a "five-sense" orientation, or Realist philosophical assumptions about the world, that most of us operate with, and different from the theological positions held by Christians. Those ideas are not always said out boldly or honestly, and we would be well off if we were to ask many kinds of tough questions if we are presented with a novel experience to try, or some alternative way of dealing with reality. Not everything new will harm us, but as St. Paul suggests, we should "test all things."

A vast array of "new" spiritual experiences are offered by an equally large group of practitioners. Some of these have a validity tested by time and stand up to close scrutiny. Many do not. Many persons with professional credentials have unwittingly bought into systems they either do not understand or choose not to consider critically. Not every credentialed person offers only good things.

Particularly significant among these are altered states of consciousness exercises. These are strikingly easy to produce. Almost anyone can learn to do them. But not everyone who knows how to guide people through them knows what to do when something goes awry for particular individuals sensitive to particular stimuli. Nor does having the ability to open the door to someone's unconscious mean that the material to be placed there is valuable.

Because of the ubiquitous tendency toward guilt found in all people, the same traps that we find so often in cults also abound in the New Age milieu. All of the cautions about cults found elsewhere in this book can be applied here in varying degrees as well:

> — Ask lots of tough questions *and* validate the given answers through sources you know and trust.
> — Anyone who causes you to feel guilty may have something to gain by it.
> — Your feelings, whatever they are, are "okay" and you have a right to them.
> — Take particularly good care of yourself when you are feeling down or depressed. That's when we are most vulnerable.

We can see, then, that much of the New Age isn't all that new, and not all of it is potentially threatening. But it presents a new and very broad opportunity for deviant groups and individuals to abuse the minds of others. Let us keep our eyes open and our minds alert.

XII

Countering the Cults

Like alcoholism and drug addition, it has taken many years to recognize the seriousness of the cult problem. Even today there are people who will defend a person's right to drink as much as he or she desires, regardless of whether or not such an action produces drunkenness. The traffic in addictive drugs and the freedom for individuals to use them are also defended by some as an inherent right, not to be curtailed in any way, at any time.

The cult phenomenon has not escaped its share of "freedom" defenders either. One of the first objections raised against any effort to counter the cult problem is that such efforts restrict the freedom of the individual to participate in the cultic group.

As a conclusion to this consideration of the cults, sects and new religious movements, this final chapter will be devoted to a look at three major documents that promote religious and individual freedoms. For an American, of course, the Constitution of the United States is the foremost guarantee of religious freedom and human rights. For the Catholic Church there is

Dignitatis Humanae, the Declaration on Religious Freedom of the Second Vatican Council, promulgated on December 7th,. 1965. For the world-community, there is the 1949 Universal Declaration of Human Rights of the United Nations.

Before examining these documents in relation to the problem of cults, sects and new religious movements, it will be helpful to review the activity of cult protagonists, and some of the groups themselves who expend every effort to discredit those who oppose cults, sects, and new religious movements. Misguided emphasis on statements of the above documents quite often confuse the ordinary person seeking to evaluate the cult phenomenon. Some cult protagonists, for example, will imitate the tactics of the cults as meanings of words are changed. The intentions of the opponents of cults are questioned at the same time the protagonists proclaim their own purity of intention. Often individuals skilled in specialized academic or professional disciplines will exceed the boundaries of their own competence in applying principles of their own familiar discipline improperly to another one. Sociologists, for example, often use the same principles of data gathering and evaluation of measurable items, as they attempt to explain the values of religious activities, which are immeasurable.

In addition, some cult protagonists seek to apply the principles of the Second Vatican Council on ecumenism, to dealings with the cultic group, and severely criticize those who oppose the cults as violating the spirit of the Council and the Church. Joseph H. Fichter, a Jesuit priest eminently known as a sociologist, crossed over into the realm of cults with his book *The Holy Family of Father Moon* (Leaven Press, Kansas City, Mo. 1985). He writes:

> I have two objective reasons for making a study of the Moonies. The first is my deep desire to promote the ecumenical outreach which has been a modern feature of the Catholic Church since the Second Vatican Council. This I see as an obligation for the fully committed religious believer. The second motive is my concern about the prevalent religious bigotry that is being expressed against the so-called "cults," the new religious movements, especially the Unification Church. To replace bigotry with tolerance and ignorance with information seems a worthy objective in a democratic society (p. 4).

However, he seems to ignore the concerns of many religious leaders when he states:

> There seems to be an almost systematic program of defamation of groups like Hare Krishnas, Children of God, the Unification Church, the Forever Family, and the Way International. These were specifically singled out for a warning by the General Secretary of the United States Catholic Conference in a letter to the American Bishops. He said that "the rise and propagation of various kinds of religious and semi-religious cults has been a growing phenomenon in the United States over the last decade or more. . . ."
>
> This kind of polite warning by one Catholic bishop was expanded to a collective condemnation of the cults after the mass wedding of 2042 Moonie couples at Madison Square Garden. The "New York Times" headlined the news "Major Faiths in City Undertaking First United Effort Against Cults." We read that Jews, Catholics, and Protestants "have joined together this summer for the first time to combat what they call destructive cults, mentioning in partiuclar the Unification Church of the Reverend Sun Myung Moon." We have here an unholy alliance, publicly endorsed by prominent religious leaders to conduct a deliberate religious persecution (p. 6).

Unfortunately, actions speak louder than words. Father Fichter sets himself up against the General Secretary of the United States Catholic Conference, Bishop Thomas F. Kelly (now the Archbishop of Louisville). He fails to note that the "undertaking" in the "New York Times" article is the Interfaith Coalition of Concern about Cults, founded in 1982. In addition, Father Fichter's book is quite favorable to the Unification Church, and he himself has been a professor at the Unification Church Seminary in Barrytown, New York, as recently as 1986.

In an article in "U.S. Catholic" magazine (November, 1984), William J. Whalen, author of a number of books on cults, seems to have changed his position, for his article is entitled "Christians Shouldn't Condemn Cults." In this article he takes all the usual accusations against the cults, and ridicules the reasoning behind the accusations, and then shows (erroneously

— in my view, at least) that the Catholic Church is guilty of an identical procedure. In making his comparison, Whalen ignores all the evidence gathered over the past decade and more, both about the cults and about human behavior. To quote a typical piece of unsupported generalization will be sufficient to indicate Whalen's approach to the problem:

> Should Christians applaud people who decide to devote their lives to God as monks or Salvation Army officers or missionaries, but condemn young people who decide, albeit mistakenly, to find salvation or save the world by following one of the new cults? Christians had best think twice before trying to deny a young man or woman the right to pursue a spiritual goal and accept the sacrifice it entails.
>
> "But cults recruit new members through deception!" Do they? How dull-witted would young people have to be to sign on with the Hare Krishna, shave their heads, wear Indian garb out on the streets, spend hours chanting and beating drums to the amusement of passersby, and still imagine that they had somehow gotten involved with the YMCA or the Catholic Youth Organization? (p. 13).

Anyone familiar with the problem of cults, sects, and new religious movements, should be able to punch holes in the above reasoning, particularly if he or she has been reading this book.

The key word in Whalen's argumentation in the first quotation is DECIDE. No one will argue with anyone's free decision to follow a particular way of life, religious or not. But the only free decision made in the pathway to a cult is the initial decision to listen to the group, enjoy the free meal, or take the free trip. The techniques of manipulation, love bombing, and tunnel vision (or isolation) make the decision-making process meaningless. It is not the result of a free and informed choice.

With regard to the second item, we have an example of ridicule and transference. No one would try to state that one who joined a cult thought they were joining the YMCA or the CYO. No one would call such a person dull-witted either. What astute people recognize though, is that young people are idealistic and are willing to follow a leader who promises good results. Meditation, self-improvement goals, and promises of success are what motivate a person to go along with the invitations despite the fact that the individual may be lacking sufficient knowledge about the group.

173

In the above example, we would heartily agree that no one would join the Hare Krishnas if they knew they were to shave their heads, wear Indian garb and spend hours chanting. We know that these things were not told to them on the first day that they expressed interest in the group. We would also disagree as to what made them join. Mr. Whalen calls it a free decision. Those who truly understand the workings of the cults see it as manipulation in its most severe form.

More recently, a new sound has come from the cult arena, a cry for dialogue. Using as their facade, the Vatican Document of May, 1986 (cf. Appendix IX) one group has been quite active in this matter. Since the Catholic Church did not immediately jump at the "opportunity" for dialogue with the cults, the Unification Church decided to take the matter into their hands.

They arranged to have the Catholic University of America to host and sponsor the event in conjunction with the National Council of Catholic Women and Church Women United, on April 27, 1987. They assembled a planning committee of Catholics, Protestants, and the Unification Church President in America.

They had several planning meetings, and considered in great detail the people to be invited. To lend further credence to their project, they asked Father Remi Hoeckman, O.P., from the Pontifical University of St. Thomas Aquinas in Rome — the Angelicum, to be the keynote and principal speaker.

However, they neglected to invite anyone (clergy or laity) who has been actively involved in the counseling of parents and young people involved in cults.

In the letterhead used for the conference, "The Catholic University of America" was in prominent type on the second line. The co-sponsors were listed. However, only in the small print on the bottom does the name of Dr. Durst and the Unification Church appear.

According to some of the participants, the program was informative and interesting. There was a heavy emphasis on dialogue and understanding, but little discussion of the real problems the cults present, the problems that concern many parents and educators, particularly those whose children become involved in cults, sects and new religions.

In fulfillment of one of the recommendations of this conference, a second conference was planned for December 12th in Los Angeles, but was rescheduled for January 11-12, 1988, when some of the new cosponsors withdrew. This time the location was Loyola Marymount University.

According to a report of the meeting sent to participants this program had "two main emphases: the theological, pastoral, ecumenical aspects, and the public or court issues."

A companion page stated, "This announces the formation of the AMERICAN CONFERENCE ON RELIGIOUS MOVEMENTS based on the support engendered by the above named conferences, the need for continued consultation and dialogue, and most importantly, the expressed enthusiasm of so many participants."

Note how manipulation and deception is present once again. A handful of people have decided that the words "cult," "sect" or "new religious movement" are no longer to be used. The report on page 2 reads:

> Over the next 12 months, ACRM plans to:
> — Foster dialogue among religious leaders, the media, the bar, the judiciary, theologates, and those responsible for church programming — to achieve better understanding of respective beliefs, modes of operation and mutual problems.
> — Analyze opposition to religious movements (RMs) (RMs rather than "NRMs, cults or sects") and to blunt or obliterate that opposition insofar as it it unjustified.

Here again, nine months later, the real pastoral problems are not addressed but seen only as opposition.

Some people, however, identified the strategy of the cult protagonists quite accurately. As early as 1982, Jack C. Ross, a sociologist from the University of Minnesota, who at that time had been in the Department of Sociology at Memorial University of Newfoundland for fourteen years, recognized that a group of self-glorifying intellectuals had arisen. He wrote:

> First there was a cult movement, then there was the anti-cult movement, then there were the intellectuals against the anti-cult movement, and then there's me. This is essay No. 4, about what No. 3 is doing to undermine No. 2 in favor of No. 1. So much for this game plan.
> Actually nothing is quite so simple. There are many intellectuals opposed to thought-control religions, and the largest number who use the work of the apparent apologists for the cults are simply neu-

tral or removed from the human issues by ivory tower isolation. . . .

The leaders of the major cluster of writers, whose work I think is gravely deficient, consist of James T. Richardson, Dick Anthony, Thomas Robbins, Anson D. Shupe, Jr., and David Bromley. . . .

Each of these writers has a number of students or colleagues forming a larger network of a score of people who cite each other, usually favorably or uncritically. They favorably review each other's work (e.g., Robbins on Bromley & Shupe's "New vigilantes" in "Journal For The Scientific Study Of Religion," 1982, 21, 1, pp. 80-81; Shupe on the essays of Robbins, Anthony, and others on pp. 81-82; Bromley praises Robbins on p. 83 — when I was in Chicago politics the ward politicians used to call this "one hand washes the other." These authors would no doubt protest any accusation of complicity, and indeed I doubt there is any. Rather, what I see here is a community of authors whose frequent collaboration has led to a complacent assumption of the adequacy of each other's work, and a centrality of views and values that has produced a willingness to overlook or down play the problems with cults that their opponents think vital (taken from the "Citizens Freedom Foundation News," Vol. 7, No. 11, November 1982).

The authors of this present work would, I suppose, logically be included in the term "oppponents" that Mr. Ross uses. The problems that we see as vital are such things as the freedom of the individual BEFORE entrance into the group; the ability and opportunity to evaluate their position when they themselves, or their parents or other family members request it; and the right to retain and practice all the basic human and religious rights. Our active involvement with people involved in cults and their families shows no such alternatives in the cults. We see freedom and choice from a practical, not a theoretical point of view.

The very first article of the Universal Declaration of Human Rights is therefore pertinent: "All human beings are born free and equal in dignity and rights. They are endowed with reason and conscience and should act toward one another in a spirit of brotherhood." (Do cult leaders respect this right and act accordingly when they deprive members of proper food, lodging, and family relationships?)

The Catholic Church's Pastoral Constitution on the Church in the Modern World, *Gaudium et Spes*, issued on December 7th, 1965 during the Second Vatican Council, speaks in a similar manner when it states that, "Since all men possess a rational soul and are created in God's likeness, since all have the same nature and origin, have been redeemed by Christ, and enjoy the same basic equality and destiny, obviously the basic equality of all must be respected" (No. 29). This spiritual and rational foundation is denied in many of the cults, sects and new religious movements.

There is a real concern when cult members are held in virtual slavery, performing tasks for the cult leader, for many hours each day. The Fourteenth Amendment of the United States Constitution prohibited slavery in the nation. Article Four, of the Universal Declaration condemns it for the rest of the world: "No one shall be held in slavery or servitude; slavery and the slave trade shall be prohibited in all their forms." (Several cults have been cited by the U.S. government for failure to pay adequate wages, for holding people in servitude and coercing children to do heavy work.)

When we consider the religious freedom of individuals involved in cults, sects, and new religious movements, the Vatican Decree on Religious Liberty states that "the human person has a right to religious freedom. Freedom of this kind means that all men should be immune from coercion on the part of individuals, social groups and every human power, so that, within due limits, nobody is forced to act against his convictions in religious matters in private or in public, alone or in association with others. The Council further declares that the right to religious freedom is based on the very dignity of the human person, as known by the revealed word of God, and by reason itself" (No. 2).

The universal Declaration in Article 18 states the same thing in this way: "Everyone has the right of freedom of thought, conscience and religion; this right includes freedom to change his religion or belief, and freedom, either alone or in community with others and in public or private, to manifest his religion or belief in teaching, practice, worship and observance." Pope John XXIII in his encyclical *Pacem in Terris* continued the theme when he wrote: "By the natural law, every human being has the right to . . . freedom in searching for truth and . . . within the limits laid down by the moral order and the common good . . . in expressing and communicating his opinions. . . Every human being has the right to honor God according to the dictates of an upright conscience, and the right to profess his religion privately and publicly" (No. 12, 14).

Cults, sects, and new religious movements hinder this process with their heavy manipulation, isolation and indoctrination. The fact that cult members are prohibited from discussing their cult affiliation with family, friends and at times, even an outside evaluator, is an outright violation of this basic human right.

There is little doubt that the cults, sects and new religious movements will be with us for a long time. The Catholic Church is not interested in forcing any one of them out of existence. The Catholic Church does however, have an obligation to teach the truth.

The Second Vatican Council Declaration on Religious Liberty, *Dignitatis Humanae*, (December 7th, 1965), states this quite clearly:

> It is in accordance with their dignity that all men, because they are persons — that is, beings endowed with reason and free will and therefore bearing personal responsibility, are both impelled by their nature and bound by a moral obligation to seek the truth, especially religious truth. They are also bound to adhere to the truth, once they come to know it and to direct their whole lives in accordance with the demands of truth. But, men cannot satisfy this obligation in a way that is in keeping with their own nature unless they enjoy both psychological freedom and immunity from external coercion. . . .
>
> The search for truth, however, must be carried out in a manner that is appropriate to the dignity of the human person and his social nature, namely, by free inquiry with the help of teaching or instruction, communication and dialogue. It is by these means that men share with each other the truth they have discovered, or think they have discovered, in such a way that they help one another in the search for truth. Moreover, it is by personal assent that men must adhere to the truth they have discovered (No. 2, 3).

The more that a particular group deviates from the above norms the more closely it approaches the classification as a cult, or a sect. When this happens, not only does society have a right and duty to speak out, but so does the Church. And it is incumbent upon the Church to understand where the deprivation of freedom really happens. The Church is entrusted too, with the responsibility of letting its members know when there is danger to their faith or morals.

That is what this book has attempted to do. Through examples, definitions, case histories, and chief characteristics, the problems of cults, sects, and new religious movements have been examined and has been found in need of attention.

In the words of Jesus Himself: "Let him who has ears to hear, let him hear" (Mark 4:9).

Appendix I

Outline for a Talk on Cults, Thought Reform and Mind Abuse

By Rev. Wm. Kent Burtner, O.P.

Virtually every former member of a cult, thought reform or mind abuse group will tell you that if they had only known what they were coming close to, they would never have gotten involved. The authors of this present volume believe that programs of information about thought reform and mind abuse should be a part of virtually every eductional program.

The aim of our education is not to say "this group is good," or "that group is bad." Even if this were the best method of teaching, the groups about which we are concerned have such a variety of front names, and the phenomenon of mind abuse, cults, etc., is so widespread, that one could never provide an adequate catalog. Rather, we wish to give to people the tools they will need to judge for themselves whether being part of a given group will be in their best interests.

What follows here is a sample talk or lecture on the topic. It is intended as a guide that can be adjusted, abridged, augmented or otherwise changed to meet the needs of a particular audience. Certainly, every example, sub-heading or the bracketed examples, need not be included. Rather, the speaker should consider the audience and gauge the talk specifically to it.

The topics covered here include an introduction, *the* definition *of a cult, and* reasons why cults pose a problem *today for us. In addition there is material on recruitment, and a consideration of* what keeps people in the cult *after they find themselves involved. Also included is what is new about the cults, and what we might learn about ourselves, our world, and our church, as a result of reflecting on the phenomenon of cultism.*

I. Introduction of the program.
"Cults" defined.
Why is it a problem.

The word "cult" describes a relationship between a leader and a group, or less commonly between a pair of individuals, where the leader utilizes the techniques of thought reform. A cult will be characterized by these two behaviors:

1. It does not tell the truth about itself.
2. By means of unrestricted use of psychological and social control techniques, it makes its members unable to resist its influence and authority.

The result is that members of cults cannot make their own life decisions, determine their future goals, feel their own feelings, or make their own choices.

If the ability to use one's gift of reason is what makes us human, then these groups rob their members of their basic humanity.

Not all cults are "religious": There are political cults, psychological cults, health cults, sports cults, etc.

Also, particular individuals who are qualified leaders of respectable groups or institutions may break out of their socially approved roles and use thought reform techniques without the sanction of their superiors.

Cults exist all over the world, but most especially in countries with rapidly changing social structures. There are millions of people affected worldwide.

While most cult leaders become wealthy, the aim of these groups is to acquire power over others.

While most cults have wealth or seek it aggressively, money

is valuable to such a group only because it will help it attain the power which the leader believes that he/she ought to have by right of divine (or some other special agency) appointment.

Most cult leaders are seeking to dominate the lives of other people, rather than to do any altruistic works in the world. Cults that do these works usually do them in order to gain credibility.

Cults are a problem because they deprive people of their God-given rights to self-determination and rob them of their human freedom.

Telling the truth:

Most people want us to believe the best about their group. They are also willing to tell the truth about their:
— ideology,
— the meaning of becoming a member,
— what the goal of the group is,
— what is expected of new members.

But Cult groups are NOT willing to do so. Cult leaders know that if they do, people might not join, or might leave.

The deception is within the system of recruiting, not simply a reflection of an over-enthusiastic member trying to help a cause.

What Cults Ultimately Do to Members

Thought Reform:

The term "thought reform" was used originally in China in the early part of this century. The Chinese ideographic characters were originally mis-translated as "wash brain," and hence the term often used, "brainwashing." Dr. Margaret Singer, an American psychologist, refers to thought reform programs as those programs developed in the earlier part of this century by such persons as Mao Tse Tung, who developed the programs used in "thought reform universities and camps" in order to effect a change in the individual's political beliefs. These she speaks of as "first generation" thought reform programs. Subsequently, other people have used the same techniques in a more refined way in order to go beyond the intents of the political reformers. The aim of these "second generation" thought reform programs is to change the *personality functioning* of the individuals brought under the program of thought reform.

Dr. Singer has listed six characteristics of thought reform programs that are applied by cults to their members:

1. Gain social control over the person.

Get them to come to more and more events given by the group, to attend long seminars, to begin doing mental exercises that allow for little or no quiet time, or time to think by one's self, or place them in a controlled environment that does these things consistently.

The aim is to get control of the time one spends inside one's mind.

2. Reduce the person's self-esteem.

People begin to see their own lives as less valuable, less meaningful, to see their own life experiences and lessons they have learned as less valuable, to doubt the truth of what they have learned in the past, to feel that the new group knows them better than anyone else, that the leadership of the group is very powerful, knows a lot, or everything. Recruits think of themselves as being inadequate, become less able to clearly understand what they are in the face of constant pressure to conform, to be socially acceptable, to accept the warmth of others in the group.

3. Reduce old ways of functioning, choosing, behaving.

The individual begins to think of the group as very powerful, themselves as powerless. Older ways of acting are discouraged. Individuals come to believe that they are not as good as the group in which they find themselves.

4. Induce new ways of functioning, choosing, behaving.

Models of behaving are shown by older members, rewards are given for new behaviors, punishments for failure to conform are meted out.

5. A closed system of logic is used to keep the person from questioning the group's beliefs, or its particular behaviors. If the premises are wrong, so too are the conclusions.

6. A special, non-informed state exists in the mind of the prospective recruit. Specific information which they would otherwise require to decide

whether or not to affiliate with a group is *deliberately* withheld from prospective recruits. They may belong to the group for an extended period of time before such information is given to them, if at all.

II. How people get recruited
Who could get involved? (Everyone!)

A. Cult recruiters have a target population that varies from group to group, and from time to time within a group.

1. Each group focuses on a few "types" to seek out.

2. Since the recruiters themselves are usually from that "type" themselves, they can spot someone else from that category easily.

B. A Typical Recruit is a normal, well-functioning member of society.

1. Profile of a typical recruit:
    a. Mentally healthy, normal social skills for their age.
        1) More than 70% of cult indoctrinees do not have any psychological problems before they meet their group.
    b. At a time of some temporary sadness, disappointment, or of major change in their lives.
        1) Often between the ages of 18-26, a period of great change for most young people. [Social roles have changed dramatically in the last years. Once it was common to use the phrase "to go out on a date," and it had a specific meaning. That phrase has very little denotative meaning today. In fact, a woman newspaper reporter told this author of being asked out on a date and she had to reply "What do you mean?"]
        2) Older people are also susceptible. [Persons of a more mature age are likely to have some funds set aside for their retirement years and are more likely to suffer from loneliness as their long-time friends become infirm or deceased. When someone comes along who is friendly, does them favors or chores, and offers them some means of future security, the defenses acquired over many years may yield to the need for companionship, and leave them vulnerable.]
    c. Generally above average intelligence.
    d. Tendency toward high ideals, commitment to making the world a better place.

2. The typical recruit is *not* seeking a new "group experience" at the time he is recruited.

a. Important: The recruiter "finds" the recruit, not the other way around.

b. The recruit would otherwise recover from the temporary "low" period, as we all normally do.

3. The recruiter manages to invite the person to come to a group activity.

a. Each group offers something of value to attract the new member.

1) Referred to as a "hook" by some groups.

2) If these groups offered nothing of value, who would ever join?

a) the recruit's "mistake" may well be presuming that the things offered subsequently by the group will be as good as those he or she received in the beginning.

b. This is geared to bring the person into the group slowly, while providing friendship and seeming comfort to the inductee.

c. Examples of group activities include: Bible study programs, training in meditation, lessons in some skill from yoga to cooking, a free personality test, an invitation from a stranger to smoke a "joint," a chance to get a very good job (but the demand is to attend some workshop or obscure training program whose goals are not clearly spelled out), or the chance to join some special people for a trip to the woods or to another city. As one former cult member put it, "If you have found the most wonderful people you have ever met, belonging to the most dedicated and friendly group you could ever have come across, if it answers all the questions you've ever had, if it has a very special place just for you, if it all seems too good to be true, then it probably is!"

4. Virtually *anyone* can be caught in a similar situation.

a. Many people believe that they could not be the victim of thought reform, mind abuse, or "brainwashing." To believe this about yourself makes you much more vulnerable. If you believe that it couldn't happen to you, you are less likely to protect yourself from it.

b. A person without a temporary period of sadness or disappointment finds an advertisement in a newspaper or magazine inviting him, or meets a co-worker or friend who invites him, to come to learn a new skill in his trade or profession, interpersonal communications, or other benefits. The program is in reality run by some cult or thought reform group. In the course of the program, the group induces the feeling of sadness or disappointment, and begins the thought reform process.

C. The group provides an environment that discourages a recruit from being his or her "normal self."

1. New recruits will be separated from friends, surrounded by new people, who are all part of the program.

2. New recruits will be given lots of love, shown a great deal of emotional "openness," and will be expected to return in kind.
   a. The "openness" of such groups is usually staged for the benefit of the new member.
   b. The new recruit may not be aware that some or all of those who are "sharing" are, in fact, committed members of the group.
   c. The group asks a great deal of trust of the recruit, without giving the new recruit an opportunity to be sure that the group is itself trustworthy.
      1) The overwhelming sense of warmth, interest in the person, flattery, etc., serves to defuse challenging questions.

3. A tremendous amount of new information is given to the new recruit over a very short period of time, so that the person has no chance to analyze it.
   The information appears logical, but is actually full of enormous gaps in logic. [The appearance of logic is given by moving carefully from one point to another and another, and then making a large leap, which the listener is prone to think is just due to his or her lack of understanding. This is precisely what the group wants them to think. No opportunity is given to go back over and analyze the data at close range.]

4. Recruits are compelled to participate in activities that require them to depend on the members of the group in order to fulfill their role. [One well known group in California plays a variation of the children's game, "dodge ball." But instead of the game they grew up with, the game is full of very complicated rules, forcing new visitors to depend on the members of the group to understand their role. Another group teaches

people lessons in communication, and each time recruits come to the class, they find that there is a different routine to begin, involving going from one person to another for a variety of instructions. Once again, the person is dependent on the group for the ability to do very basic activities.]

5. The recruit finds increasing demands made upon his or her time. [A group doesn't need to have a live-in situation to take control of a person's time. Rather, one can begin with, for example, a cultic Bible study program that at the beginning meets only once a week, and slowly finds pressure to come twice a week, to another set of activities, and eventually spends every free moment with the group.]

6. Certain interference with the individual's diet and sleep cycles occurs.
   a. In some groups, it is impossible to get a balanced diet.
   b. Some period of sleep deprivation is common to cults in general.
   c. These elements need not be present at all times. Only an occasional reinforcement will be needed.

III. What keeps People in Cults?

A. The pressures listed above are continued and will increase.

1. These pressures continue in varying degrees, increasing or decreasing what psychologists call "ego function."
   a. These individuals are under varying pressures and given varying degrees of ability to function autonomously depending on what the group needs of them from one time to another, and the degree of commitment the group perceives in the individual.
   b. Persons who reach "middle level management" positions in the group tend to become aware of the pressures they are using and which are being used on them. At this point they will either rationalize that what they are doing is "for God" or their higher purpose, or they will decide that their position, power and influence is more important than questioning the program of the group.

B. Two Important Dynamics of Coercion:
   The rational and emotional faculties of an individual are at-

tacked by a cult or any group using thought reform techniques in this manner:

1. *Suspension of the individual's ability to analyze* is accomplished by means of:

a. Logical fallacies. ["The world is so full of negativity, won't you try to be objective?" Except that "objective" now means to reject *anything* that might be construed as negative.]

b. Suspension of questioning. ["Your question is really a good one, but we will be talking about that in a later presentation. Won't you hold your question till then?" Except that the question is never dealt with. Another variation is to make questioners feel as if they "should have been able to figure that out" for themselves and that they are stupid for asking.]

c. The assumption that your own life experience is not sufficient to provide criteria by which to judge the program. ["The new truth we have received is more powerful than anything you have ever heard. We will show you the 'spiritual' way to understand it." This author was told by members of one group at a presentation I was to make, that if I didn't base my comments about that group on the material they gave me, that was obviously being slanderous and they would have to "take the appropriate legal action." Neither my own experience counseling members of the group, nor research into it was creditable.]

d. Sensory overload. [Human beings can take in only so much new information in an analytical way at a time. When too much information is given, they begin to simply absorb it uncritically. With gross overstimulation, the person may have a psychotic episode. Sometimes cults will cause these so that the person will feel a greater sense of dependence upon them.

e. Use of body/brain physiology to simulate "mystical" experiences. [The followers of one guru will breathe deeply while chanting and dancing. When the music stops, they feel the great elation that was promised them. In fact, they are hyperventilating, and would feel just as "high" by chanting, dancing and breathing without the guru.]

f. Mystification. [One group says it can teach you to see "divine light," but after months of meditation sessions and a trip to another city to be "inducted," they have you gently apply pressure to your eyeballs. This is the "light" they spoke of. But after months of "preparation," it feels like something tremendous has happened.]

g. Trance induction. [Did you ever hear a speaker who started to speak slowly, rhythmically, in a monotone, and everyone seemed to drift off a bit? It is possible to put a large group of people into a light trance state. And once you do it often enough, you can teach people how to go into trances and give messages to themselves that they would not ordinarily do. And, it is all done under the aegis of "therapy," "spirituality," or some other good.]

2. *Using GUILT as a key tool of manipulation.*

Certain, or all, of a person's emotions are targeted by the group and are considered to be intrinsically evil. When the group stimulates these same emotions, the resulting emotion is *guilt.*

For the cultist, the belief is, "Your feelings are moral actions for which you are responsible."

Feelings in and of themselves are morally neutral. What we do with them makes all the difference. To be angry, unhappy, tired, or even have a sexual feeling is by itself not a moral or immoral act.

What we do as a result of having those feelings makes all the difference. We have always distinguished between a sin and a temptation. [If someone were very angry with you and decided to harm you physically, that would not be a very good use of his anger. On the contrary, if being angry at you, one were to sit down and have a long talk with you and work out your differences, that would be a virtuous use of the anger. The problem is not whether or not one is angry, but what one does on account of it. A cultic group will target on one or a whole cluster of feelings, label them as intrinsically evil, and make you feel guilty for having them.]

To have any doubts about the leader, or the truth or validity of the mission, doctrine, or behavior of the group is proof positive that some evil exists in the recruit.

C. Robert J. Lifton's Concept of *Ideological Totalism.*

NOTE: Recommended for a more advanced group, or where more detailed information is needed, see Robert J. Lifton's *Thought Reform and the Psychology of Totalism,* specifically chapter 22 and his discussion of the eight areas of human dynamic that denote ideological totalism and which, when all are maximally utilized, the individual cannot assert himself or herself over against the group. Regarding subsequent issues in counseling, see Margaret T. Singer's article, *Coming Out of the Cults,* "Psychology Today," January, 1979.

IV. Are Cults New to our time?

A. Cults as revitalization movements, historical precedents.

1. In a way cults are not new. There have been periods of significant social change throughout the history of human civilization. When these intense periods of change come about, in every group there arise movements that attempt to bring about some kind of reintegration of the social fabric.

Some such groups become positive groups, and are helpful to people, others not so.

2. Such groups are helpful insofar as they help people understand the new stresses of the changing social fabric as comprehensible and meaningful.

Groups also can attempt to deal with contemporary stresses by reducing understanding and awareness, and making up a new "myth" which reduces the real issues to simple ones.

B. Modern cults as thought-reform programs.

1. The first generation of modern thought reform programs began with "thought reform universities" and "thought reform camps" established by Mao Tse-Tung after his ascendency in China.

The aim of the psychological and social manipulation at work there was to cause the individuals within them to change their political ideology.

2. Based on the technology evolved in China and Korea, second generation thought reform programs came into existence beginning in the 1950s.

These modern programs have as their aim the alteration of the psychological functioning of the individual.

C. Using the second generation thought reform techniques, modern cults deal with the many intense stresses of modern life by closing off awareness and reducing individuals to mere functionaries in groups led by persons with ulterior motives.

1. Five areas of special stresses today are evident:

a. *Political:* our modern political system seems to leave individuals powerless to effect any change or growth.

b. *Economic:* the world economic system seems to be

beyond anyone's control and people feel powerless and totally at its mercy.

    c. *Technological*: with ninety percent of the scientists who have ever lived alive now, the technological revolution has just begun.

        1) The computer age is just dawning.

        2) The way in which we do business, education, etc., will never be the same as it was even thirty years ago.

    d. *Societal*: Roles and social structures have changed so much that it is difficult for people to know and understand their place in society, or in the world.

    Social relationships have changed drastically also, and one is never quite sure what is expected from others, whether in formal business relationships, friendships, or romances.

    e. *Psychological*: The world has never known as much about the function of the mind as it does today.

        1) That includes how to stimulate, motivate and control others.

        2) Because we can easily label our own or other's emotional and mental states according to this understanding, we can also easily "judge" them, and thus we create enormous, unfulfilled expectations for ourselves.

    2. These five areas leave individuals feeling powerless and less able to cope generally in society.

    Institutions which help people understand their place in the world, especially the Church, are by their nature reactive to any given set of social circumstances, and hence, people will need to struggle for some time before new social understandings and new social structures come to be, and lessen that feeling of uncertainty and powerlessness that we find in society.

    3. Cults make life simpler for their members, by eliminating awareness of the social stresses, rather than by making the stresses meaningful.

D. Similar applications of the techniques of thought reform exist as Mind Abuse:

    1. Cultic relationships at work in families.

    a. Abuse of spouses and children can take place emotionally, and these may be partly understood under the same *rationale* as mind abuse occuring in cultic relationships.

    2. There is a great similarity between the kind of counseling used with victims of cultic mind abuse and that used for those caught up in the abuse of drugs or alcohol, or the counseling given to abused spouses or children.

V. Lessons for Ourselves, Our World, the Church.

A. Protecting ourselves and our young people.

1. Information is the best way to directly prevent the involvement of people in cults. Virtually every former cult member says something like, "If I had only known there were groups like this, I would never have come near to it."

2. We need to know and understand that:

a. When someone offers you something for free, it probably isn't. Few people from ghettos become involved, because they are "street wise" and can "see a con artist coming at twenty yards."

b. You have the right to information! Anyone who would deprive you of that is suspect.

1) Someone presenting an idea or solution should be able to defend his idea directly to you without appeal to other "higher ups" or be able to give you places to go to get that information outside the group.

2) You have the right not only to question the presenter about new information, but to *validate* it from sources you trust outside of the group.

c. When we are tired, under stress, suffering a loss of some kind, we are vulnerable.

1) Your feelings, whatever they are, are valuable and are not evil. You have the right to choose what you will do with them, and moral choices follow from that.

2) If someone causes you to feel obligated and/or guilty, they may have an ulterior motive. Back away and take time to evaluate the situation.

3) Check with your trusted friends, family, clergy, counselors, teachers when someone makes a new offer under these circumstances. This is true *especially* if you are feeling depressed or sad.

3. Realize that everyone, at one time or another, is vulnerable to the mind abuse of cults and other thought reform programs. So that they can work their programs on your mind, cults and other thought reform programs *need* you to believe that you couldn't be taken in.

B. Lessons for Our World

1. Cults and thought reform programs want our respect and to be seen as just another part of society no different from other segments.

In fact, when they claim for themselves the protection

granted to other institutions for social good, we would do well to demand of them the same criteria of proof as we do for established groups.

2. Cults place their own ethics above the law, and ask of society some special treatment. The laws should be enforced equitably for all.

3. Tragedies such as those at Jonestown, Guyana, in 1978, can be prevented in the future by simple attention to the activities of such groups.

C. Lessons for the Church

1. It is clear that the spirituality of religious cults is counterfeit. But people hunger for genuine spirituality. They also need to live in community, to experience the love and care of others in immediate and practical ways. Oftentimes, the first time a person is able to live in a context where spirituality is overtly permitted is a cult environment, even if it will later be taken away. [For this reason, we need to provide a multitude of opportunities for young people to be with each other, to learn that spirituality and being a socially acceptable person are not mutually exclusive. Young people thrive on group interaction that is energetic, positive, genuine, and which allows for reflection.]

2. We often talk of community, but rarely deliver to our young people an authentic experience of community.

Hence the need for retreat experiences, group collaboration, etc., that give young people, and adults as well, an authentic experience of Christian community.

3. We tragically undervalue the contributions young people can make. Because adolescence is extended so long in western countries, the fulfillment of deep yearnings for meaningful contribution are often postponed. Cults challenge people and give them opportunities to feel that they are making a contribution that is of value.

4. The cults present a microcosmic world to us. From the study of cults and their relationship to society, it should be clear to us that we are in the midst of rebuilding the very fabric of the world's society. It will be from the resources of the Church and the great wisdom traditions in the world that this will be accomplished. We need to pay attention to this task with equal diligence.

5. In the last analysis, one does well to recall the words of St. Paul: ". . .where sin increased, grace abounded all the more" (Romans 5:20).

Appendix II

Teacher Lesson Plan

The following plan is designed to be used in four sessions. Much of the material listed here is a summary form. More complete information can be found by consulting the subject within the text.

This program was used for several years in the Archdioceses of Philadelphia and New York, especially in the Catholic Schools.

OBJECTIVE: To inform junior and senior high students about pseudo-religious destructive cults, their origins, their ideologies, their methodologies, their activities, and their ultimate aims.

Goals: Class I
Sociology of Cults
1963-1981

The American institutions of family, church, school, and government — the traditional pillars of authority and stability — have been gradually undermined for 18 years beginning with the assassination of President John Kennedy. What cultural circumstances must be analyzed and understood? How did cults begin during this period? What description of cults must be made?

―――――――――

"According to their own reports many participants joined these religious cults during periods of depression and confusion when they had a sense that life was meaningless."

Dr. Margaert Singer

Class II
Cults Ideologies
Philosophy or Theology

During the 1963-1981 period the more developed and well known cults were establishing their roots among idealistic, young, searching Americans.

What are the names of these groups? What are some of their beliefs? Where are these groups located? Who are their leaders?

"I will state that coercive persuasion and thought reform techniques are effectively practiced on naive, uninformed subjects with disastrous health consequences."

Dr. John Clark
Harvard Medical School

Class III
Cults Methodologies
Recruitment and
Mind Control

The cults employ a heavy emotional process called "love-bombing" to lure idealistic but many times naive and unsuspecting young people into their web. Once re-

cruited, the cults apply on the recruits, a systematic technology of mind control and behavior modification that is subtly deceptive.

What is "love-bombing"? What is meant by "mind control and behavior modification"? How are these processes employed by the cults? What is deprogramming?

"As necessary as ideals and aims are, utopian 'magic formulas' will not get us anywhere, since they are usually accompanied by totalitarian power or the destructive use of violence."

Pope John Paul II
Address to German Youth,
November, 1980

Class IV
Cult Guilt and
Fear Addiction

The cults engage the indoctrinated and mind-controlled members in a host of fundraising and recruiting activities that keep them "on-the-move," tired, confused, nonthinking and "always busy."

What about the psychological violence of "guilt, fear, and the power of satan" the cult imposes on the members? How do the cults use philosophical dualism, i.e. good vs. evil to their benefit?

I — Sociological Background — 1963-1981

1. The four pillars of American life, the family, the Church, the school, and the government have seen their integrity and their authority undermined gradually during the period between 1963-1981.

2. More than a president was lost on November 22, 1963 when John F. Kennedy was assassinated. Respect for human life and a sense of the sacred were also attacked in Dallas. Security in leadership, permanency and stability in authority were brutally stripped away from the American psyche in a few brief moments.

3. Subsequent political assassinations such as Robert Kennedy, Martin Luther King, Jr., Malcolm X, and the attempts on former Presidents Ford and Reagan continue to give the impression that democracy and constitutionality may not even survive, let alone govern us.

4. The Vietnam conflict and its attendant protest marches redefined authority and patriotism in all their spiritual and moral nuances as well as splitting the American soul in half.

5. The credibility of the presidency itself was undermined by Vietnam, the bombings in Cambodia, and the culmination of lost presidential authority and integrity in Watergate.

6. Our major cities exploded literally in fireballs and riotous looting because minority groups and the poor felt disenfranchised and leaderless. Detroit, Watts, Harlem, and North Philadelphia were aflame in frustration and leaderless anarchy.

7. The high priest of LSD, Timothy Leary, and company spread the message of chemically induced hallucination as the way to inner awareness. The Beatles legitimatized this inward movement by providing the musical "theology" of peace, love, and brotherhood garnered largely from Eastern Mysticism and peppered with pot. But the flower children did not see the contradiction between supposed self-discovery and blown away rectitude.

8. The perceived impersonalism of American higher education and our computerized technology turned many young people inward to drugs, meditation, yoga, and individual gurus.

9. Counter-cultures and sub-cultures were gradually eroding the sense of belonging to family, church, school, and government. Hippies, yippies, and new communes — "new parents" and "new families" — were displacing traditional authority figures and established communities.

10. American youth entered the 1970s disillusioned and deceived. The full-blossoming of the flower children generation would be seen in the free-to-be-me movements of the 1970s with their accepted but not critiqued motto, "Do your own thing."

11. Jim Jones in the Peoples' Temple, Mr.Moon in the Unification Pseudo-Church, Charles Dederich in Synanon, Swamit Probhupada in Hare Krishna. Guru Maharaj Ji in Divine Light Mission, L. Ron Hubbard in Scientology, David Moses Berg in Children of God, Victor Paul Wierwille in The Way International, Elizabeth Clare Prophet in The "Church" Universal and Triumphant, Stewart Traill in The "Church" of Bible Understanding (Lamb House), are the more pominent cult leaders who have stepped into the spiritual and moral vacuum of the last 18 years.

12. Characteristics of a Cult:

a) the presence of a living, charismatic leader, usually a male but not always, who controls the movement;

b) the demand of absolute loyalty and obedience, with no allowance for dissent or direct input from the followers regarding philosophy or ideology;

c) the severing of family ties with one's natural parents, siblings, relatives and friends (this varies in degree and intensity among the many cults, keep in mind that psychological alienation is every bit as insidious as physical alienation);

d) the selling of merchandise and/or courses as a means of fund-raising; the leadership elite benefits the most from the raised monies, most especially the cult founder;

e) the carefree control of the total environment, i.e. the eating, sleeping, thinking, informational flow, and the activities of all recruits and members are systematically coordinated;

f) cult societies are undemocratic and absolutist, many are even facist;

g) cults practice fraud and deception both in their recruiting and fund-raising activities;

h) the 'new truths' of the cults must not be questioned but blindly accepted, meditated upon or studied, and mediated only by trained leaders and directors.

"When the irreverant intellectual has done his work, the best lack of all conviction, while the worst are full of passionate intensity. Surely some revelation is at hand. Surely the Second Coming is at hand."

William Butler Yeats — "The Second Coming"

II — Cults Ideologies — Philosophy or "Theology"

1. The combination of technology, secular humanistic sociology and psychology, and moral relativism all conspired to debunk traditional spirituality, morality, especially religious experience, and traditional theologies right across denominational lines.

2. A whole generation of young people has grown up and may still be growing up without a biblical, dogmatic and historical sense of the transcendent, of mystery, and the sacred.

3. And a whole generation of young people has grown up and is still growing up with the onslaught of pseudo-religions which purport to offer the stability and permanence that the four pillars of family, church, school and government may have temporarily lost.

4. CULTS and the DIETY of CHRIST

a) **Ananda Marga Yoga** — Leader: Shrii Shrii Anadamurti. "Be constantly absorbed in the thought of god and you too will become God." (Baba's Grace — Discourse of Anadamurti.) This Indian Cult's terrorist arm attempted to assassinate John Paul II on his recent trip to the Far East. **Ananda Marga** ironically means "Path of Bliss."

b) **Baha'i** — an independent world religion based on a "unique revelation of God" traces its roots to a 9th-century division within Islam. God called by different names, is one but unknowable. Christ was a "manifestation" of God and a way to God.

c) **Bawa Muhaiyaddeen Fellowship** — Leader Bawa Muhaiyaddeen. "God is a secret and a mystery, but man is also a mystery. Only God can see God. So if man is to see God he must become God. Man becomes God and God becomes man. It is no big deal" (Bawa).

d) **Children of God** — Leader: David Moses Berg. Started as a fundamentalist counterculture ministry but degenereated into belief in the occult, reincarnation, and sexual permissiveness. The COG believes that Berg is the only end-time prophet; that it is the remnant church of the last days; that its authority is absolute; and in the use of blasphemy, profanity, prostitution, vulgarity, and pornography.

e) **Church of the Living Word** — Leader: John Robert Stevens. (Also called **The Walk**) "Jesus Christ came to participate in humanity and make the bridge of communication so that God could communicate himself into our very beings. What he is, we become." According to Stevens, this begins with contemporary revelations which make them the Living Word (Christ) to the world. Although some acknowledgment is made of the inspiration and authority of Scripture, in practice, the source of teaching is current revelation, not the Bible. Stevens considers himself God's chief intercessor.

f) **Church Universal and Triumphant** — Leader: Elizabeth Clare Prophet. Also called Summit Lighthouse or Summit International. The Church is a mixture of eastern religions, theosophy, Christianity and many other elements of thought. Elizabeth is recognized as one of the two witnesses in Revelation 11. Her late husband and the founder, Mark, is considered the other. Jesus is considered as a man that had the Christ Consciousness within Him. He was one of many who achieved the "God self" witness.

g) **Divine Light Mission** — Leader: Guru Maharaj Ji is the living perfect master. Jesus was the Perfect Master of his time but Ji has replaced him. Ji claims the world needs the knowledge of Reality, and he claims to be the source of that knowledge and of peace in the world.

h) **Eckankar** — Leader: Sri Darwin Gross — Eckankar says it is the wellspring and essence of all religions, philosophies, realization via the "ancient science of soul travel." Eckankar makes the biblical God into a demon who as Creator is responsible for the evil in the world and declines Christ as "god as all men are god."

i) **Hare Krishna** — Founder: Chaitanya Mahaprabru. Also called **International Society of Krishna Consciousness** (ISKCON). To the Krishnaite, the world is not real, it's illusion. Salvation comes by chanting the name of their God, Hare Krishna, at least 1780 times daily. They consider Jesus only as a guru.

j) **Inner Peace Movement** — Leader: Rev. Francisco Coll, D.D. A form of Spiritualism and spiritism, combining ESP astro-projection, psychic phenomena, etc. They introduce seven levels of consiousness. Christ consciousness is the highest. Jesus had reached Christ consciousness while on earth. Jesus was a man. They separate Jesus and Christ. God is impersonal and spoken of as the All, The Cosmos, the Universal.

k) **Rosicrucianism** — Jesus was a reincarnated man, the highest luminary possible. The Christ spirit in Him was a manifestation of the cosmic Christ.

l) **Scientology** — Founder: L. Ron Hubbard claims to have found the spiritual technology to dispense the one "true way" to man. It is a process working through levels of self-knowledge and knowledge of past lives to awaken the primordial deity within until a person is able to regain total godhead. Christ is a man who achieved a "state of Clear" but not the higher state of "Operating Tretan."

m) **The Unification Church** — Founder/Leader: Sun Myung Moon, says that God has dual qualities — spirit and energy. God is a personal being with consciousness, intelligence, love and purpose. Salvation can come only through a Messiah who achieves perfection, marries and has perfect offspring. Christ, Moon says, was to do this, but he failed because he died before he could marry. Because he was resurrected, Moon says, Jesus did redeem man spiritually. The physical redemption of man will happen through a second Messiah who is, of course, by implication the "Reverend" Moon. Moonies are represented by CARP — Collegiate Association For The Research of Principles (Moon's Divine Principle) on college campuses.

n) **T.M. — Transcendental Meditation** — Leader: Maharishi Mahesh Yogi says that anyone can practice his technique of deep meditation in order to achieve "bliss consciousness of Absolute Being." Incorporated in 1959 in California as a non-profit religious organization called spiritual growth, peace and happiness through a system of deep meditation. The Beatles, Mia Farrow, Shirley MacLaine, and The Rolling Stones helped to spread this movement. By 1976 TM could claim a following of 6,000 teachers and an annual income of $2 million. Beliefs: The purpose of life is happiness sought through an endless cycle of incarnation and reincarnation. Through the liturgy of the mantra, we dive within ourselves to discover the creative intelligence within us, ridding ourselves of indifference and ignorance thus discovering "bliss consciousness."

o) **The Forum — formerly EST — Erhard Seminar Training** — Founder: Werner Erhard (born Jack Rosenberg) a former automobile salesman, a former Scientologist with extensive occult involvement, studied and involved in Mind Dynamics, Zen Buddhism, hypnosis, Subud, Yoga, Silva Mind Control, psychobernetics, Gestalt, encounter therapy and transpersonal psychology. EST is the fruit of his "conversion" experience and personal research into these disciplines, EST training is designed to change a person's epistemology i.e. their way of relating to reality, radically and permanently. People are "voluntarily" conditioned to the point of "epistemological vulnerability" and then the EST philosophy is conveniently provided as "the answer" and "the truth" about life and how to live it.

EST is a subjective experience and people can "get" different things from it. "Getting it" is the term used by estians to describe what they learned from the seminar training. According to Erhard, my Self equals your Self equals the same Self. All is One. "Self is all there is. I mean that's it." "As you can see, this universe is perfect. Don't lie about it. You're god in your universe. You caused it. You pretended not to cause it so that you could play in it" (Erhard). About 20% EST graduates are in the field of education. Erhard pays special attention to clergy; they receive special discount rates on "scholarships" to attend his seminar training.

p) **LIFESPRING** — founded by John Hanley, like EST, a genre of the human potential movement. Attempts to focus on what the "individual" needs to function, communicate, and make choices in a more personal way. Like EST, Lifespring prescinds from spiritual and moral viewpoints (objectivity) and results in subjectivism, a form of secular humanism. The Catholic Christian viewpoint of "humanity redeemed in the blood of Jesus Christ" is not the starting point, the focus, or the end point of Lifespring. Such groups go counter to message, community, worship and service in the Roman Catholic understanding.

q) **Church of Bible Understanding** (COBU), or "Lamb House," like the Way International, a bible cult. Founded by Stewart Traill as the Forever Family. Traill offers his color-coded interpretation of the Bible and sets himself up as the ultimate authority for "doctrine" and discipline.

"Stress if strong enough can, produce a marked increase in hysterical suggestibility so that the individual becomes susceptible to influences in his environment to which he was formerly immune. It can happen to anybody."

Konrad Lorenz
"On Aggression"

III — Mind Control Techniques Used By Pseudo-Religious Cults

Mind control is a strategy used by cult leaders for their own expansion of influence and control.

First, the person is conditioned or softened up.

Second, the person is persuaded or indoctrinated into new beliefs. The cult leaders have three objectives in mind:

First, to win converts;

Second, to secure teaching disciples;

Third, to make money.

The factors used to "educate and condition" a person are:

First, Isolation;

Second, Hunger;

Third, Fatigue;

Fourth, Tenseness;

Fifth, a Fear-Love Relationship;

Sixth, Repetition;

Seventh, Threats you do not even realize are threats;

Eighth, Lack of privacy, both physical and mental.

Depending on which pseudo-religious cult you are talking about, these factors are used more or less in producing mind control. Brainwashing is the name of the game. And by brainwashing, we mean simply thought reform — reform to what the leader wants you to think.

During the time when the person is being indoctrinated, he does the following things.

1. He studies diligently.

2. He listens hour after hour with no questions allowed.

3. He self-examines himself and what he stands for.

4. He becomes self-critical.

5. Then he re-examines himself.

6. He now comes across new thought conclusions.

7. He learns by doing.

8. There is no reality testing with anyone outside the group. His questions are only answered within the group.

9. The most important and last phase is impressing the person with the infallibility of the cult leader. The cult leader has had God revealing great things to him, or God has come in visions to him — and the cult leader has had things revealed to him from God like no other person ever known.

After awhile of being with cult members, teachers, leaders, etc. the person will gradually be won from the ability to make a decision and will be an integral part of the group and cannot function alone. When this finally happens the mind control is complete. The person will obey faithfully all God has revealed to the cult leader. The cult leaders use certain phrases over and over and they are woven into speeches, materials, teachings, and conversation and everyday living so that the member repeats them audibly to himself or others day after day. This reinforces the mind control.

The person finally cannot think except as far as the group thinks. And the terrible thing — the person does not even know his mind is controlled. He thinks he has a free will to believe what he wants, while in fact he thinks only as far as the teachers and leaders of the group suggest. A person does not know that he is brainwashed! One cannot feel brainwashing! Just as one cannot smell carbon-monoxide.

IV — Cults Guilt, Fear, and Emotional Addiction

1. Almost all of the cults, especially the bible cults (COBU, The Way International, "The Walk") and the Moonies play heavily on the philosophical dualism of good versus evil, light versus darkness and their kingdom versus Satan's kingdom and the impending doom of Armageddon. These groups are shot through with apocalypticism.

2. All people, including family and friends, not belonging to the cult are evil, of Satan. That is why you and I must overcome, why we can be lied to, we are of Satan. ("Heavenly deception.")

3. When philosophical dualism is coupled with emotional apprehension, fear, and guilt, the combination can explode with the ferocity of mass destruction such as that of Jonestown.

4. In the closed controlled environment of the cult and the cult-like world the potential for self-destruction, i.e. suicide or psychosis and destructive behavior is intensified by fear, guilt, and peer-pressure with the catalyst being the "new truth." The real and the imagined spiritual warfare between good and evil of the new truth becomes played-out like Jones' Peoples' Temple.

5. Catholic educators must point out that these groups: cults, cult-like experiences, and pseudo-evangelical groups all employ:

a. Abuse of Authority — They replace old authority with new authority. The come-on may be "a hope of glory" in the coming world promised by this "new prophet" or "Messiah." Or the come-on may be the promised "power" or "money" that will follow from the new truth.

b. Abuse of Intimacy — The "new parents" and the "new family" must coordinate a member's every move even to eating, sleeping, and bathroom privileges.

c. Abuse of Time — Lack of sleep, deprivation of privacy, diet modification, and ideological indoctrination all conspire under systematic application and emotional "highs" and "lows" to produce confused, tired, passive, obedient and committed sheep.

d. Abuse of Discipline — Whether the abuse is physical or psychological the end result to the victim is equally devastating. Robotized automatons on the streets, in bars, in airports, bus terminals, offices, and local neighborhoods are pathetic in hawking their "wares" and their "gospels according to. . . ."

e. Abuse of Money — Suffice it to say that all collected monies are turned over to the cult-leaders and their "elite" leadership.

Recommendations for Teachers

1. That every educator read Flo Conway and Jim Siegelman's book on sudden personality change, a book titled, *Snapping,* as well as Robert J. Lifton's book, *Thought Reform and the Psychology of Totalism,* especially chapter 22 is a must. All educators should have a bibliography for themselves and their students and direct them to reading and research projects.

2. That all teachers seriously study the sociology, theology, spiritual and mental health, legal, and political dimensions of cult groups and include their information wherever possible in the courses they teach.

3. That school assemblies, church youth groups, PTA meetings and home and school associations all receive information about cults and hear from former cult members and their families.

4. That interdenominational and interdisciplinary study groups and task forces be set up and mobilized since the cult threat cuts across denominational and ethnic lines.

5. That religious communities must study the reasons why growing numbers of their members are drifting towards human potential groups such as EST and Lifespring.

6. That a thorough re-studying of our Catholic biblical roots and dogmatic developments be undertaken by all educators. The danger of large numbers of Catholic youth possessing an abiblical, adogmatic, and ahistorical sense of their specific Roman Catholic identity can be the fertile soil for later cult enticements.

7. That any Catholic educators who are substituting the teachings of Christ and His Church with new found "truths" have the decency and honesty to move out of formal Catholic education positions.

8. That the doctrinal writings of Pope John Paul II, especially *Redemptor Hominis* become an integral part of our personal spirituality as well as our preaching and teaching. These writings represent a brilliant compendium and synthesis of our Catholic Doctrine.

9. That all parish ministry team members pastorally address through preaching and teaching programs the serious personal and family tensions, ambiguities, and frustrations of many of our people young and old. The need to affirm our people lovingly and remind them of our fundamentally optimistic Catholic theology of God's grace and mankind's response-in-faith will give them a sense of belonging to us and to one another.

Suggestions for Avoiding
Cult Recruiters at Vacation Spots

1. Travel in small groups at all times (i.e. 3 or 4 not 1 or 2). A teenager walking or traveling alone is a very "vulnerable" target for a cult recruiter.

2. Be aware that cult recruiters will be present in large numbers during Senior Week, (also throughout the summer).

3. If approached, do not under any circumstances give out the address or phone number of where you are staying, or the number of kids at your place.

4. Do not engage in prolonged discussions. If alone, no conversations at all should take place. Your beliefs and allegiances will be assaulted.

5. Do not accept any party or dinner invitations whatsoever from cult recruiters. Boys should be aware of girl recruiters and girls of boy recruiters. (They may look like nice clean smiling "Happy" faces; in fact, they are under mind control and severe pressure "to get" warm bodies.)

6. If excessively bothered by recruiters or fund raisers on the streets, in bus terminals, on the boardwalk, or at your place, do not hesitate to call the police. (Your privacy is being invaded. Tell them to "bug off" or you will call the police.)

7. Lonely, confused, upset kids are the easiest but not the only "victims" of trained cult recruiters. Stay together and protect one another, not just your friends and classmates, but any and all kids you see being "manipulated."

Appendix III

Following is the 1984 Pastoral statement of His Eminence, Jaime Cardinal Sin, Archbishop of Manila, on certain doctrinal aspects of the Maharishi Technology of the Unified Field, held after consultation with theological experts.

The Basic Conflict Between Maharishi and Christianity

The Maharishi's doctrine and teaching on (1) God, (2) man, (3) the way to go to God, (4) pain and suffering, and (5) sin is in open contradiction to Christian Doctrine.

1. The 'God' of the Maharishi is *impersonal*, as opposed to the God manifested in Christian revelation where God is a personal God who loves each human person in an intimate way.

By denying the Creator as Supreme and teaching that "All is One" Maharishi removes the distinction between the Creator and the creature. This directly leads to, or is an equivalent form of pantheism.

The 'mantras' given to the followers of the Maharishi have been discovered to be invocations, in most of the cases, to deities of the Hindu pantheon, thus in a real sense denying the oneness of God and fostering *polytheism*.

2. *Man* is considered capable of attaining unlimited perfec-

tion, of being totally liberated from all pain and suffering through the instrumentality of Transcendental Meditation practiced in the Maharishi way. Similarly through this, TM man can find solution to all human problems ranging from control of the elements to the attainment of indestructibility and immortality.

Two flaws, among others, appear clearly in this doctrine: (a) It does not accept the *immortality of the soul*, nor life beyond, as belonging to the nature of the soul; (b) ignores completely the existence of *original sin*, a Christian dogma, and the consequences for the realities of life.

3. The way to God is placed by Maharishi in TM as understood by him, his books, and his followers, and it is placed on TM as the exclusive way to God.

Two flaws, again, are hidden in these affirmations: (a) the abuse of the *term TM* which has been appropriated by them as if theirs was 'the' TM par excellence, the only authentic one (there is Christian mysticism, even authors speak of Hindu and Buddhist mysticism, and certainly there is also the well-known za-zen method of meditation); and (b) the way to God in the present economy for all is the way of the *Cross* as long as we are pilgrims, as explicitly preached by Christ himself, accepted in Christian doctrine and life. The heroism of Christian faithful suffering with the greatest courage and dignity appears to be absent in the Maharishi way to God.

4. Implicit in the Maharishi approach to the problem of pain and suffering is the rejection of the redemptive value of suffering and of the existence of *Christ as the Redeemer*. In fact, Maharishi in his book, *Meditations of Maharishi Mahesh Yogi* (Bantam Books, New York, 1968, p. 23), writes explicitly: "I don't think Christ ever suffered or Christ could suffer." (This statement has been repeated in many places by the Maharishi followers.)

5. *Sin.* Maharishi tries to ignore the existence of sin. In this Maharishi follows the Vedic doctrine that regards sin as a bodily matter and has nothing to do with the spirit or soul of man. The whole concept of 'sin,' if implicitly accepted is considered as something external, and legalistic. The real sense of freedom and responsibility is absent and the 'effects' of sin are the object of rituals, mantras, and TM. There is no interior conversion, but a rather manipulative use of TM to attain liberations.

At the basis of this concept and approach is the concept of God, man, way to God, pain and suffering described above. From this point of view, one cannot be a Christian and a Maharishi.

6. As for TM, it may be considered as doctrine (content) or as technique (method). From this point of view of *doctrine* it is not acceptable to a Catholic, or a Christian at that. As for TM as technique, in the way the Maharishi group presents it, it is not acceptable either because of its intrinsic connections with the doctrine (cf. 'mantras' and 1 and 2 above).

This kind of TM is to be *distinguished* from various forms of prayer proper to the Oriental religious attitudes, some of which may be acceptable, and even beneficial, if properly scrutinized and used. TM, however, as proposed by Maharishi and as the end-result looked at by the Maharishi doctrine and followers is, to say the least, quite risky. It becomes not a remedy but an escape. Its unavoidable result, within the Maharishi doctrine context, is the desensitization of conscience by trying to relieve not the guilt and the real disorder but only its symptoms and its accompanying restlessness.

Appendix IV

The Bayside Movement has been resisting the authority of the local bishop since it began in 1968. We reproduce here. the November 4, 1986 letter of Bishop Francis Mugavero of Brooklyn in which he states quite clearly that there is no substance to the alleged apparitions, and that the Bayside Movement is dangerous to the Faith.

Declaration Concerning The "Bayside Movement"

In recent months, doubts have been raised by members of the so-called "Bayside Movement" concerning the official position of the Diocese of Brooklyn on the alleged "apparitions" of the Blessed Virgin Mary, and other heavenly beings, to a woman by the name of Veronica Lueken.

Moreover, erroneous claims have been made by a number of followers of Mrs. Lueken concerning the legitimacy of their position, in order to justify their activities on behalf of the "Movement." These have taken the form of statements in their publications that "since Articles 1399 and 2218 of (the 1917 Code of) Canon Law were abrogated by Pope Paul VI in 1966, no ecclesiastical permission is required, neither can anyone incure censure, for the publication or dissemination of information dealing with revelations, visions or miracles, provided these do not endanger Faith or morals."

As a result of the above-mentioned doubts and claims, a number of Christ's faithful continue to attend the regularly-scheduled "vigils" held at Flushing Meadow Park, and to disseminate or receive propaganda literature on this matter.

I, the undersigned Diocesan Bishop of Brooklyn, in my role as the legitimate shepherd of this particular Church, wish to confirm the constant position of the Diocese of Brooklyn that a thorough investigation revealed that the alleged "visions of Bayside" completely lacked authenticity.

Moreover, in view of the confusion created by published reports of messages and other literature by this "Movement," I consider it my obligation to offer Christ's faithful pastoral guidance, lest their faith be endangered by "messages" and "teachings" relayed by "visionaries," which are contrary to the Faith of our Catholic Church.

Therefore, in consultation with the Congregation for the Doctrine of the Faith, I hereby declare that:

1. No credibility can be given to the so-called "apparitions" reported by Veronica Lueken and her followers.

2. The "messages" and other related propaganda contain statements which, among other things, are contrary to the teachings of the Catholic Church, undermine the legitimate authority of bishops and councils and instill doubts in the minds of the faithful, for example, by claiming that, for years, an "imposter (sic) Pope" governed the Catholic Church in place of Paul VI.

3. Those who persistently maintain that "no ecclesiastical permission is required for the publication or dissemination" of information concerning "revelations, visions or miracles," are erroneously interpreting the directives of the Holy See when they attempt to justify the publication of the propaganda literature on the "Bayside Messages."

In view of my declaration concerning the authenticity of the "visions of Bayside," the Congregation for the Doctrine of the Faith has confirmed that the principles governing the publication of such religious material still maintain authoritative moral value prohibiting the endangering of faith and good morals (Cf. Response of *SCDF* of June 14, 1966, in *AAS* 58, 1186).

As a result, those publishing or disseminating this propaganda literature are acting against the judgment of legitimate Church authority.

4. Because of my concern for their spiritual welfare, members of Christ's faithful are hereby directed to refrain from participating in the "vigils" and from disseminating any propaganda related to the "Bayside apparitions." They are also discouraged from reading any such literature.

5. Anyone promoting this devotion in any way, be it by participating in the "vigils," organizing pilgrimages, publishing or disseminating the literature related to it, is contributing to the confusion which is being created in the faith of God's people, as well as encouraging them to act against the determinations made by the legitimate pastor of this particular Church (c.212, §1).

It remains my constant hope that all the faithful spend their time and energies in promoting devotion to our Blessed Lady, in the many forms which have been approved by the Catholic Church.
(Signed):

Bishop Francis Mugavero
Bishop of Brooklyn

Appendix V

Because of the confusion the Fatima Crusaders, also known as the Tridentine Latin Rite Church, have caused to the Church, especially in the Spokane, Washington and western Idaho area, we reprint here the statement of Bishop Lawrence Welsh in which he warns people of the errors of this group.

Statement on TLRC

By Bishop Lawrence Welsh

After much consultation and prayer, I have given approval for the *Inland Register* to publish the series of articles regarding the Fatima Crusaders, which begins in this issue. In the history of the Catholic Church, after almost every general Council there have been groups which have broken away from the mainstream of the church. They have done this in reaction to the restatement of the Christian tradition by the Fathers of that particular Council.

It is a very sad phenomeon but also very human. In faith we grieve to see the fabric of the church so divided. Our life as Christians is directed toward the unity of all men and women in Christ. Whatever divides the church is to be mourned because it divides Christ himself.

Sincere

We are sure that the Catholics who have joined the Fatima Crusaders are sincere in their belief. The *Inland Register* series presents the sorrows, the traumas, and the difficulties they have experienced for the sake of their belief. They are seeking to do God's will as they understand it.

Yet, as Bishop of Spokane, I do not feel that I can stand by silently while people from this group cause confusion in the minds of some of our Catholic people.

The Fatima Crusaders or the Tridentine Latin Rite Church cannot be identified as a legitimate expression of the Roman Catholic faith. Their denial of the papacy as incorporated in the lives of the last four popes is a denial of the church itself. How can one believe in the presence of Christ in the church and the power of his Spirit while denying the concrete presence of the office of the Pope?

Not legitimately Catholics

There is no such thing as a legitimate expression of the Catholic tradition that is not in union with the Holy Father. The Fatima Crusaders are therefore not legitimately Catholics. Their celebration of the sacraments is not a legitimate part of the life of the church. Bishop Schuckardt has received no mission from the church universal and does not accept the unity of the apostolic office. Yet these are some of the very elements which make the Church Roman Catholic.

The past 18 years have been very challenging for the church. Given the direction by the bishops of the church in union with the Holy Father, Catholics have been about the difficult task of reform and renewal. There have been extreme reactions at times and clearly abuses at times, but guided by the official teaching office of the church it has sought to live by and to teach the mainstream of Catholic tradition as it has been known for 2,000 years.

As your bishop, I must caution you, the faithful of this diocese, to protect yourselves from any error including this effort by the Fatima Crusaders. Their presentation of Catholic tradition distorts the mainstream of Catholic faith by a certain selected historical perception of Catholic life. They take a far too pessimistic view of world order.

Teaching authority denied

Furthermore, they deny the teaching authority of the Second Vatican Council and the last four popes. Implicitly Bishop Schuckardt has set himself up as the final and last arbiter of

Catholic tradition. This follows the pattern used by all so-called reformers of the past.

They are above the then current expression of Catholic tradition. History over and over again has demonstrated that such movements are not from the Holy Spirit. Whatever the admitted weaknesses and sinfulness of the Roman Cathoic Church, the Fatima Crusaders stand opposed to the unity, Catholicity, and apostolicity of the church. I truly believe the series that begins this week helps to identify this more clearly. I am grateful to Bob Cubbage and the *Inland Register* staff for their very competent and professional efforts to bring this story to the Catholic people of our diocese.

Appendix VI

This Pastoral letter was sent December 31, 1985 by Bishop Daniel P. Reilly to parishes in the Norwich, Connecticut diocese which had been affected by the Apostolic Formation Center and its activity.

It gives a good summary of the history of the movements and why the center was closed by direction of the Bishops.

My brothers and sisters in the Lord:

On this first Sunday of the New Year, I extend to each of you and all of your loved ones best wishes for a blessed, peaceful and happy 1986.

I am writing to you about a matter of importance to the Diocese of Norwich and especially to this area of Tolland County, the Vernon Deanery of our Diocese. Today in many of the Catholic Churches in this area this pastoral letter is being read. It concerns the former Mary, Queen of the Apostles Center which was situated in Somers. Until a few years ago, it was known as the Apostolic Formation Center for Renew-All and also for a brief period of time was apparently called Our Lady of Grace Center. The mission of this Center was the religious formation of lay-catholics by lay-catholics.

In recent months articles appeared in the media alleging that some teachings and practices contrary to the Catholic faith had taken place at the Center. I wish to speak to you in the context of those allegations.

Mr. J. Roy Legere was the founder of the Apostolic Formation Center. He came to Somers from Warren, Massachusetts, where he began his apostolate. The original Center and its successor never enjoyed the official approval of the Church. However, over the years of its existence the leaders of the apostolate informed the Bishops of the Diocese of Norwich about their general work listing the number of retreats held and the numbers of people who attended them. The priests who ministered at the Center, although neither invited nor appointed by the Bishop, received the faculties of the Diocese of Norwich when their Superiors and/or Bishops indicated they were priests in good standing.

The sudden death of Mr. J. Roy Legere in December of 1978 was a cause of discord and division among some of those associated with the Center and much angry emotion surfaced. In mid-1980 I appointed a committee of three priests of the Diocese of Norwich to hold a series of public hearings to determine the nature of and reasons for this division. The findings were inconclusive but apparently the death of Mr. Legere had left a vacuum of leadership at the Center. Subsequently, Mr. Charles Shattuck became President of the Center. Its name was changed to Mary, Queen of the Apostles Formation Center in the hope of producing a new sense of unity and purpose. However, the problems continued and on June 1, 1985, I informed Mr. Shattuck that I was withdrawing the privilege of priest and Blessed Sacrament from the Center. This was done. On June 3, 1985, the Board of Directors closed the Center and it was subsequently sold. I informed Mr. Shattuck that he would not be allowed to re-open the Center in the Diocese of Norwich. Shortly thereafter, I also informed the Bishops of seventeen other dioceses where branches of the Center were said to exist that the Center had been closed at my initiative.

Shortly thereafter, a series of articles appeared in the media about practices alleged to have occurred at the former Apostolic Formation Center when Mr. J. Roy Legere served as its President.

I have investigated these allegations from a theological, moral, legal and psychological perspective. I have concluded that moral and theological breaches did occur by a small number of people involved in the former Apostolic Formation Center. Identifying publicly who these people were and what these breaches were serves no valid purpose. However, I have taken steps to insure that these breaches of religious and moral conduct have ceased and will not re-occur. I am very grateful to those who have assisted me and the Diocese of Norwich in this matter. A number of very competent and concerned people have given much time and effort to insure that a proper investigation was made for the welfare of all concerned.

In dealing with this matter, I have a very genuine pastoral concern for those hundreds and hundreds of good and sincere people who came to the Center seeking spiritual nourishment and counsel in the context of Catholic Church teaching. These people have been very disappointed and disillusioned by the adverse publicity which the Center has recently received. They were unaware of any problems at the Center and are incredulous about them today. Many of them have written letters to me and others stressing the good the Center has done for their Christian living. I would not want this to be harmed in any way.

However, my decision made last June 1, 1985, to withdraw the privilege of priest and Blessed Sacrament from Mary, Queen of the Apostles Formation Center in Somers stands firm and final. Neither it nor its predecessor, The Apostolic Formation Center, will be permitted to re-open in the Diocese of Norwich.

But I do wish to reach out to those people of good will who have found stronger faith and spiritual sustenance at the Center. The Diocese of Norwich stands ready to help any of them needing assistance at this time. Therefore, I am forming a Diocesan Committee to assist those people who found the Mary, Queen of Apostles Formation Center and the former Apostolic Formation Center for Renew-All to be a positive source of personal growth and holiness in their lives. In the near future an announcement will be made concerning the membership, the purpose, and the program of this commitee.

As we begin this New Year, let us pray that the Lord will fill each of us with His love and peace and that together we may do our best for His greater glory and the salvation of His people.

Sincerely yours in Christ,
(Signed:)

Daniel P. Reilly
Bishop of Norwich

Appendix VII

This April 2nd, 1986 letter from Johannes Cardinal Willebrands, President of Secretariat for Christian Unity, to Archbishop Peter Gerety, Archbishop of Newark, is an explanation of the proper relationship of Catholic people who are nonmembers of ecumenical organizations to their Bishops.

Dear Archbishop Gerety,

I am writing in response to the questions you have formulated in relationship to the activity in the Archdiocese of Newark of the group known as the Sword of the Spirit. The basic question you raise is whether an organization which describes itself as ecumenical can for that reason replace your jurisdiction over Catholics in your Archdiocese who belong to it, in matters such as teaching these Catholics the fundamentals of a life of holiness, commitment to Christ, and in Christian training and formation.

Our response to the issue you raise is, of course, from the perspective of ecumenism. In this regard, we would affirm your authority as Archbishop in matters concerning teaching, evangelization, spiritual formation and ecumenism in your Archdiocese. In regard to ecumenism, documents of the Second Vatican Council, authoritative post-conciliar documents published by the Secretariat for Promoting Christian Unity, and the new Code of Canon Law (1983) clearly affirm the responsibility of bishops in general and of local ordinaries in particular, for both the fostering and the guidance of ecumenism. Enclosed you will find excerpts from the documents I refer to. They illustrate clearly the *jurisdiction* bishops have, in union with the Holy See, in matters of ecumenism. I cite here three passages from the list as examples:

I. *The Decree on Ecumenism*, n 4, after giving description of ecumenical activities, says "Such actions, when they are carried out by the Catholic faithful with prudent patience and *under the attentive guidance of their bishops*, promote . . . unity" (UR, 4).

II. *Ecumenical Directory, Part II: Ecumenism in higher Education* (1970): "It belongs. . . *to bishops* and episcopal conferences both *to translate general principles into practice* and to adjust undertakings already on foot to existing conditions as these affect men and matters — and even, as occasion offers, to start new undertakings."

III. *Ecumenical Collaboration at the Regional, National and Local Levels* (SPUC, 1975):
1. *The Ecumenical Task*: "Ecumenical initiatives should be true expressions of the life of the local Church, and not simply the work of individuals. They should be carried on *under the guidance of the bishop* and in close association with the ecumenical commission of the diocese or of the episcopal conference".

Sound ecumenical initiatives are always welcome. It is also true that there can be ecumenical action "by means of informal groups of a spontaneous kind" (*Ec. Coll.*, 7). Such groups can bring their own contribution to the ecumenical movement but it remains that "where there are groups of this kind under Catholic responsibility, it is necessary that they function in full communion with the local bishop if they are to be authentically ecumenical" (*ibid.*).

But such initiatives and such organizations cannot replace the jurisdiction of a bishop over the Catholics in his diocese, or the place of the bishop as the "visible fundamental principle of unity in their particular churches" (*LG* 23). They cannot replace the bishop as the chief shepherd of his flock, or as the chief teacher of his diocese, who is charged with the Christian formation of all members of his flock. They cannot replace the responsibility of the bishop to foster ecumenism, and his authority to guide it in his diocese. As *Lumen Gentium* 22 notes, "the order of bishops is the successor of the college of the apostles in their role as teachers and pastors, and in it the apostolic college is perpetuated."

And even more explicitly:

"For the bishops . . . are the authentic teachers, that is teachers endowed with the authority of Christ, who preach the faith to the people assigned to them, the faith which is destined to inform their thinking and direct their conduct" (*LG* 25).

In his letter to you, Father Herbert Schneider S.J. states that SOS is an ecumenical branch "not under your jurisdiction" and therefore they "see no reason to stop . . . teaching these new members the fundamentals of a life of holiness, commitment to Christ and loyal committed service to God's people in their own local Church situation". Father Schneider seems here to overlook two essential factors: (1) First, it is the bishop who still has primary responsibility for such teaching in regard to Catholics in his diocese. (2) Secondly, if Catholics join an ecumenical organization, the organization does not replace the jurisdiction of their bishop, who remains for Catholics the "authentic teacher endowed with the authority of Christ" (*LG* 25).

Father Schneider also states: "We also see no reason to stop allowing people to accept the Covenant of the Sword of the Spirit after *training and formation is complete*, if they wish to do so, and *we* think that this is right for them in the Lord". The training and formation spoken of is obviously long term, and directed towards a lifetime commitment. Again, for Catholics, it is their bishop who has primary responsibility for this Christian training and formation. Speaking of the responsibility of bishops, *Lumen Gentium* (27) says that "the pastoral charge, that is, the *permanent* and *daily care* of their sheep, is entrusted to them fully". If the bishop decides to work with an ecumenical organization in this regard, that is fine. But he is the one who has to decide. And if he does so, he still cannot relinquish his pastoral responsibility for the people entrusted to him in his diocese.

According to Catholic teaching, Bishops must promote every authentic approach to ecumenism. But we can see no circumstances in which the fact that a Catholic belongs to an ecumenical group, means that the bishop of his diocese no longer has primary jurisdiction and responsibility for that person in regard to teaching the fundamentals of a life of holiness, commitment to Christ, and seeing to their Christian training and formation. The bishop may not have jurisdiction over the ecumenical group. But he does have jurisdiction over the members of his diocese who belong to the ecumenical group.

Furthermore, according to Catholic ecumenical norms, the bishop must provide and guide ecumenism. Therefore, he has the responsibility and the right to evaluate, in light of Catholic principles on ecumenism, the purpose and the program of a given independent ecumenical organization Catholics in this diocese are being invited to join. If, after serious evaluation, he makes the assessment that the organization is in some way detrimental to the well-being of the people, or seriously falls short in regard to its ecumenical approach, he has the right to direct the people of his diocese not to participate in it. They in turn owe him their obedience. For the bishops, to which order he belongs, are "the authentic teachers", according to *Lumen Gentium* (25), "teachers endowed with the authority of Christ, who preach the faith to the people assigned to them."

If an organization, ecumenical or otherwise, gets approval from the Holy See, it is still the local Bishop who has responsibility to see the proper implementation of its procedures in his diocese.

I hope that these comments respond to the question that you raise in regard to ecumenical dimensions of the difficult problem that has emerged in the Archdiocese of Newark regarding the People of Hope and the Sword of the Spirit. Please feel free to contact us if further information or clarification is needed.

With best wishes and personal regards, I remain,
    fraternally yours in Christ,

                                        Johannes Card. Willebrands
                                        President

A. *Examples from Documents of the Second Vatican Council*
    I. *The Decree on Ecumenism*
       Texts illustrating the responsibility and authority of Bishops in Ecumenical Matters

    N. 4 After giving description of ecumenical activities,

says "Such actions, when they are carried out by the Catholic faithful with prudent patience and *under the attentive guidance of their bishops*, promote . . . unity" (UR, 4).

N. 4 "This sacred Council is gratified to note that the participation by the Catholic faithful in ecumenical work is growing daily. It commends this work to the *bishops everywhere in the world for their diligent promotion and prudent guidance.*"

N. 8 In speaking about principles relating to *communicatio in sacris*: "The concrete course to be adopted, when all the circumstances of time, place and persons have been duly considered, *is left to the prudent decision of the local episcopal authority*, unless the bishops' conference according to its own statutes, or the Holy See, has determined otherwise."

II. *Ad Gentes* (1965)

N. 15 On ecumenical cooperation: "There should be collaboration of this type not only between private persons, but also, *subject to the judgment of the local ordinary*, between churches or ecclesiastical communities in their undertakings".

B. *Post Conciliar Documents*
I. *Directory Concerning Ecumenical Matters*, Part I (SPUC 1967)

N. 3 fosters the setting up of Ecumenical Commissions: "charged to promote ecumenical activity *by the episcopal conferences or of the local ordinary*. In those dioceses which cannot have their own commission there should at least be one person *delegated by the bishop* for these duties"

N. 28 vs. indifferentism: "In some places and with some communities, sects and persons, the ecumenical movement and the wish for peace with the Catholic Church have not yet grown strong."

(N. 28) (Therefore) "*the local ordinary* or, if need be, *the episcopal conference* may indicate suitable measures for preventing the dangers of indifferentism and proselytism among the faithful. It is hoped that through the grace of the Holy Spirit *and the prudent pastoral care of bishops*, ecumenical feeling . . . will . . . increase."

N. 32 Concerning prayer in common:
"Where Catholics are concerned, this kind of participation is committed to the guidance and encouragement of *local ordinaries*.

N. 36b The *place* for prayer in common could be "the church of one or other of the communities concerned, if there is need for this and the *local ordinary approves*".

N. 42 "It is particularly opportune that the *Catholic authority*, whether the *local* one, the synod or the episcopal conferences, does not extend permission for sharing in the reception or administration of the sacraments . . . except after satisfactory consultations with the competent authorities (at least local ones) of the separated Oriental Church.

N. 50 "Because of the close communion referred to earlier (n.40) *local ordinaries can give permission* for a Catholic to read lessons at a liturgical service if he is invited".

N. 52 "It is recommended that with the *approval of the local ordinary* separated Eastern priests and communities be allowed the use of Catholic church buildings and cemeteries and other things necessary for their religious rites. . .".

N. 53 "As far as circumstances allow, and with *the local ordinary's permission*, these facilities (Orthodox spiritual and sacramental ministrations to their own faithful in Catholic institutions) can be offered in the Catholic premises, including the Church".

N. 55 Concerning access to the Eucharist, penance and anointing of the sick, by separated brethren in cases of urgent necessity: "In other cases, the judge of this urgent necessity must be the *diocesan bishop* or the episcopal conference".

N. 56 Concerning the question of a Catholic preaching or reading Scriptures at the celebration of the Lord's Supper by separated Christians:

"At other services, even liturgical ones, it is allowable to exercise some functions, *with the previous permission of the local ordinary. . .*".

N. 61 "If the separated brethren have no place in which to carry out their religious rites properly and with dignity, *the local ordinary* may *allow* them the use of a Catholic building, cemetery or church".

II. Ecumenical Directory, Part II: Ecumenism in Higher Education

N. 65 "Bishops have a special responsibility for promoting the ecumenical movement and it is *for them to lay down the required guiding principles*".

"It belongs. . . *to bishops* and episcopal conferences both *to translate general principles into practice* and *to adjust undertakings already on foot* to existing conditions as these affect men and matters — and even, as occasion offers, to start new undertakings".

III. Ecumenical Collaboration at the Regional, National and Local Levels (SPCU, 1975)

1. *"The Ecumenical Task"*: "Ecumenical initiatives should be true expressions of the life of the local church, and not simply the work of individuals. They should therefore be carried on under *the guidance of the bishops* and in close association with the ecumenical commission of the diocese or of the episcopal conference.

2. *The Catholic Understanding of local church. . . relation to the Ecumenical Movement*: Quotes LG 23: "*Individual bishops* are the visible, fundamental principle of unity in their particular churches".

3. *Various Forms of Local Ecumenism* lists areas and forms of local ecumenical action in this chapter, and they "remain always subjected to the pastoral authority of the *diocesan bishop* or the episcopal conference".
   — Concerning *"common bible work"*, many of the 56 national Bible societies "working in agreement with a number of *episcopal conferences*

and diocesan bishops", have developed programs of cooperation with Catholics.

— Concerning *"shared premises":*

"Clearly, initiatives in the matter of shared premises can be undertaken only under the authority of the bishop of the diocese.

6. *Pastoral and Practical Reflections for Local Ecumenical Action:*

    b. "Ultimately, it is always the responsibility of the regional or national episcopal conference to decide on the acceptability and the appropriateness of all forms of local ecumenical action".

    i. decision to join a council depends on the highest ecclesiastical authority. (If only one diocese, it would be the Ordinary of the diocese).

7. *Other Forms of Ecumenism.*

    Concerning the emergence of "informal" groups: "In connection with the hierarchy of the Church, these informal groups can offer original and inspiring ideas, whereas without such a contact and apart from ecclesiastical direction, they run the risk of becoming unfaithful to Catholic principles of ecumenism and even of endangering the faith".

    "At the same time, where there are groups of this kind under Catholic responsibility, it is necessary that they function *in full communion with the local Bishop*, if they are to be authentically ecumenical."

C. *Cases When Other Christians May be Admitted to Eucharistic Communion in the Catholic Church* (SPUC, 1972)

    N. 6 What Authority Decides Particular Cases? — The meaning of N. 55 of the *Directorium Oecumenicum.*

    "If cases of the same pattern recur often in a given region, episcopal conferences can give general directions. More often however it falls to the bishop of the diocese to make a decision. He alone will know all the circumstances of particular case".

Concerning Certain Interpretations of the "Instructio, June 1972" (SPUC, 1973)

N. 6 "It is the local Ordinary's responsibility to examine these exceptional cases and make concrete decisions. The Instruction (N.6) recalls that the Directorium Oecumenicum gives the episcopal authority power to decide whether in these rare cases the required conditions are present or not".

D. *Code of Canon Law* (1983)

Canons illustrating the bishops' jurisdiction in matters relating to ecumenism are:

N. 755 §§ 1 and 2	N. 1125
N. 463 § 3	N. 316 § 1
N. 383 § 3	N. 312 §§ 1 and 3.
N. 844 § 5	

(April 2, 1986)

Appendix VIII

There are several professional groups that are conscious of the cult phenomenon, and offer help in this field. In addition, there are groups of parents throughout the country who will assist people with a cult problem. Information, referrals, counseling and speakers can be obtained from any of the listings below.

American Family Foundation
P.O. Box 336
Weston, MA 02193
617-893-0930

An organization of professional people who share a common concern about the effect of the mental health of victims. AFF produces a bi-monthly publication, "The Cult Advisor," keeping everyone up-to-date on the cult problem. The authors are all members of the Advisory Board.

Archdiocese of New York
1011 First Avenue
New York, N.Y. 10022
212-371-1000

Provides assistance through the Chancery Office and the Consultant on Cults, Father James LeBar, (914-471-2537).

Catholic Answers
P.O. Box 17181
San Diego, CA 92117

Provides assistance and information on problems with fundamentalism, (and by extension, some of the shepherding problems, as well).

Center for Christian
Information
P.O. Box 5616
Santa Fe, NM 87502

Catholic group which deals
with theological issues. It
publishes newsletter.

Cult Awareness Network
National Office
2412 West Pratt Blvd. — Suite
1173
Chicago, IL 60626
312-267-7777

There are approximately 40
local affiliates of CAN in the
U.S. Call or write for the one
near you. Produces news-
letter, "CAN NEWS."

CULT HOT LINE & CLINIC
1651 Third Avenue
New York, NY 10028
212-860-8533 (24 hours) also

6505 Wilshire Blvd.
Los Angeles, CA 90048
213-852-1234

Provides immediate as-
sistance to cult victims, parents, and others.

Interfaith Coalition of
Concern about Cults
711 Third Avenue
New York, NY 10017
212-983-4977

Composed of clergy and lay
church leaders of six major
faith groups in the N.Y. Metropolitan area. It produces
quarterly newsletter.

Positive Action Center
P.O. Box 20997
Portland, OR 97220
503-252-0997

Provides counseling for a variety of mental health problems, especially cults. Produces newsletter.

Spiritual Counterfeits Project
P.O. Box 4308
Berkeley, CA 94704
415-540-0300; 540-5767 (access)

A Christian group with a
wealth of information on
many groups — often with an
in-depth look at the operations from a Christian view
point.

Appendix IX

The Vatican Report
Sects or New Religious Movements:
A Pastoral Challenge

May 3rd, 1986
(Reprinted with permission)

Foreword

In response to the concern expressed by Episcopal Conferences throughout the world, a study on the presence and activity of "sects," "new religious movements," [and] "cults" has
been undertaken by the Vatican Secretariat for Promoting
Christian Unity, the Secretariat for Non-Christians, the Secretariat for Non-Believers and the Pontifical Council for Culture.
These departments, along with the Secretariat of State, have
shared this concern for quite some time.

As a first step in this study project, a questionnaire (cf. Appendix) was sent out in February, 1984, to episcopal Conferences
and similar bodies by the Secretariat for Promoting Christian
Unity in the name of the forementioned departments of the

Holy See, with the aim of gathering reliable information and indications for pastoral action, and exploring further lines of research. To date (October, 1985), many replies have been received by Episcopal Conferences on all continents, as well as from regional Episcopal bodies. Some replies include detailed information from particular dioceses and were accompanied by copies of pastoral letters, booklets, articles, and studies.

It is clearly not possible to summarize the vast documentation received, and which will need to be constantly updated as a basis for a constructive pastoral response to the challenge presented by the sects, new religious movements, and groups. The present report can only attempt to give a first overall picture, *and is based on the replies and documentation received.*

This report is divided as follows:
1. Introduction
2. Reasons for the spread of these movements and groups.
3. Pastoral challenges and approaches.
4. Conclusion.
5. Invitation from the 1985 Synod.
6. Questions for further study and research.
7. Selected bibliography.
8. Appendix

1. Introduction

1.1 *What are "Sects"? What Does One Mean by "Cults"?*

It is important to realize that there exists difficulties in concepts, definitions, and terminology. The terms *sect* and *cult* are somewhat derogatory and seem to imply a rather negative value judgment. One might prefer more neutral terms such as *new religious movements, new religious groups.* The question of the definition of those movements or groups as distinct from *church* or *legitimate movements within a church* is a contentious matter.

It will help to distinguish sects that find their origin in the Christian religion from those which come from another religious or humanitarian source. The matter becomes quite delicate when these groups are of Christian origin. Nevertheless, it is important to make *this distinction.* Indeed, certain sectarian mentalities and attitudes, i.e., attitudes of intolerance and aggressive proselytizing, do not necessarily constitute a sect, nor do they suffice to characterize a sect. One also finds these attitudes in groups of Christian believers within the churches and ecclesiastical communities. However, these groups can change positively through a deepening of their Christian formation and through the contact with other fellow Christians. In this way they can grow into an increasingly ecclesial mind and attitude.

The criterion for distinguishing between *sects* of Christian origin, on the one hand, and *churches and ecclesial communities*, on the other hand, might be found in the sources of the teaching of these groups. For instance, sects could be those groups, which apart from the Bible, have other "revealed" books or "prophetic messages," or groups which exclude from the Bible certain proto-canonical books, or radically change their content. In answer to Question 1 of the Questionnaire, one of the replies states:

> For practical reasons, a cult or sect is sometimes defined as 'any religious group with a distinctive worldview of its own derived from, but not identical with, the teachings of a major world religion. As we are speaking here of special groups which usually pose a threat to people's freedom and to society in general, cults and sects have also been characterized as possessing a number of distinctive features. These often are that they [groups] are often authoritarian in structure, that they exercise forms of brainwashing and mind control, that they cultivate group pressure and instill feelings of guilt and fear, etc. The basic work on these characteristic marks was published by an American, Dave Breese, *Know the Marks of Cults* (Victor Books, Wheaton, IL, 1985).

Whatever the difficulties with regard to distinguishing between sects of Christian origin and churches, ecclesial communities or Christian movements, the responses to the Questionnaire reveal at times a serious lack of understanding and knowledge of other Christian churches and ecclesial communities. Some include among sects, churches and ecclesial communities which are not in full communion with the Roman Catholic Church. Also, adherents of major world religions (Hinduism, Buddhism, etc.) may find themselves classified as belonging to a sect.

1.2 However, and apart from the difficulties mentioned, almost all the local churches do see the *emergence* and rapid *proliferation* of all kinds of "new" religious or pseudo-religious movements, groups, and practices. The phenomenon is considered by almost all responses as a *serious matter*, by some as an alarming matter; in only a very few countries does there not seem to exist any problem (e.g., in predominantly Islamic countries).

In some cases the phenomenon appears within the mainline churches themselves (*sectarian attitudes*). In other cases it occurs outside the churches (independent or free churches; messianic or prophetic movements), or against the church-like patterns. However, not all are religious in their real content or ultimate purpose.

1.3 The phenomenon develops fast, and often quite successfully, and often poses *pastoral problems*. The most immediate pastoral problem is that of knowing how to deal with a member of a Catholic family who has been involved in a sect. The parish priest or local pastoral worker or advisor usually has to deal first and foremost with the relatives and friends of such a person. Often, the person involved can be approached only indirectly. In those cases when the person can be approached directly in order to give him or her guidance, or to advise an ex-member on how to reintegrate into society and the Church, psychological skill and expertise is required.

1.4 *The Groups that are Most Affected*
The most *vulnerable* groups in the church, especially the youth, seem to be the most affected. When they are "footloose," unemployed, not active in parish life or voluntary parish work, or come from an unstable family background, or belong to ethnic minority groups, or live in places which are rather far from the Church's reach, etc., they are a more likely target for the new movements and sects. Some sects seem to attract mainly people in the middle-age group. Others thrive on membership from well-to-do and highly educated families. In this context, mention must be made of university campuses which are often favorable breeding grounds for

sects or places of recruitment. Moreover, difficult relations with the clergy, or an irregular marriage situation, can lead one to break with the Church and join a new group.

Very few people seem to join a sect for evil reasons. Perhaps the greatest opportunity of the sects is to attract good people and good motivation in those people. In fact, they usually succeed best when society or Church have failed to touch this good motivation.

1.5 *The reasons for the success* among Catholics are indeed manifold and can be identified on several levels. They are primarily related to the needs and aspirations which are seemingly not being met in the mainline Churches. They are also related to the recruitment and training techniques of the sects. They can be external either to the mainline Churches or to the new groups: economic advantages, political interest or pressure, mere curiosity, etc.

An assessment of these reasons can be adequately done only from *within the very particular context* in which they emerge. However, the results of a general assessment (and this is what this report is about) can, and in this case do, reveal a whole range of "particular" reasons which as a matter of fact turn out to be almost universal. A growing interdependence in today's world might provide us with an explanation for this.

The phenomenon seems to be symptomatic of the *depersonalizing structures* of contemporary society, largely produced in the West and widely exported to the rest of the world, which create multiple crisis situations on the individual as well as on the social level. These crisis situations reveal various needs, aspirations, and questions which, in turn, call for psychological and spiritual responses. The sects claim to have, and to give, these responses. They do this on both the effective and cognitive level, often responding to the affective needs in a way that deadens the cognitive faculties.

These basic needs and aspirations can be described as so many expressions of the human search for wholeness and harmony, participation and realization, on all the levels of human existence and experience, so many attempts to meet the human quest for truth and meaning, for those constitutive values which at certain times in collective as well as individual history seem to be hidden, broken, or lost, especially in the case of people who are upset by rapid change, acute stress, fear, etc.

1.6 The responses to the Questionnaire show that the phenomenon is to be seen not so much as a threat to the Church (although many respondents do consider the aggressive proselytism of some sects a major problem), but rather as a pastoral challenge. Some respondents emphasize that, while at all times preserving our own integrity and honesty, we should remember that each religious group has the right to profess its own faith and to live according to its own conscience. They stress that in dealing with individual groups we have the duty to proceed according to the principles of religious dialogue which have been laid down by the Second Vatican Council and in later church documents. Moreover, it is imperative to remember the respect due to each individual, and that our *attitude* to sincere believers should be one of openness and understanding, not of condemnation.

The responses to the Questionnaire show a great need for information, education of believers, and a renewed pastoral approach.

2. Reasons for the Spread of Those Movements and Groups

Crisis situations or general vulnerability can reveal and/or produce needs and aspirations which become basic motivations for turning to the sects. They appear on the cognitive as well as on the affective level, and are *relational* in character, i.e., centered upon "self" in relations with "others" (social), with the past, present, and future (cultural, existential), with the transcendent (religious). These levels and dimensions are *interrelated.* These needs and aspirations can be grouped under nine major headings, although in individual cases they often overlap. For each group of "aspirations" we indicate what the sects seem to offer. The main reasons for their success can be seen from that point of view, but one must also take into account the recruitment practices and indoctrinational techniques of many sects (cf. below 2.2).

2.1 *Needs and Aspirations*

2.1.1 Quest for Belonging (sense of community)

The fabric of many communities has been destroyed; traditional lifestyles have been disrupted; homes are broken up; people feel uprooted and lonely. Thus the need to belong.

Terms used in the responses: belonging, love, community, communication, warmth, concern, care, support, friendship, affection, fraternity, help, solidarity, encounter, dialogue, consolation, acceptance, understanding, sharing, closeness, mutuality, togetherness, fellowship, reconciliation, tolerance, roots, security, refuge, protection, safety, shelter, home.

The sects appear to offer: human warmth, care and support in small and close-knit communities; sharing of purpose and fellowship; attention for the individual; protection and security, especially in crisis situations; resocialization of marginalized individuals (for instance, the divorced or immigrants). The sect often does the thinking for the individual.

2.1.2 Search for Answers

In complex and confused situations people naturally search for answers and solutions. The sects appear to offer: simple and ready-made answers to complicated questions and situations; simplified and partial versions of traditional truths and values; a pragmatic theology, a theology of success, a syncretistic theology proposed as "new revelation"; "new truth" to people who often have little of the "old" truth; clearcut directives; a claim to moral superiority; proofs from "supernatural" elements: glossolalia, trance, mediumship, prophecies, possession, etc.

2.1.3 Search for Wholeness (Holism)

Many people feel that they are out of touch with themselves, with others, with their culture and environment. They experience brokenness. They have been hurt by parents or teachers, by the church or society. They feel left out. They want a religious view that can harmonize everything and everybody; worship that leaves room for body and soul, for participation, spontaneity, creativity. They want healing, including bodily healing (African respondents particularly insist on this point).

Terms used in response: healing, wholeness, integration, integrity, harmony, peace, reconciliation, spontaneity, creativity, participation. The sects appear to offer: a gratifying religious experience, being saved, conversion; room for feelings and emotions, for spontaneity (e.g., in religious celebrations); bodily and spiritual healing; help with drug or drink problems; relevance to the life situation.

2.1.4 Search for Cultural Identity

This aspect is very closely linked with the previous one. In many Third World countries the society finds itself greatly dissociated from the traditional cultural, social, and religious values; and traditional believers share this feeling.

The main terms used in the responses are: inculturation/incarnation, alienation, modernization.

The sect appears to offer: plenty of room for traditional cultural/religious heritage, creativity, spontaneity, participation, a style of prayer and preaching closer to the cultural traits and aspirations of the people.

2.1.5 Need to be Recognized, to be Special

People feel a need to rise out of anonymity, to build an identity, to feel that they are in some way special and not just a number or a faceless member of a crowd. Large parishes and congregations, administration-oriented concern and clericalism, leave little room for approaching every person individually and in the person's life situation.

Terms used in response: self-esteem, affirmation, chances, relevance, participation.

The sects appear to offer: concern for the individual; equal opportunities for ministry and leadership, for participation, for witnessing, for expression; awakening to one's own potential, the chance to be part of an elite group.

2.1.6 Search for Transcendence

This expresses a deeply spiritual need, a God-inspired motivation to seek something beyond the obvious, the immediate, the familiar, the controllable, and the material to find an answer to the ultimate questions of life and to believe in something which can change one's life in a significant way. It reveals a sense of mystery, of the mysterious; a concern about what is to come; an interest in messianism and prophecy. Often the people concerned are not aware of what the Church can offer or are put off by what they consider to be a one-sided emphasis on morality or by the institutional aspects of the Church. One respondent speaks of "privatized seekers":

Research suggests that a surprisingly large proportion of the population will, if questioned, admit to having some kind of religious or spiritual experience, say that this has changed their lives in some significant way and most pertinently add that they have never told anyone about the experience . . . Many young people say that they have frequently known difficulty in getting teachers or clergy to discuss, let alone answer, their most important and ultimate questions.

Terms used in the responses: transcendence, sacred, mystery, mystical, meditation, celebration, worship, truth, faith, spirituality, meaning, goals, values, symbols, prayer, freedom, awakening, conviction.

The sects appear to offer: the Bible and Bible education; a sense of salvation; gifts of the Spirit; meditation; spiritual achievement.

Some groups not only offer permission to express and explore ultimate questions in a "safe" social context, but also a language and concepts with which to do so, as well as the presentation of a clear, relatively unambiguous set of answers.

2.1.7 Need of Spiritual Guidance

There may be a lack of parental support in the seeker's family or lack of leadership, patience, and personal commitment on the part of church leaders or educators.

Terms used: guidance, devotion, commitment, affirmation, leadership, guru.

The sects appear to offer: guidance and orientation through strong, charismatic leadership. The person of the master, leader, guru, plays an important role in binding the disciples. At times there is not only submission but emotional surrender and even an almost hysterical devotion to a strong spiritual leader (messiah, prophet, guru).

2.1.8 Need of Vision

The world of today is an interdependent world of hostility and conflict, violence and fear of destruction. People feel worried about the future; often despairing, helpless, hopeless, and powerless. They look for signs of hope, for a way out. Some have a desire, however vague, to make the world better.

Terms used: vision, awakening, commitment, newness, a new order, a way out, alternatives, goals, hope.

The sects appear to offer: a "new vision" of oneself, of humanity, of history, of the cosmos. They promise the beginning of a new age, a new era.

2.1.9 Need of Participation and Involvement

This aspect is closely linked with the previous one. Many seekers not only feel the need of a vision in the present world society and toward the future; they also want to participate in decision making, in planning, in realizing.

The main terms used are: participation, active witness, building, elite, social involvement.

The sects appear to offer: a concrete mission for a better world, a call for total dedication, participation on most levels.

By way of summary, one can say that the sects seem to live by what they believe, with powerful (often magnetic) conviction, devotion, and commitment; going out of their way to meet people where they are, warmly, personally, and directly, pulling the individual out of anonymity, promoting participation, spontaneity, responsibility, commitment..., and practicing an intensive follow-up through multiple contacts, home visits, and continuing support and guidance. They help to reinterpret one's experience, to reassess one's values and to approach ultimate issues in an all-embracing system. They usually make convincing use of the word: preaching, literature, and mass media (for Christian groups, strong emphasis on the Bible); and often also of the ministry of healing. In one word, they present themselves as the only answer, *the* "good news" in a chaotic world.

However, although all this counts mostly for the success of the sects, other reasons also exist, such as the recruitment and training techniques and indoctrination procedures used by certain sects.

2.2 *Recruitment, Training, Indoctrination*

Some recruitment, training techniques, and indoctrination procedures practiced by a number of the cults, which often are highly sophisticated, partly account for their success. Those most often attracted by such measures are those who, first, do not know that the approach is often staged and, second, who are unaware of the nature of the contrived conversion and training methods (the social and psychological manipulation) to which they are subjected. The sects often impose their own norms of thinking, feeling, and behaving. This is in contrast to the church's approach, which implies full-capacity informed consent.

Young and elderly alike who are at loose ends and are easy prey to those techniques and methods, which are often a combination of affection and deception (cf. the "love bombing," the "personality test," or the "surrender"). These techniques proceed from a positive approach, but gradually achieve a kind of mind control through the use of abusive behavior-modification techniques.

The following elements are to be listed:

— Subtle process of introduction of the convert and his gradual discovery of the real hosts.
— Overpowering techniques: love bombing, offering "a free meal at an international center for friends," "flirty fishing" technique (prostitution as a method of recruitment).
— Ready-made answers and decisions are being almost forced upon the recruits.
— Flattery.
— Distribution of money, medicine.

— Requirement of unconditional surrender to the initiator, leader.

— Isolation: control of the rational thinking process, elimination of outside information and influence (family, friends, newspapers, magazines, television, radio, medical treatment, etc., which might break the spell of involvement and the process of absorption and feelings and attitudes and patterns of behavior.

— Processing recruits away from their past lives; focusing on past deviant behavior such as drug use, sexual misdeeds; playing upon psychological hang-ups, poor social relationships, etc.

— Consciousness-altering methods leading to cognitive disturbances (intellectual bombardment); use of thought-stopping cliches; closed system of logic; restriction of reflective thinking.

— Keeping the recruits constantly busy and never alone; continual exhortation and training in order to arrive at an exalted spiritual status, altered consciousness, automatic submission to directives; stifling resistance and negativity; response to fear in a way that greater fear is often aroused.

— Strong focus on the leader; some groups may even downgrade the role of Christ in favor of the founder (in the case of some "Christian" sects).

3. Pastoral Challenges and Approaches

A breakdown of traditional social structures, cultural patterns and traditional sets of values caused by industrialization, urbanization, migration, rapid development of communication systems, all-rational technocratic systems, etc., leave many individuals confused, uprooted, insecure, and therefore vulnerable. In these situations there is naturally a search for a solution, and often the simpler the better. There is also the temptation to accept the solution as the only and final answer.

From an analysis of the responses, some symptoms of the pathology of many societies today can be listed. Many people suffer from them. They feel anxious about themselves (identity crisis), the future (unemployment, the threat of nuclear war). Questions about the nature of truth and how it is to be found, political uncertainty and helplessness, economic and ideological domination, the meaning of life, oneself and others, events, situations, things, the "hereafter."

They suffer a loss of direction, lack of orientation, lack of participation in decision making, lack of real answers to their real questions. They experience fear because of various forms of violence, conflict, hostility: fear of ecological disaster, war and nuclear holocaust; social conflicts, manipulation.

They feel frustrated, rootless, homeless, unprotected; hopeless and helpless and consequently unmotivated; lonely at home, in school, at work, on the campus, in the city; lost in anonymity, isolation, marginalization, alienation, i.e., feeling that they do not belong, that they are misunderstood, betrayed, oppressed, deceived, estranged, irrelevant, not listened to, unaccepted, not taken seriously.

They are disillusioned with technological society, the military, big business, labor, exploitation, educational systems, church laws and practices, government policies.

They might have learned to want to see themselves as conscientious "doers," not worthless drifters or self-seeking opportunists, but often do not know what to do or how to do it.

They are at a loss at various "in-between" times (between school and university, between school and work, between marriage and divorce, between village and city).

They become empty, indifferent or aggressive, or they may become "seekers."

In summary, one could say that all these symptoms represent so many forms of alienation (from oneself, from others, from one's roots, culture etc.). One could say that the needs and aspirations expressed in the responses to the questionnaire are so many forms of a search for "presence" (to oneself, to others, to God). Those who feel lost want to be found. In other words, there is a vacuum crying out to be filled, which is indeed the context in which we can understand not only the criticisms toward the church which many responses contain, but foremost the pastoral concerns and proposed approaches. The replies to the questionnaire point out many deficiencies and inadequacies in the actual behavior of the church which can facilitate the success of the sects. However, without further insisting on them, we will mainly emphasize the positive pastoral approaches which are suggested or called for. If these are acted upon, the challenge of the sects may prove to have been a useful stimulus for spiritual and ecclesial renewal.

3.1 *Sense of Community*

Almost all the responses appeal for a rethinking (at least in many local situations) of the traditional parish-community system; a search for community patterns which will be more fraternal, more "to the measure of man," more adapted to people's life situation; more basic ecclesial communities: caring communities of lively faith, love (warmth, acceptance, understanding, reconciliation, fellowship), and hope; celebrating communities; praying communities; missionary communities; outgoing and witnessing; communities open to and supporting people who have special problems: the divorced and remarried, the marginalized.

3.2 *Formation and Ongoing Formation*

The responses put strong emphasis on the need for evangelization, catechesis, education and ongoing education in the faith — biblical, theological, ecumenical — of the faithful at the level of the local communities, and of the clergy and those involved in formation. (One reply advocates "reflective courses" for teachers, youth leaders, clergy, and religious.) This ongoing process should be both informative, with information about our own Catholic tradition (beliefs, practices, spirituality, meditation, contemplation, etc.) about other traditions and about the new religious groups, etc., and formative, with guidance in personal and communal faith, a deeper sense of the transcendent, of the eschatological, of religious commitment, of community spirit, etc. The church should not only be a sign of hope for people, but should also give them the reasons for that hope; it should help to ask questions as well as to answer them. In this process there is an overall emphasis on the centrality of Holy Scripture.

Greater and better use should be made of the mass media of communication.

3.3 Personal and Holistic Approach

People must be helped to know themselves as unique, loved by a personal God, and with a personal history from birth through death to resurrection. "Old truth" should continually become for them "new truth" through a genuine sense of renewal, but with criteria and a framework of thinking that will not be shaken by every "newness" that comes their way. Special attention should be paid to the experiential dimension, i.e., discovering Christ personally through prayer and dedication (e.g., the charismatic and "born again" movements). Many Christians live as if they had never been born at all! Special attention must be given to the healing ministry through prayers, reconciliation, fellowship, and care. Our pastoral concern should not be one-dimensional; it should extend not only to the spiritual, but also to the psychological, social, cultural, economic, and political dimensions.

3.4 Cultural Identity

The question of inculturation is a fundamental one. It is particularly stressed on the responses from Africa, which reveal a feeling of estrangement from Western forms of worship and ministry which are often quite irrelevant to people's cultural environment and life situation. One respondent declared:

Africans want to be Christians. We have given them accomodation but no home . . . They want a simpler Christianity, integrated into all aspects of daily life, into the suffering, joys, work, aspirations, fear, and needs of the African . . . The young recognize in the independent churches a genuine vein of the African tradition of doing things religious.

3.5 Prayer and Worship

Some suggest a rethinking of the classic Saturday evening/Sunday morning liturgical patterns, which often remain foreign to the daily life situation. The word of God should be rediscovered as an important community-building element. "Reception" should receive as much attention as "conservation." There should be room for joyful creativity, a belief in Christian inspiration and capacity of "invention," and a greater sense of communal celebration. Here again, inculturation is a must (with due respect for the nature of the liturgy and for the demands of universality).

Many respondents insist on the biblical dimension of preaching; on the need to speak the people's language; the need for careful preparation of teaching and liturgy (as far as possible done by a team, including lay participation). Preaching is not mere theorizing, intellectualizing, and moralizing, but presupposes the witness of the preacher's life. Preaching, worship, and community prayer should not necessarily be confined to traditional places of worship.

3.6 Participation and Leadership

Most respondents are aware of the growing shortage of ordained ministers and of religious men and women. This calls for stronger promotion of diversified ministry and the ongoing formation of lay leadership. More attention should perhaps be given to the role that can be played in an approach to the sects — or at least to those attracted by the sects — by lay people who, within the church and in collaboration with their pastors, exercise true leadership, both spiritually and pastorally. Priests should not be identified mainly as administrators, office workers, and judges, but rather as brothers, guides, consolers, and men of prayer. There is too often a distance that needs to be bridged between the faithful and the bishop, even between the bishop and his priests. The ministry of bishop and priest is a ministry of unity and communion which must become visible to the faithful.

Conclusion

In conclusion, what is to be our attitude, our approach to the sects? Clearly it is not possible to give one simple answer. The sects themselves are too diverse; the situations — religious, cultural, social — too different. The answer will not be the same when we consider the sects in relation to the "unchurched," the unbaptized, the unbeliever, and when we are dealing with their impact on baptized Christians and especially on Catholics or ex-

Catholics. Our respondents are naturally concerned mainly with this last group.

Clearly too, we cannot be naively irenical. We have sufficiently analyzed the action of the sects to see that the attitudes and methods of some of them can be destructive to personalities, disruptive to families and society, and their tenets far removed from the teachings of Christ and his church. In many countries we suspect, and in some cases know, that powerful ideological forces, as well as economic and political interests, are at work through the sects, which are totally foreign to a genuine concern for the "human" and are using the "human" for inhumane purposes.

It is necessary to inform the faithful, especially the young, to put them on their guard and even to enlist professional help for counseling, legal protection, etc. At times we may have to recognize and even support appropriate measures on the part of the state acting in its own sphere.

We may know too from experience that there is generally little or no possibility of dialogue with the sects; and that not only are they themselves not open to dialogue, but they can also be a serious obstacle to ecumenical education and effort wherever they are active.

And yet, if we are to be true to our own beliefs and principles — respect for the human person, respect for religious freedom, faith in the action of the Spirit working in unfathomable ways for the accomplishment of God's loving will for all humankind, for each individual man, woman, and child, we cannot simply be satisfied with condemning and combating the sects, with seeing them perhaps outlawed or expelled and individuals "deprogrammed" against their will. The "challenge" of the new religous movements is to stimulate our own renewal for a greater pastoral efficacy.

It is surely also to develop within ourselves and in our communities the mind of Christ in their regard, trying to understand "where they are" and, where possible, reaching out to them in Christian love.

We have to pursue these goals, being faithful to the true teaching of Christ, with love for all men and women. We must not allow any preoccupation with the sects to diminish our zeal for true ecumenism among all Christians.

5. Invitation From the 1985 Synod

5.1 The extraordinary synod of 1985 called to celebrate, assess, and promote the Second Vatican Council, gave certain orientations concerning the renewal of the church today. These orientations, which address themselves to the general needs of the church, are also a reply to the needs and aspirations which some people seek in the sects (3.1). They underline the pastoral challenges and the need for pastoral planning.

5.2 The final report of the synod notes that the world situation is changing and that the signs of the times be analyzed continually (II, D7). The church is often seen simply as an institution, perhaps because it gives too much importance to structures and not enough to drawing people to God in Christ.

5.3 As a global solution to the world's problems, the synod's invitation is to an integral understanding of the council, to an interior assimilation of it, and putting it into practice. The church must be understood and lived as a mystery (II, A; cf. 3.1.6) and as communion (II, B; cf. 4.1; 4.6). The church must commit itself to becoming more fully the sign and instrument of communion and reconciliation among men (I, A2; cf. 4.1; 3.1.6). All Christians are called to holiness, that is, to conversion of the heart and participation in the trinitarian life of God (II, A4; cf. 3.1.1; 3.1.5). The Christian community needs people who live a realistic and worldly holiness. Since the church is a communion, it must embody participation and co-responsibility at all levels (II, C6; cf. 4.6; 3.1.9). Christians must accept all truly human values (II, D3) as well as those specifically religious (II, D5) so as to bring about enculturation, which is "the intimate transformation of authentic cultural values through their integration in Christianity and in the various human cultures" (II, D4; cf. 3.7.4; 4.4). "The Catholic Church refuses nothing of what is true and holy in non-Christian religions. Indeed, Catholics must recognize, preserve, and promote all the good spiritual and moral, as well as sociocultural, values that they find in their midst" (II, D5). "The church must prophetically denounce every form of poverty and oppression, and everywhere defend and promote the fundamental and inalienable rights of the human person" (II, D6; cf.3.2).

5.4 The synod gives some practical orientations. It stresses spiritual formation (II, A5; cf. 3.1.7;4.2), commitment to integral and systematic evangelization, and catechesis to be accompanied by witness which interprets it (II, Ba2; cf. 3.1.8; 3.1.3) precisely because the salvific mission of the church is integral (II, D6; cf. 4.3) securing interior and spiritual participation in the liturgy (II B6; cf. 3.1.9; 4.5); encouraging spiritual and theological dialogue among Christians (II, C7) and dialogue "which may open and communicate interiority"; fostering concrete forms of the spiritual journeys such as consecrated life, spiritual movements, popular devotion (II, A4; cf. 3.1.7), and giving greater importance to the word of God (II, Ba1), realizing that the Gospel reaches people through witness to it (II, Ba2).

6. Questions for Further Study and Research

N.B. Where possible, the study and research should be undertaken in ecumenical cooperation.

6.1 *Theological Studies*

a) The different types of sect in the light of *Lumen Gentium*, No. 16, *Unitatis Redintegratio* and *Nostra Aetate*.

b) The "religious" content of "esoteric" and "human potential" sects.

c) Christian mysticism in relation to the search for religious experience in the sects.

d) The use of the Bible in the sects.

6.2 *Interdisciplinary Studies*

(Historical, sociological, theological, anthropological.)

a) The sects and the early Christian communities.

b) The ministry of healing in the early church and in the sects.

c) The role of the prophetic and charismatic figures (during their lifetime and after their death).

d) The sects and "popular religiosity."

6.3 *Interdisciplinary Studies*

(It is in this field that most work seems to have been done already)

a) Recruitment techniques and their effects.

b) After-effects of sect membership and deprogramming.

c) Religious needs and experiences of adolescents and young adults and their interaction with sexual development, in relation to the sects.

d) Authority patterns in the sects in relation to the lack of a need for authority in contemporary society.

e) The possibility or impossiblity of "dialogue" with the sects.

6.4 *Sects and the Family*

a) Reactions in the family to sect membership.

b) Family breakups or irregular family status in reaction to the attraction of the sects.

c) Sect membership and the solidity of the family; family pressures on children of sect members.

d) Family patterns and conjugal morality in the sects.

6.5 *Women in the Sects*

a) Opportunities for self-expression and responsiblity (cf., sects founded by women).

b) Inferior position of women in different types of sect: Christian fundamentalist groups, Oriental sects, African sects, etc.

6.6 *Acculturation and inculturation* of sects and their evolution in different cultural and religious contexts: in traditional Christian cultures, in recently evangelized cultures, in totally secularized societies or those undergoing a rapid process of secularization (with its diverse impact on Western and "non-Western" cultures). Migration and the sects.

6.7 *A comparative historical and sociological study of youth movements* in Europe before World War II and youth membership in contemporary cults and sects.

6.8 *Religious freedom* in relation to the sects: ethical, legal, and theological aspects. Effects of government action and other social pressures. Interaction between political, economic, and religious factors.

6.9 *The images of sects in public opinion* and the effect of public opinion on sects.

Selected Bibliography

General Reference Works

Bibliographies and Dictionaries

A Selected Bibliography on New Religious Movements in Western Countries, IDOC. International Documentation and Communication Center. Rome, 1979.

Barrett, David B. World Christian Encyclopedia. A comparative survey of churches and religious in the modern world. Oxford, 1984.

Blood, Linda Osborne. Comprehensive Bibliography on the Cult Phenomenon. Weston (MA): American Family Foundation, 1982.

Crim, Keith, ed. Abingdon Dictionary of Living Religions. Nashville (TN): Abingdon, 1981.

Foucart, Eric. Repertoire Bibliographique. Sects and marginal religious groups of the contemporary East (Studies and documents on the science of religion). Quebec, 1982.

Plume, Christian and Xavier Pasquini. Encyclopedie des sectes dans le monde. Nice, 1980.

Poupard, Paul. Dictionnaire des Religions. Paris, 1984, 2nd ed., 1985. Spanish trans. Barcelona: Herder, 1986.

Turner, Harold W. Bibliography of New Religious Movements in Primal Society. Vol. I: Black Africa. Boston, 1977.

Specialized Periodicals

Aagard, Johannes, ed. New Religious Movements Update: A Quarterly Journal of New Religious Movements. Aarhus, Denmark (1977-).

Bulletin Signaletique — Section 527, 528: Sciences Religeuses. Paris. Centre de Documentation du CNRS, 1970-

Missionalia. The South African Missiological Society. Pretoria (see from Vol. 8, No. 3, November 1980 to date).

Pontifical Library Propaganda Fide. Bibliographia Missionaria. Rome (see from Anno XL - 1976 to Anno XLVII - 1983).

Secretariat for Non-Believers. Ateismo e Dialogo. Vatican (see from Anno XIV - June 2, 1979 to date).

Valentin, Frederike. Sekten und religiose Sondergemeinschaften in Osterreich. Verkmappe: Vienna (from 1977 to date).

General

Bartz, W. *Le Sette oggi. Dottrina, organizzazione, diffusione.* Queriniana: Brescia, 1976.

Batz, K. *Weltreligionen heute.* Hinduism. Zurich-Koln, 1979.

Batz, K. *L'Attrait du mysterieux. Bible et esoterisme.* Ottowa: Novalis, 1980.

Cereti, G. *I Nuovi Movimenti Religiosi, le sette e i nuovi culti.* Rome, 1983.

Cournault, Fanny. *La France des Sectes.* Paris: Tchou, 1978.

Eggengerger, O. Die Kirchen, Sondergruppen und religiose Vereinigungen. A Handbook. Zurich, 1983.

Gibon, Yves de. *Des Sectes a notre porte.* Paris, 1979.

Gregoire, M. *Histoire des sectes religieuses. Paris:* Baudouin Freres, 1828—1829 (5 vols).

Grundler, J. *Lexikon der Christlichen Kirchen und Sekten.* Vol. I-II. Vienna: Herder, 1961).

Haack, F.W. *Des Sectes pour les Jeunes.* Mame, 1980.

Hoff, Eugene von. *L'Eglise et les Sectes.* Quelques dissidences religieuses de notre temps. Paris: Societe centrale d' Evangelisation, 1951.

Hutten, K. *Scher-Grubler-Enthusiasten.* The book of traditional sects and religious special groups. Stuttgart, 1982.

Needleman, Jacob. *Understanding the New Religions.* Seabury Press, 1978.

Reller, H. *Handbuch Religiose Gemeinschaften, Freikirchen.* Special groups, sects, philosophies of life, and new relgions. Gutersloh: VELKD-Arbeitskreis, 1978.

Rudin, James and Rudin, Marcia. *Prison or Paradise? The New Religious Cults.* Philadelphia: Fortress Press, 1980.

Vernette, Jean. *Des chercheurs de Dieu "hors-frontieres."* Paris, 1979.

Vernette, Jean and Rene Girault. *Croire en dialogue.* — The Christian before religions, churches, sects. Limoges: Ed. Droguet-Ardant, 1979.

Wilson, Bryan. *Contemporary Transformations of Religion.* London: Oxford University Press, 1976.

Wilson, Bryan. *Religious Movements.* New York: The Rose of Sharon Press, 1981.

Woodrow, A. *Les Nouvelles Sectes.* Paris: Seuil, 1977.

Works on Different Parts of the World

Africa

Andersson, E. *Messianic Popular Movements in the Lower Congo.* Uppsala, 1958.

Baeta, C.G. *Prophetism in Ghana: A Study of Some Spiritual Churches.* London: SCM Press, 1962.

Barrett, David B. *Schism and Renewal in Africa. An Analysis of 6,000 Contemporary Religious Movements.* Oxford, 1968.

Barrett, David B. (ed.) *Kenya Churches Handbook* (The development of Kenya Christianity.) Kisinu, Kenya.

Batende, M. "Les perspectives dans les communautes messianiques africaines." Second Annual Colloquium in Kinshasa, 1983.

Benetta, Jules-Rosette (ed.). *The New Religions of*

Africa. Norwood, NJ: Ablex Publishing Corp., 1979.

Fashole-Luke, E.W., Gray, R., Hastings, A. and G.O.M. Tasle (eds.). *Christianity in Independent Africa* London: Collings, 1978.

Hebga, M. "Interpellation des mouvements mystiques." Second Annual Colloquium in Kinshasa, February 1983.

Holas, Bohumil. *Le Separatisme religieux en Afrique noire. L'example de la Cote d'Ivoire*. Paris: PUF, 1965.

Muanza Kalala, E. *Les sectes au diocese de Mbujimayi (Zaire)*. Rome, Pontifical Lateran University, 1980.

Sundkler, B. *Bantu Prophets in South Africa*. Oxford, 1961.

Europe

Bosch, J. *Iglesias, sectas y nuevas cultos*. Madrid: Ed. Bruno, 1981.

Denaux, A. *Godsdienstsekten in Vlaanderen*. Leuven, DF, 1982.

Guizzardi, Gustavo. "New Religious Phenomena in Italy. Towards a Post-Catholic Era?" Archives des sciences sociale des religions. Vol. 21, No 42 (July-Dec. 1976), 97-116.

Haack, F.W. *Jugendreligionen*. Munich, 1979.

Hernando, J. Garcia. *Pluralismo Religioso*. Vol II. Sects and non-Christian religions. Madrid, 1983.

Hummel, R. *Indische Mission und neue Frommigkeit im Westen*. Stuttgart, 1982.

O'Cuinn, C. *Why the New Youth Religions?* Ireland, 1980.

Schreiner, L. and Mildenberger, M. *Christus und die Gurus. Asiatische religiose Gruppen im Westen*. Stuttgart-Berlin, 1980.

Terrin, Aldo Natale. *Nuove Religioni. Alla Ricerca della Terra Promessa*. Editrice Morcelliania-Brescia, 1985.

Vernette, Jean. *Au pays de nouveau-sacre. Voyage a l'interieur de la juene generation.* (Centurion edition), 1981.

Vernette, Jean. *Sectes et reveil religieux* (Salvator edition, Cedex) 1976.

Asia

Earhart, Byron H. *The New Religions of Japan: A Bibliography of Western-Language Materials.* Michigan Papers in Japanese Studies 9. Center for Japanese Studies. 8 XXVI. Michigan, 1983.

Elwood, D. *Churches and Sects in the Philippines.* [n.d.]

Lee, Raymond L.M., and Ackerman, S.E. "Conflict and Solidarity in a Pentecostal Group in Urban Malaysia." *The Sociological Review, Vol. 28*, No. 4, 1980.

Lacombe, Olivier. "Les 'Sectes' dans l'hindouisme." *Axes, Vol. X/2* (Dec. 1977-Jan. 1978).

Van Des Kroef, Justus M. "Mouvements religieux modernes d'acculturation en Indonesie." *Histoire des Religions, Vol. III*, under the direction of Henri-Charles Puech. Paris: Gallimard, 1976.

Latin America

Council of Latin American Bishops' Conferences (CELAM). *Sectas en America Latina.* Bogota, 1982.

Glazier, Stephen D. "Religion and Contemporary Religious Movements in the Caribbean: A Report." *Sociological Analysis, Vol. 41*, No. 2 (Summer 1980).

Metraux, A. "Les Messies de l'Amerique du Sud." *Archives de Sociologie des Religions, Vol. 2, No. 4 (July-Dec. 1957).*

Oliveira Filho, Jose Jeremias. Notas de Sociologia das Seitas. Cuadernos de ISER, 1975.

Prado, Juan Guillermo. *Sectas Juveniles en Chile.* Covadonga edition: Santiago, 1984.

Samain, Etienne. "Bibliographia Sobre Religiosidade popular." *Reli-giao e Sociedade, No. 1.* Hucitec: Sao Paulo, 1977.

Schlesinger, Hugo and Porto, Humberto. *Crencas, Seitas e Simbolos Religiosos.* Paulinas ed: Sao Paulo, 1982.

Willems, Emilio. *Followers of a New Faith* (Brazil and Chile). Nashville (TN) 1968.

Oceania and the Pacific Islands

Burridge, K.O.L. "Mouvements religieuses d'acculturation en Oceanie." *Histoire des Religions, Vol. III.* Gallimard: Paris, 1976.

Hodee, Paul. "Culture moderne, sectes, problems familiaux et non-croyence en Polynesie francaise." *Ateismo e Dialogo, Vol. 15,* No. 4 (1980).

Verity, Leslie. *Dangerous Trends: An Analysis of the Social Repercussions of the "New" Religions and the Anti-religious Movement.* Auckland, 1977.

Worsley, Peter. *The Trumpet Shall Sound: A Study of Cargo Cults in Melanesia.* Schocken Books: New York, 1968.

North America

Anthony, D., et al. *The New Religious Movements: Conversions, Coercion and Commitment.* Crossroad: New York, 1983.

Appel, W. *Cults in America: Programmed for Paradise.* New York, 1983.

Bergeron, Richard. *Le Cortege des Fous de Dieu.* Montreal, 1982.

Bird, F. and Reimer, B. "A Sociological Analysis of New Religions and Para-Religious Movements in the Montreal Area." *Canadian Journal,* 1976.

Clark, S.D. *Church and Sect in Canada.* Toronto, 1948.

Hill, D.C. *A Study of Mind Development Groups, Sects and Cults in Ontario.* Govt. Publ: Ottawa, 1980.

Stipelman, S. *Coping with Cults.* (a course for students) Jewish Education Council of Montreal, 1982.

Zaretsky, E.J. and Leone, M.P. (eds.). *Religious Movements in Contemporary America.* Princeton (NJ), 1974.

Appendix X

Two articles from the "Cultic Studies Journal," (Vol. 2, No. 2, 1985) of the American Family Foundation (Weston, Massachusetts) which appeared in a special issue devoted to the ethics of excessive proselytizing. They are included here to provide a better understanding of this subject, which affects cultic and non-cultic groups who seek new members through recruitment and conversion. Reprinted with permission.

Evangelization and Freedom in the Catholic Church

By James LeBar

Twenty years ago — October 28, 1965, to be exact — the Catholic Bishops of the world, in the final section of the Second Vatican Council, promulgated a document that revolutionized the attitude of Catholics toward other religions. Known by its first words in Latin, *Nostra Aetate* ("In our age"), this document has provided the basis for dialogue and collaboration among the non-Christian religions.

During the year 1985 the Jewish community throughout the world joined with the Catholic Church to mark the anniversary of this document and the progress in understanding and brotherhood that has been achieved over the past twenty years. There were interfaith meetings at the Vatican in the spring and fall, and the Thanksgiving Square Foundation sponsored a symposium in Dallas, Texas, at which the President of the Vatican Secretariat for non-Christians, Francis Cardinal Arinze, was the principal participant. After a day of discussions, a banquet was held during which leaders of seven world religions expressed thanksgiving to God and to the Catholic Church for this document.

Less than two months after the release of *Nostra Aetate*, on December 7, 1965, this same Vatican Council issued the decrees *Dignitatis Humanae* (of Human Dignity) and *Ad Gentes Divinitus* (Divinity Sent to the Nations). The first is usually called the Decree on Religious Liberty and the second is the Decree on Missionary Activity in the Church. These two documents, coupled with *Nostra Aetate*, provide the schema for missionary activity of the Catholic Church at the present time.

The Founders of the Second Vatican Council could scarcely have known, twenty years ago, how different the missionary scene would be in the 1980's, with the rise of the cults, gurus, and self-proclaimed messiahs in the United States and other countries. Although fundamentalism did exist at that time, its rapid expansion, often in the form of cult-like groups, could not have been predicted.

In the midst of its own efforts at renewal the Catholic Church experienced both positive and negative reactions to the many changes decreed by the Vatican Council. Many could not understand the new relationship of openness and dialogue with other Christian Churches, with Jewish leaders, and with other non-Christian groups. At the same time that the cults and gurus were increasing their influence, society found itself in a very materialistic period. In reaction to this materialism, many persons began to seek goodness, peace and God; however, they looked outside the framework of the Churches, Catholic and otherwise. They were ripe for the cult leaders and the gurus.

Other enterprising people saw the Bible as a drawing card for followers, and many biblically oriented cultic groups arose. Nevertheless, there were then, and are now, many biblically based churches and other organizations that are not cults, even though they do not resemble traditional churches. Many Catholics have become involved with such groups, and the Church, although concerned about their departure, respects this choice. The Decree on Religious Liberty states:

> The Vatican Council declares that the human person has a right to religious freedom. Freedom of this kind means that all men should be immune from coercion on the part of individuals, social groups and every human power so that, within due limits, nobody is forced to act against his convictions in religious matters in private or in public, alone or in associations with others. The Council further declares that the right to religious freedom is based on the very dignity of the human person as known by the revealed word of God and by reason itself.

This particular idea is repeated in the Decree on Missionary Activity with a different emphasis:

> The Church strictly forbids that anyone should be forced to accept the faith, or be induced or enticed by unworthy devices; as it likewise strongly defends the right that no one should be frightened away from the faith by unjust persecutions.

The Church does object, however, when it becomes obvious that many of its members are deceitfully enticed *away from* the Church of their heritage without the individual person making a conscious, free choice to *move to* a new religious group.

With the above concepts in mind, let us examine a problem that has become prevalent in the present time: the excessively aggressive missionary activities of some religious groups and the problems they cause for themselves and for other groups who seek to exercise freedom of religion and freedom of speech.

There are many factors to consider whenever one discusses religion and freedom, especially in America. Americans are particularly sensitive to their First Amendment freedom and will tolerate no intrusions in this area. Americans are used to making choices, and they resent any group or individual who places restrictions on their ability to do so. In addition, Americans have developed a sense of fair play and mutual respect, even in areas of intense competition. Thus, while we may witness a fierce political campaign, when it is over we all accept the results of the election, and respect and honor are given to the elected officials, even by members of the opposition party.

However, when matters of religion and faith are concerned, all these influences converge with a tenacity that defies explanation.

For the Christian, Catholic or otherwise, the impetus for missionary activity comes from the Gospel, from the words of Jesus himself. Sometimes called the "Great Commission," these three passages are significant:

> Thus it is written that the Messiah must suffer and rise from the dead on the third day. In his name, penance for the remission of sins is to be preached to all the nations, beginning at Jerusalem. (Luke 24:46-47)
>
> Jesus came forward and addressed them in these words: "Full authority has been given me both in heaven and earth; go therefore and make disciples of all the nations. Baptize them in the name of the Father, and of the Son, and of the Holy Spirit. Teach them to carry out everything I have commanded you." (Matthew 28:18-20a)
>
> Then he told them: "Go into the whole world and proclaim the good news to all creation. The man who believes in it and accepts baptism will be saved; the man who refuses to believe in it will be condemned." (Mark 16:15-16)

Concentrating on the early Christians for the moment, we note that the Apostles did follow this Great Commission and saw to it that the Gospel — the Good News — was proclaimed and preached to the whole world. Ancient secular history attests to the fact that the followers of Jesus, first called Christians at Antioch, were quite enthusiastic about their faith, and as such converted many to this "new way."

In later centuries the Church continued to expand through missionary activity, more formalized and organized than in the days of primitive Christianity. Great men such as St. Patrick in Ireland, Saints Cyril and Methodius in the Slavic lands, and Saint Boniface in Germany appeared on the scene to spearhead missionary efforts. Religious communities were also formed to bring the message of Christ to foreign lands through health care, education, and pastoral care. For the most part, Christianity prospered and spread far and wide.

Opposition to the spread of Christianity was not long in coming, however. The Romans persecuted the Christians, for example, by throwing them to the lions. Later, Islam took a fanatical, warlike position that saw the Moslems and Christians engaged in fierce wars for many years, particularly over the custody of the holy shrines in Jerusalem.

For the most part, however, the spread of Christianity and opposition to it operated well within the realm of proper social influence and custom. There were influences, to be sure, sometimes even intimidation, but the causes for the most part that influenced decision making were practical and sensible. However, some were not always reasonable. The early Christians were often faced with the choice of adhering to their new faith or being put to death. Later, Christians were faced with the possibility of expulsion from their homelands if they did not adhere to the religion of the king. Modern Christians in some Communist countries are forced to choose between their Christian faith and their very existence.

All this may seem to be a rather long way to the heart of the problems caused by some groups which use high-pressure methods to proclaim the Good News. But it is a necessary preamble if one is to understand the dangers in these groups.

It is not difficult to recognize the more prominent cult leaders and their followers. But when a particular group purports to use the Bible as its source of information and authority, and has a leader who is energetic, enthusiastic, and motivating, the true value of the group is more difficult to ascertain.

Today's society has a large number of self-appointed people who seek to fulfill the Great Commission according to their own designs, without recourse to any higher human authority. Sometimes their enthusiasm slips from proper boundaries and a problem ensues. Many missionary groups have centered their activities on college campuses, and utilize high-pressure tactics to secure recruits. Such methods are quite successful because so many students today lack a basic religious education — of whatever faith group — and either do not know how to counter the efforts or, perhaps, not having had true religious experiences in the past, are open to whatever is suggested. Furthermore, they are not aware of the manipulation of their freedom of choice and their power to evaluate ideas properly.

Joseph Cardinal Bernardin, Archbishop of Chicago, in an address to the opening session of the then newly-founded National Council for Catholic evangelization on June 12, 1983, defined true evangelization in these words:

So as not to spend all my time explaining what evangelization is not, allow me to make a few positive statements about what I believe it to be. In the Scriptures, Jesus never evangelized through coercion. Rather, he did it by invitation. Jesus evangelized by inviting people to embrace several realities . . . all of which are connected and interrelated. . .

Let me summarize. Evangelization is always an invitation — to the Kingdom, to conversion, to discipleship. Jesus evangelized through word and deed. At times, His very presence evangelized. When Jesus evangelized, He offered meaning to people. He joined words and meanings to gestures of healing . . . Evangelization is not just a piece of the Church's educational ministries. It is surely that, but it is much more. It is the integrating force and thrust of all the Church's ministries.

How different this attitude is from groups which thrust the Bible or biblical verses at people so fast that they scarcely have time to think before an answer is required. The Catholic Church does indeed recognize the rights of others to evangelize, and in many instances cooperates in some activities where it is possible. But when any individual or group exceeds the boundaries of proper behavior, the Church is concerned, not only because some of its members may be lost, but also because the recruits for such a group, be they from the Catholic Church or any other Church, have no opportunity to make a free decision in the matter.

To determine whether a particular biblical group is helpful or harmful, several questions need to be addressed:

1. Is excessive pressure put on a recruit to become a member immediately?

2. Are members allowed to evaluate the teaching of the group with other groups, or with their own present church?

3. Are biblical texts used in persuasion quoted accurately and in context?

4. What are the purposes of the group? Can the recruit observe these purposes in action?

5. Who are the leaders of the group and where do they get their guidance, instruction, and leadership responsibility?

6. Regarding the group itself, what category of student is being recruited: the unchurched, the believer, the alienated, the members of other churches?

7. What relationship does the group have with other religious groups on campus, citywide, or nationally? Does it participate in ecumenical activities?

8. How does the particular group regard members of other denominations with regard to salvation?

If, for example, a particular group on a college campus — or elsewhere, for that matter — transforms a recruit into a "born-again Christian" overnight, talks against the previous faith of the recruit, and wants nothing to do with any other group, claiming they have the only way to salvation, then there is a high degree of probability that the group is a dangerous one.

Nor is there assurance that established churches are immune from such unethical behavior. An isolated small congregation might have a manipulative pastor who leads the flock astray. Within the Catholic Church, for example, there have been problems with Charismatic groups that have become too authoritarian and have refused to listen to the authority of the bishop. (The Bishop of Cleveland and the Archbishop of Newark have recently had to take action in this regard.) The very traditional and loyal Opus Dei organization has been criticized as well, and in Great Britain, Basil Cardinal Hume issued guidelines for the group in his Archdiocese. Thus, the Catholic Church's hierarchical system permits such abuses to be corrected when detected. Two additional instances, one recent, the other from a century ago, can serve as examples of this process:

A year or two ago in the Archdiocese of Miami, Florida, the archbishop declared null the baptism of a Jewish child. The baptism had been done during a child custody case, against the will of the parents. His reasoning for the action was that the parents had indicated a desire to raise the child as Jew, and thus the baptism, done at the instigation of an outside party, was improper, unwarranted and invalid.

In the nineteenth century, Theodore Ratisbonne, after a rather stormy early life, converted from Judaism to Catholicism, and in 1830 became a priest. He had a rather renowned life as a priest, gaining fame for his preaching, scholarship, and evangelization, specializing in the conversion of the Jews. In this latter capacity, two scandals occurred which involved Abbe Ratisbonne and damaged his reputation considerably. One of them was clearly a case of excessive proselytization. A Jewish child, whose mother died in childbirth, was raised with the consent of the father by a Jewish foster family who had her educated in Catholic Schools. When her foster parents died, her father claimed her guardianship, and the girl, by now eighteen years of age, claimed she had been pressured to become Catholic. The civil government and the Church both stepped in to rectify this situation, though this was not always the case.

In both these instances, the civil and/or the ecclesiastical authorities stepped in to rectify a situation gone astray. Religious groups which recognize no authority but their own, on the other hand, can easily fall into excessive practices that violate moral and ethical codes. If there is no safeguard through accountability, an individual leader can be mesmerized by success, adulation of the community, or other factors and use more and more controlling means to rule the flock.

Proselytizing has been a part of society since the beginning of the Christian era, if not before. Our concern here is not proper use of this tool, but its inordinate application coupled with other psychological and psycho-social techniques. No one can realistically prohibit or place restrictions on proselytizing without being accused of restricting freedom. In a pluralistic society such as ours in America, groups have the right to seek new members, but they have no right to use deception, high pressure, and guilt to force the decision of an individual.

True evangelization (evangelism) is done according to the norms that Jesus used. He invited. He invited people to hear His message, to decide to follow Him, and then to do so. The choice to stay or depart must be up to the individual. When Jesus taught a difficult doctrine, He saw many walk away, so many in fact that He asked His disciples, "Will you also go away?" (John 7:66-69) Any group wishing to be faithful to the Great Commission must do likewise.

As a final thought, the example of Mother Teresa and the Missionary Sisters of Charity comes to mind. Here is a woman who wanted the religious life as a Catholic Sister. She left her homeland of Yugoslavia and went to India. There she was so moved by the extreme poverty of the "unwashed" that she received permission to work with these people. Eventually she left the teaching order she had joined, and after other young women joined her, some from the order she had left, she founded her own community dedicated to the service of the poor. And today, more than fifty years later, the community prospers, and has more applicants than it can handle.

In October, 1984, Mother Teresa, at the invitation of Pope John Paul II, addressed the international priests' retreat at the Vatican, at which I was present. There I heard her give what I consider to be the most perfect example of evangelization. No pressure, no compulsion, no deception — just the life of a good person and the desire of a good ruler to help his people. Transcribed excerpts from her talk follow.

> I remember some time ago, some years back, when the President of Yemen asked for our Sisters to come to Yemen. And I was told that for so many, many years there has been no public chapel, public Mass, or publicly known fact that a person is a priest. . . So I told the president, "I am willing to give you the Sisters, but without a priest, without Jesus, we don't go."

> Then, they must have had a consultation between them, and they decided, "Yes." (And something struck me so much.) And the priest came. There was the altar. There was the tabernacle, there was Jesus. And only he (the priest) could bring Jesus there.

> After that the government built the building for us when we went there to take care of the street people, the dying, and the destitute; and they built a convent for us also. And then the governor who had sponsored the building — (Sister asked him, "Kindly make sure that one room be beautifully done because Jesus is going to be there") — built our chapel. And this governor asked Sister, "Sister, show me how to build the Roman Catholic Church right here." (He meant the little chapel, and instead of saying chapel, he said "Roman Catholic Church right here!") And they built that chapel so beautifully, and it is there today, and the Sisters are there.

> And then they asked us to open [a center] — they gave us a whole mountain — to rehabilitate the lepers, the many,

many lepers. So, we went to see the place, and I saw there an open grave. The smell, the awfulness of the bodies . . . I cannot express what I saw. And I was thinking, "Jesus, how, how can we leave you like that?" And then, I accepted that place. And if you went now, you would see quite a different place. And then I asked — they were all Muslims, not a single Catholic there — one of the rich men. . . I said, "These are all Muslim people. They need to pray. Kindly build a Mosque for them that they can pray." And the man was surprised that I, a Catholic Sister, would ask such a thing, but he built a most beautiful Mosque for the people. And you see those lepers, crawling, crawling, going there to pray. And then, when that Mosque was completely open, he turned to me and he said, "I give you my word. The next thing I will build is the Catholic Church for the Sisters."

These are beautiful examples of the hunger of people, of our poorest of the poor: the ignorant, the unwanted, the unloved, the rejected, the forgotten . . . yes, their hunger for God.

If only all missionaries could follow this model, this world in which we live would be a different place. Evangelicals, Protestants, Catholics, and others would be truly fulfilling the Great Commission, which after all is to preach the commandment of love: "Love one another, such as my love has been for you, so must your love be for each other. This is how all will know you for my disciples: your love for one another." (John 13:34-35)

A Catholic Viewpoint on Christian Evangelizers

By James E. McGuire

My purpose in the following article is to address some of the specific concerns that I hear Roman Catholic clergyman, parents, and young people express with respect to "Christian" evangelizers who seem more concerned with winning converts to their particular group than with witnessing to Christ.

It is not my intention at this time to focus on the more global and discursive point of guaranteed religious freedom in the United States today. The first amendment guarantees of religious belief and practices, so often discussed in general terms, are not usually at the heart of the matter when Christians and non-Christians discuss controversial evangelizing or proselytizing activities. People are usually more caught up in the impact that sudden conversions have on an individual's inner peace and previous religious commitment, as well as the family's reaction to a member's sudden conversion to "Christianity."

Personal Faith and Religious Anthropology

Four years ago, an eighteen-year-old friend of mine, a graduate of twelve years of traditional Roman Catholic education, went South to begin her college education. Having chosen a small Baptist school in South Carolina, Kim suddenly found herself rooming with a Baptist student who "witnessed" constantly, reading from the Bible and questioning Kim's commitment to Christ almost daily.

Kim called me several times, deeply upset and agitated that her fundamental structure of personal faith and confessional experience were under constant attack. I advised her to make the statement, "Yes, I am saved. As a Roman Catholic, I have encountered Jesus as my personal Savior, and the Holy Spirit is in my life."

My reasons for this counsel were twofold: first, I am genuinely convinced that Kim did then and still does believe in Jesus as her Lord, and second, her present vocation as a radiologist is a definite manifestation of the inner goodness and Christian concern that was observable in her life four years ago.

Unfortunately for Kim, my suggestion had little impact on her roommate, who then shifted her questioning to such Roman Catholic doctrines as devotion to Mary Mother of the Lord, the sacraments, the office of the Papacy, and the centrality of the Eucharist.

Why? That's what Kim and I both wanted to know at the time. I am sure that we will never answer the question as concerns this particular case, because Kim had to withdraw from the school after one semester — and one roommate later. We were both one hundred percent certain that the context of this particular campus was not conducive to her spiritual, mental, and physical well-being.

This case, while not absolutely paradigmatic, is typical of such encounters as experienced by both Catholic and non-Christian young people, especially those of the Jewish faith.

The main reason that such persistent proselytizing occurs, in my view, is that the proselytizers or evangelists assume that Kim and others like her "need to be saved." When a proselytizer's opening question is a direct and penetrating "Have you accepted Jesus as your personal Savior?" delivered without qualifications or regard for the other person's readiness to answer, that is too heavy a burden for a stranger to place on a young person.

Shouldn't the question be a little more protracted in order to include the necessary nuances? How about this instead: "Given your Roman Catholic background and my Baptist background, do you feel as I do that we have a common ground to discuss and share one another's understanding of and commitment to the person of Jesus Christ?"

Such wording respects what I feel is the pivotal point in this entire context: the recognition that every Christian is the sum total of each person and experience that he or she has met along the way in his or her family, church, school, and community. In other words, a person's individual, family, and religious history and church experience — his or her Christian *anthropology* — must be acknowledged and respected from the start.

The love, sweat, tears, and faith experiences of our home front — parents, friends, neighbors, parishioners, priest, minister, or rabbi — are sacred memories, constitutive of our being who we are, and should never be taken for granted or casually dismissed as no longer important, or, worse, as mistaken.

Herein lies my greatest worry, and the root of some degree of resentment of the young, zealous Christian proselytizers and/or evangelists who are taking off after the "unsaved" of this world. With little or no study of or interest in the theologies and practices of other Christian denominations or non-Christian religions, with a limited perspective on the psychological, emotional, and rational dimensions of how a person's faith is formed and develops, and with very little sensitivity to where a person "has been" in his or her quest for God, their encounters with the "unsaved" most often take place in a religious, social, cultural, and psychological vacuum.

The zealot doesn't seem concerned with the family turmoil which may result from a young person's rejection of former ways; the mandate to save must take precedent. My objection is not to this centrality of achieving salvation from the Lord, but the manner, the *modus agendi*, the over enthusiastic and even fanatical tendencies of some proselytizers and evangelizers.

The dilemma that these overly enthusiastic and somewhat fanatical evangelizers presents to the evangelical church is truly ironic.

The primacy given through the centuries to the Bible's authority over all human authorities is now theologically troublesome to evangelical Protestantism. How can you temper over-enthused or fanatical disciples without some measure of church authority and a fundamental listing of gospel teachings? But *whose* authority and *whose* list of teachings? A tradition of private interpretation of biblical truths seems to clash with the contemporary need of the evangelical churches to respect other people's God-given and constitutionally guaranteed freedom to think, to decide, and to act religiously and responsibly.

Whose evangelical voice is the "most" correct? Will authority rest with Billy Graham, Jimmy Swaggart, Jerry Falwell, Oral Roberts, the Inter-Varsity Fellowship, the Fellowship of Christian Athletes? Therein lies the dilemma for this one Roman Catholic priest.

Who is to speak authoritatively and decisively for the Christian evangelical churches? Who will be recognized as the voice of fairness, equity, and genuine Christian truth in the larger dialogue of evangelical Christianity with "mainstream" Protestant churches, Roman and Orthodox Churches, Judaism, Islam, Hinduism, Buddhism, and a hundred other confessional bodies?

If the pluralism of American religious experience is to be respected, American evangelical Christians face the serious challenge of evolving external church structures that embody authority, discipline, and doctrine. Evangelical Christians must also accept the central challenge presented by the advances in ecumenism and interdenominational dialogue. These absolutely necessary conditions must be met if mutual witnessing and evangelization are to occur without mistrust and misunderstanding.

My spirit and intent in this article has been polemical — not in the manner of provocation and disunity, but intellectually polemical; more, I trust, in the manner of a Christian apologist.

The issue needing our immediate attention is the discomfort, unhappiness, and, at times, resentment felt by many Christians and non-Christians towards what they perceive as the unwholesome and troubling activities of Christian evangelicals who choose not to recognize and respect an individual's previous religious history, but act from some self-proclaimed divine mandate to save us guys out here in the chaos.

Appendix XI

Pastoral Responses of the U.S. Catholic Bishops

Pastoral Statement for Catholics on Biblical Fundamentalism

Archbishop John Whealon of Hartford, Connecticut, chaired the ad hoc Committee on Biblical Fundamentalism of the National Conference of Catholic Bishops which issued this statement on March 27, 1987. It is designed to assist Catholics in understanding the problems caused by fundamentalism.

It is reprinted here with permission of the copyright owners, the United States Catholic Conference.

This is a statement of concern to our Catholic brothers and sisters who may be attracted to biblical fundamentalism without realizing its serious weaknesses. We Catholic bishops, speaking as a special committee of the national Conference of

Catholic Bishops, desire to remind our faithful of the fullness of Christianity that God has provided in the Catholic Church.

Fundamentalism indicates a person's general approach to life which is typified by unyielding adherence to rigid doctrinal and ideological positions — an approach that affects the individual's social and political attitudes as well as religious ones. Fundamentalism in this sense is found in non-Christian religions and can be doctrinal as well as biblical. But in this statement we are speaking only of biblical fundamentalism, presently attractive to some Christians, including some Catholics.

Biblical fundamentalists are those who present the Bible, God's inspired word, as the only necessary source for teaching about Christ and Christian living. This insistence on the teaching Bible is usually accompanied by a spirit that is warm, friendly and pious. Such a spirit attracts many (especially idealistic young) converts. With ecumenical respect for these communities, we acknowledge their proper emphasis on religion as influencing family life and workplace. The immediate attractions are the ardor of the Christian community and the promises of certitude and of a personal conversion experience to the person of Jesus Christ without the need of church. As Catholic pastors, however, we note its presentation of the Bible as a single rule for living. According to fundamentalism, the Bible alone is sufficient. There is no place for the universal teaching church — including its wisdom, its teachings, creeds and other doctrinal formulations, its liturgical and devotional traditions. There is simply no claim to a visible, audible, living, teaching authority binding the individual or congregations.

A further characteristic of biblical fundamentalism is that it tends to interpret the Bible as being always without error or as literally true in a way quite different from the Catholic Church's teaching on the inerrancy of the Bible. For some biblical fundamentalists, inerrancy extends even to scientific and historical matters. The Bible is presented without regard for its historical context and development.

In 1943 Pope Pius XII encouraged the church to promote biblical study and renewal, making use of textual criticism. The Catholic Church continued to study the Bible as a valuable guide for Christian living. In 1965 the Second Vatican Council, in its Constitution on Divine Revelation, gave specific teaching on the Bible. Catholics are taught to see the Bible as God's book — and also as a collection of books written under divine inspiration by many human beings. The Bible is true — and to discover its inspired truth we should study the patterns of thinking and writing used in ancient biblical times. With Vatican II, we believe that "the books of Scripture must be acknowledged as teaching firmly, faithfully and without error that truth which God wanted put into the sacred writings for the sake of our salvation" (Dogmatic Constitution on Divine Revelation, 11). We do not look upon the Bible as an authority for science or history. We see truth in the Bible as not to be reduced solely to literal truth, but also to include salvation truths expressed in varied literary forms.

We observed in biblical fundamentalism an effort to try to find in the Bible all the direct answers for living — though the Bible itself nowhere claims such authority. The appeal of such an approach is understandable. Our world is one of war, violence, dishonesty, personal and sexual irresponsibility. It is a world in which people are frightened by the power of the nuclear bomb and the insanity of the arms race, where the only news seems to be bad news. People of all ages yearn for answers. They look for sure, definite rules for living. And they are given answers — simplistic answers to complex issues — in a confident and enthusiastic way in fundamentalist Bible groups.

The appeal is evident for the Catholic young adult or teenager — one whose family background may be troubled; who is struggling with life, morality and religion; whose Catholic education may have been seriously inadequate in the fundamentals of doctrine, the Bible, prayer life and sacramental living; whose catechetical formation may have been inadequate in presenting the full Catholic traditions and teaching authority. For such a person, the appeal of finding *the answer* in a devout, studious, prayerful, warm, Bible-quoting class is easy to understand. But the ultimate problem with such fundamentalism is that it can give only a limited number of answers and cannot present those answers, on balance, because it does not have Christ's teaching church nor even an understanding of how the Bible originally came to be written and collected in the sacred canon, or official list of inspired books.

Our Catholic belief is that we know God's revelation in the total Gospel. The Gospel comes to us through the Spirit-tradition of the church and the inspired books: "This sacred tradition, therefore, and Sacred Scripture of both the Old and New Testament are like a mirror in which the pilgrim church on earth looks at God" (Dogmatic Constitution on Divine Revelation, 7).

A key question for any Christian is, Does the community of faith which is the Lord's church have a living tradition which presents God's word across the centuries until the Lord comes again? The Catholic answer to this question is an unqualified yes. That answer was expressed most recently in the Constitution on Divine Revelation of the Second Vatican Council. We look to both the church's official teaching and Scripture for guidance in addressing life's problems. It is the official teaching or magisterium that in a special way guides us in matters of belief and morality that have developed after the last word of Scripture was written. The church of Christ teaches in the name of Christ and teaches us concerning the Bible itself.

The basic characteristic of biblical fundamentalism is that it eliminates from Christianity the church as the Lord Jesus founded it. That church is a community of faith, worldwide, with pastoral and teaching authority. This non-church characteristic of biblical fundamentalism, which sees the church as only spiritual, may not at first be clear to some Catholics. From some fundamentalists they will hear nothing offensive to their beliefs, and much of what they hear seems compatible with Catholic Christianity. The difference is often not in what is said — but in what is not said. There is no mention of the historic, authoritative church in continuity with Peter and the other apostles. There is no vision of the church as our mother — a mother who is not just spiritual, but who is visibly ours to teach and guide us in the way of Christ.

Unfortunately, a minority of fundamentalist churches and sects not only put down the Catholic Church as a "man-made organization" with "man-made rules," but indulge in crude anti-Catholic bigotry with which Catholics have long been familiar.

We believe that no Catholic properly catechized in the faith can long live the Christian life without those elements that are had only in the fullness of Christianity: the eucharist and the other six sacraments, the celebration of the word in the liturgical cycle, the veneration of the Blessed Mother and the saints, teaching authority and history linked to Christ, and the demanding social doctrine of the church based on the sacredness of all human life.

It is important for every Catholic to realize that the church produced the New Testament, not vice versa. The Bible did not come down from heaven, whole and intact, given by the Holy Spirit. Just as the experience and faith of Israel developed its sacred books, so was the early Christian Church the matrix of the New Testament. The Catholic Church has authoritatively told us which books are inspired by the Holy Spirit and are therefore canonical. The Bible, then, is the church's book. The New Testament did not come before the church, but from the Church. Peter and the other apostles were given special authority to teach and govern before the New Testament was written. The first generation of Christians had no New Testament at all — but they were the church then, just as we are the church today.

A study of the New Testament, in fact, shows that discipleship is to be a community experience with liturgy and headship and demonstrates the importance of belonging to the church started by Jesus Christ. Christ chose Peter and the other apostles as foundations of his church, made Simon Peter its rock foundation and gave a teaching authority to Peter and the other apostles. This is most clear in the Gospel of Matthew, the only Gospel to use the word *church*. The history of 20 Christian centuries confirms our belief that Peter and the other apostles have been succeeded by the bishop of Rome and the other bishops, and that the flock of Christ still has, under Christ, a universal shepherd.

For historical reasons the Catholic Church in the past did not encourage Bible studies as much as she could have. True, printing (the Latin Bible was the first work printed) was not invented until the mid-15th century, and few people were literate during the first 16 centuries of Christianity. But in the scriptural renewal the church strongly encourages her sons and daughters to read, study and live the Bible. The proclamation of the Scriptures in the liturgical assembly is to be prepared for by private Bible study and prayer. At the present time, two decades after Vatican II, we Catholics have all the tools needed to become Christians who know, love and live the Holy Bible. We have a well-ordered Lectionary that opens for us the treasures of all the books of the Bible in a three-year cycle for Sunday and holy day Masses, and a more complete two-year cycle for weekday Masses. Through the Lectionary the Catholic becomes familiar with the Bible according to the rhythm of the liturgical seasons and the church's experience and use of the Bible at Mass. We have excellent translations (with notes) in The New American Bible and The Jerusalem Bible. We have other accurate translations with an imprimatur. We have an abundance of commentaries, tapes, charts and Bible societies.

We Catholics have excellent Bible resources and scholars of

international repute. Our challenge now is to get this knowledge into the minds, hearts and lives of all our Catholic people. We need a pastoral plan for the word of God that will place the Sacred Scriptures at the heart of the parish and individual life. Pastoral creativity can develop approaches such as weekly Bible study groups and yearly Bible schools in every parish. We need to have the introduction to each Bible reading prepared and presented by the lector in a way that shows familiarity with and love for the sacred text (cf. Foreword to the Lectionary, Introduction, Nos. 15, 155, 313, 320). In areas where there is a special problem with fundamentalism, the pastor may consider a Mass to which people bring their own Bibles and in which qualified lectors present a carefully prepared introduction and read the text — without, however, making the Liturgy of the Word a Bible study class. We need better homilies, since the homily is the most effective way of applying biblical texts to daily living. We need a familiar quoting of the Bible by every catechist, lector and minister. We have not done enough in this area. The neglect of parents in catechetics and the weakness of our adult education efforts are now producing a grim harvest. We need to educate — to re-educate — our people knowingly in the Bible so as to counteract the simplicities of biblical fundamentalism.

In addition to that, we Catholics need to redouble our efforts to make our parish Masses an expression of worship in which all — parishioners, visitors and strangers — feel the warmth and the welcome and know that here the Bible is clearly reverenced and preached. The current trend toward smaller faith-sharing and Bible-studying groups within a parish family is strongly to be encouraged.

We call for further research on this entire question. We note that the U.S. Center for the Catholic Biblical Apostolate (1312 Massachusetts Avenue, N.W., Washington, D.C. 20005) will maintain an updated listing of available resources for Catholic Bible study. Any individual Catholic parish representative may write to learn the many available helps for developing Bible study and Bible teaching in accord with our long and rich Catholic tradition.

Ad Hoc Committee on Biblical Fundamentalism:
Archbishop John F. Whealon — Chairman, Bishop Alvaro Corrada del Rio, S.J., Archbishop Theodore E. McCarrick, Bishop Richard J. Sklba, Archbishop J. Francis Stafford, and Bishop Donald W. Trautman.

Responding to Proselytism
Letter of California's Hispanic Bishops

The drift of Hispanic Catholics to other religious communities is treated by the six Hispanic bishops of California in a letter they issued in May [1988]. Addressed to the Hispanic people of California, the letter expresses concern for the people, "body and soul, materially and spiritually."

The bishops pledge their "continuing efforts to help you achieve that level of dignity and respect owed you as children of a loving God." Speaking to the claims made by groups that proselytize in Hispanic communities, the bishops say: "We hope that our words will not be taken as an attack on true religious respect, on true ecumenism. . . . This drift to other religions is usually the direct result of an aggressive and disrespectful proselytism on the part of some so-called Christian sects, not the mainline denominations of Protestant Christianity."

The bishops note that Hispanic Catholics often do not find Spanish-speaking priests in U.S. parishes. But the bishops add that steps are being taken in seminaries and religious communities to change this situation. The bishops stress some of the strengths of the Catholic Church as well as the role played in the church for many centuries by Spanish-speaking Catholics. "Our Catholic faith is part of an ancient heritage of which we as Catholics of Hispanic origin should be especially proud," the bishops write. Their letter follows.

We, the Hispanic bishops of California, wish to express to you, the Hispanic people of California, by means of this pastoral letter the deep love and concern we have for you. We share the same history, culture and struggles, and your opportunities and problems are our opportunities and problems. We wish to encourage you to be all that you can be and all that God desires you to be. You are the sons and daughters of God! St. Paul expresses this marvelous truth in his Letter to the Galatians:

"You are no longer a slave but a son! And the fact that you are a son makes you an heir, by God's design" (Gal. 4:7).

Our brother bishops of California, and indeed all the bishops of the United States, share these same sentiments with us in regard to you. You are a very important part of the church in California and throughout the United States. This conviction was already expressed in the words of the pastoral letter "The Hispanic Presence: Challenge and Commitment" addressed to you by all the bishops of the United States on Dec. 12, 1983: "At this moment of grace we recognize the Hispanic community among us as a blessing from God." What we say here is meant to reinforce this conviction of ours and communicate it to you more effectively.

Your and Our Concerns Are Many

You have many concerns. Your lives are not as full, peaceful, meaningful and dignified as you would like. Some of you live in continuous fear because of your immigration status and the inadequacy of the existing immigration policies. Many of you are parents and are experiencing great confusion and difficulty in raising your children in another culture, a culture which is markedly different from our traditional Hispanic cultures. You do not always find understanding and acceptance for yourselves or your children. A growing number of your children do complete high school and go on to college and a profession, thanks to their own dedication and the support they receive from you. Many, nevertheless, are dropping out of school. An alarming number are involved with gangs and drugs. The unemployment rate is also high among you. Very large numbers work hard for low wages and often receive little or no benefits such as medical care and insurance. Your children's future is already threatened before birth by the lack of prenatal care and the anti-conception, pro-abortion mentality of many segments of society in the United States. The aged among you, our beloved *ancianos*, moreover, are forced to live in inadequate conditions because of the lack of affordable housing.

We, the Hispanic bishops of California, take all of these realities to heart. We are concerned about you, body and soul, materially and spiritually. That integral concern inspires us today as we reflect on your circumstances as immigrant people and as a minority within U.S. society. We hope that this letter will be one of many which will allow us to approach these concerns in a constructive way. At this time we wish to concentrate on a situation that especially saddens us.

One Situation Especially Saddens Us

The main concern we wish to address at this time is the drift to other religions of so many Hispanics who were baptized and often raised in the Catholic faith. We hope that our words will not be taken as an attack on true religious respect, on true ecumenism, as that wonderful movement has developed since the time of Pope John XXIII. This drift to other religions is usually the direct result of an aggressive and disrespectful proselytism on the part of some so-called Christian sects, not the mainline denominations of Protestant Christianity. The Roman Catholic Church enjoys ever-increasing mutual understanding and respect with the vast majority of Protestant Christian traditions. We are maintaining a dialogue in the pursuit of Christian unity with them. This was the prayer of Jesus Christ: "that all may be one as you, Father, are in me, and I in you; I pray that they may be one in us, that the world may believe that you have sent me" (Jn 17:21).

If you are among those who are no longer practicing Catholics, ask yourselves why and then read this letter, which is in a very special way addressed and dedicated to you because we care about you. If you are presently an active member of the Catholic Church, you should also read this letter in order to re-affirm your faith and to help us bring back those who have fallen away.

Why Some Leave the Catholic Church

What are some factors which have alienated some of our Hispanic brothers and sisters?

1. Members of religious sects might have visited you and confused you. They lead some of you to believe that the teachings and practices of our church are wrong or contrary to the spirit of Jesus Christ. They try to "prove" this to you citing texts from the Bible. Some of you may have felt that your eyes and ears were opened to the truth and that you had been deceived by priests and other Catholic teachers. Frequently those who attack Catholic doctrine do not really know what the doctrines are. They have incomplete and unfounded ideas about what the church really teaches. You are told, for instance, that it is wrong to pray to the saints or even to Mary, and to "adore" statues as they claim we do. First of all, Catholics are not taught to adore the saints or statues. We adore only

God. We do believe, however, that God has special friends, people of exceptional virtue and integrity — the saints — who have attained a level of holiness, of intense friendship with him, that allows them to be special instruments of his grace. God has always reached down to us through others, most especially through Jesus Christ. The saints can intercede for other human beings before God. This has been the ancient custom and belief of Christians from the earliest times of Christianity. It seems very strange, moreover, that these sects should attack us for venerating the saints, since it is a common and very commendable human custom to venerate the memory, the image or the photograph of family, dear friends and loved ones. Do we not keep photographs of loved ones in our wallet and lovingly contemplate them from time to time?

The church presents saints to us as heroes of virtue and as models to follow. The saints are special members of God's family. They are God's dear friends and loved ones. If great and miraculous events come about through the intercession of Mary and the saints, it is all due to God, whom we know through Jesus Christ and his followers down through the ages.

2. Another reason why you may be disenchanted with the church is that you might have felt that you were not understood by a priest or religious at some time or other. Some priests and religious are extremely tired and under stress due to the heavy demands made upon their time and human energies. Like everybody else, some priests and religious find it difficult at times to balance work, study, prayer and wholesome relaxation. Be aware that those who are called to serve in the church — in our church and in any other church for that matter — are subject to imperfections. They are men and women burdened by the same weaknesses and faults as everyone else.

Because of the heavy burdens and stress placed upon those who are called to serve in the church, we encourage you to show support and solidarity to them in a common effort to meet the spiritual and social challenges that we all face.

In many places, however, it is not a question of finding a priest who, for whatever reason, does not attend to you adequately. Rather, you do not find any Spanish-speaking priest at all and therefore you do not find the Mass and other services in Spanish. Many seminaries and religious congregations are making special appeals to Hispanic candidates for the priesthood. Learning Spanish is a requirement for ordination to the priesthood in some dioceses of California today. So there will be more Spanish-speaking priests to serve you. There are also many Spanish-speaking deacons serving you throughout California as well as committed religious men and women. There are many lay leaders collaborating with the priest. But if there is a shortage of priests, is it not due in part to the failure to cultivate vocations in the home? That is where you can help by fostering vocations, especially in the family.

3. The religious sects claim that we do not read or know the Bible in the Catholic Church. If today we and they enjoy the Bible, it is because the Catholic Church preserved it over the ages as a source of divine revelation. Our Hispanic Catholicism, for example, is permeated with a graphic and dramatic sense of the truths of Sacred Scripture. What else do you consider our religious celebrations with their Christmas pageants (*pastorelas*), our Holy Week drama and our household recitation of the rosary wherein we meditate on the major events in the Gospel story! Are not our cathedrals, churches, chapels and shrines graphic displays of biblical truths and are they not frequently more moving than words printed on a page? Finally, the eucharistic liturgy, the focal point of our prayer and worship, is permeated with scriptural elements.

Why Be a Catholic?

There are many reasons why we are blessed to be Catholic Christians. Let us consider now some of the advantages of being a Catholic:

1. We belong to a church and tradition that traces itself back to Jesus Christ, the Son of God made man. The religious sects pressuring you find their origins hundreds of years after the death of Christ. The continuity in faith and tradition that we enjoy as Catholics, in contrast, is beautifully expressed in the role of the successor of St. Peter, who is the pope. Peter unquestionably had a special function among the first apostles. Since the death of Peter, the church has maintained a historical list of the bishops of Rome who succeeded him. We Catholics should be grateful to God for this. In Matthew's Gospel we hear Jesus conferring upon Peter a special responsibility: "I say to you that you are Peter" (*rock* in the Aramaic language spoken by Jesus) "and upon this rock I will build my church" "and whatever you declare bound on earth shall be bound in heaven" (Mt. 16:18).

2. We Catholics have the privilege of enjoying a special relationship to Mary, the mother of Jesus. This is especially true of the Hispanic communities, who venerate Mary under many different titles. One of these is Blessed Mary of Guadalupe,

whose image is venerated on the *tilma* of Juan Diego preserved in the Basilica of Guadalupe in Mexico City. That image was entrusted to Juan Diego, who had only recently been baptized in the Catholic faith.

To accept the teaching of the sects is to reject Mary and what she stands for in God's wonderful plan of redemption. To join these sects is to betray the Marion tradition of our *ancestros*, who saw so clearly the terrible contradiction involved in accepting and loving Christ while rejecting or ignoring his mother.

3. The sacraments are opportunities to encounter God here and now. In the eucharist, or holy communion, we encounter Jesus Christ, body and blood, soul and divinity. This sacrament was left to us by Christ himself the night of his passion. The eucharistic liturgy, the Mass, is a biblically based celebration and incorporates almost countless biblical references in its various parts. The sects reject this marvelous sacramental encounter and therefore deprive their members of this incredible opportunity.

The sacrament of reconciliation was also instituted by Christ: "Receive the Holy Spirit. If you forgive sins, they are forgiven; if you do not forgive them, they are not forgiven" (Jn. 20:22-23). This sacrament has a long history and has been practiced in different ways from the very beginning of the church. The custom of privately confessing one's sin to the priest is very ancient. Those who take advantage of this wonderful encounter with Jesus Christ to receive absolution for sins committed after baptism can tell you how freeing and encouraging it is. Modern psychology tells us how important it is to overcome guilt and doubt in our lives. The sacrament of reconciliation, penance or confession as it is called, is a great blessing given us by Jesus Christ himself. It has been faithfully preserved in the Catholic Church.

4. Our Catholic faith is part of an ancient heritage of which we as Catholics of Hispanic origin should be especially proud. Today half the Roman Catholics of the world trace their religious and cultural heritage back to Spain and Portugal and to the rich popular Catholicism of Latin America. This Catholicism reflects the profound religious traditions of the indigenous cultures of the Americas into which it was grafted.

As Catholics we are part of a truly worldwide family of faith. The travels of our Holy Father Pope John Paul II have called attention more than ever before to the universal nature of our Catholic tradition and its vitality in a world looking for answers to so many questions about the meaning of human existence.

Conclusion

We, the Hispanic bishops of California, have addressed this pastoral letter to you, the many and diverse Hispanic communities of California. We have initiated a dialogue and have expressed our concern and real affection (*carino*) for you. Our love is only a faint shadow of God's infinite love for each and every one of you.

We wish to encourage you to assume your proper, active role in society and in the church. Remember always that the Roman Catholic Church is the church of our forefathers, of your *abuelos*. If you have left its ranks or moved away from it, we want to welcome you back. If you are a faithful member struggling to live your heritage of faith, we hope you will reaffirm others in that faith with the assistance and under the protection of the Virgin Mary, our mother.

We sincerely hope that all those involved in ministry and service in the church — your parish priests, your parish staff and your teachers — will take our words to heart. While these words have been addressed especially to you, our Hispanic brothers and sisters, it is the parish priest and his collaborators who have the primary responsibility to make our parishes and schools real communities that foster the hospitality and fellowship needed to make the concerns we express here something more than wishful thinking.

We pledge our continuing efforts to help you achieve the level of dignity and respect owed you as children of a loving God and brothers and sisters of the Lord Jesus Christ. We, as servants of that Lord, have pledged our lives to proclaim his Gospel. May you join with us in that joyful proclamation as Catholics of Hispanic origin: And may you do so with all your mind, heart and soul! *Que Dios Nuestro Senor les bendiga abundantemente.*

The six Hispanic bishops who signed this letter are: Joseph Madera; Auxiliary Bishops Juan Arzube, Gilbert Chavez, Alphonse Gallegos and Armando Ochoa; and retired Archbishop Tomas Clavel.

Appendix XII

Bibliography

(This listing of books on the subject was prepared by the BoysTown Center in Nebraska as part of their booklet CULTS and KIDS, and is used with permission of the Cult Awareness Network, who now have the reprint authority. * Best Bets)

*Alexander, Brooks et al. *The God Men: Witness Lee and 'The Local Church.'* Berkeley, CA: The Spiritual Counterfeits Project, 1977.

Allen, Steve. *Beloved Son, A Story of the Jesus Cults.* Indianapolis and New York: The Bobbs-Merrill Company, Inc., 1982.

*Appel, Willa. *Cults in America: Programmed for Paradise.* New York: Holt, Rinehart, and Winston, 1983.

Barron, Bruce. *If You Really Want to Follow Jesus.* Sycamore, IL 60178: Partners Press (from author: 644½ South Avenue), $3.75, 1981 (Shepherding).

Barrs, Jerram. *Shepherds and Sheep: A Biblical View of Leading and Following.* Downers Grove, IL 60515: Inter Varsity Press, 1983.

Belfrage, Sally. *Flowers of Emptiness: Reflections on an Ashram.* Dial Press, $10.95, 1981 (Rajneesh).

Biemiller, Lawrence. *"Campuses Trying to Control Religious Cults."* The Chronicle of Higher Education, April 6, 1983.

B'nai B'rith Cult Education Project. *The Magnetism of Cults.* Washington, D.C. 20036: B'nai B'rith, 1640 Rhode Island Avenue. NW, 1983 (videotape rent or purchase).

*Boettcher, Robert B. *Gifts of Deceit.* New York: Holt, Rinehart, and Winston, 1980.

Breeze, Dave. *Know the Marks of the Cults.* Wheaton, IL: Victor Books, 1977.

* Burtner, Rev. Wm. Kent. *Coping with Cults: How They Work in America.* Kansas City, MO 64040: N.C.R. Cassettes, Box 281, 1980. Audiocassettes, 3½ hours.

Bussell, Harold L. *Unholy Devotion: Why Cults Lure Christians.* Grand Rapids, MI: The Zondervan Publishing House, 1983.

Clark, John G. Jr., MD, et al. *Destructive Cult Conversions: Theory, Research, and Treatment.* Weston, MA 02193: Center on Destructive Cultism, P.O. Box 336, 1981.

*Congressional Information Meeting on *"The Cult Phenomenon in the United States."* Weston, MA 02193: American Family Foundation, Box 336. 161 pages. February 5, 1979.

*Conway, Flo and Jim Siegelman. *Snapping: America's Epidemic of Sudden Personality Change.* New York: J.B. Lippincott Company (also Dell Publishing), 1978.

Conway, Flo and Jim Siegelman. *"Information Disease: Have Cults Created a New Mental Illness?"* Science Digest, January 1982, 86ff.

Daner, Francine Jeane. *The American Children of Krishna: A Study of the Hare Krishna Movement.* New York: Holt, Rinehart, and Winston, 1976.

*Davis, Deborah Berg. *The Children of God: The Inside Story.* Grand Rapids, MI: The Zondervan Publishing House, 1984.

*Delgado, Richard. *"Religious Totalism: Gentle and Ungentle Persuasion Under the First Amendment."* Southern California Law Review, Volume 51, Number 1, 1977.

*Edwards, Christopher. *Crazy for God: The Nightmare of Cult Life.* Englewood Cliffs, NJ: Prentice Hall, Inc., 1979.

*Enroth, Ronald. *Youth, Brainwashing, and the Extremist Cults.* Grand Rapids, MI: The Zondervan Publishing House, 1977.

*Enroth, Ronald. *A Guide to Cults and New Religions.* Downers Grove, IL 60515: Inter Varsity Press, 1984.

*Freed, Josh. *Moonwebs: Journey into the Mind of a Cult.* Toronto, Ontario, Canada M5W 1C2: Canada Wide Feature Services, Ltd., Box 345, Station A, 1980.

Gerstel, David U. *Paradise Incorporated: Synanon* Novata, CA: Presidio Press, 1982.

Goldberg, Lorna and William. *"Group Work with Former Cultists."* Social Work, March 1982.

Hefley, James C. *The Youth Nappers,* Wheaton, IL: Victor Books, 1977.

*Heller, R.K. *Deprogramming for Do-It-Yourselfers.* Medina, OH 44258: The Gentle Press, Box 47, 1982.

*Horowitz, Irving Louis, Editor. *Science, Sin, and Scholarship: The Politics of Reverend Moon and the Unification Church.* Cambridge, MA: MIT Press, 1978.

Kaslow, Florence and Marvin Sussman. *"Cults and the Family."* Marriage and Family Review, Vol. 4, Numbers 3/4. New York: The Haworth Press, 1982.

*Kemperman, Steve. *Lord of the Second Advent: a Rare Look Inside the Terrifying World of the Moonies.* Ventura, CA: Regal Books, 1981.

Lane, David Christopher. *The Making of a Spiritual Movement — The Untold Story of Paul Twitchell and Eckankar.* Del Mar, CA: Del Mar Press, 1983.

Larson, Bob. *Larson's Book of Cults.* Wheaton, IL: Tyndale House Publishers, 1982.

*Lifton, Robert J. *Thought Reform and the Psychology of Totalism.* New York: W. W. Norton and Company, Inc., 1961. (See Chapter 22.)

*MacCollam, Joel A. *Carnival of Souls* (1978) and *Weekend That Never Ends* (1977). New York: Seabury Services/Episcopal Church Ministries.

Martin, Rachel. *Escape.* Denver, CO 80215: Accent B/P Publications, Box 15337, 1979 (Brother Evangelist cult).

Martin, Walter. *The New Cults.* Santa Ana, CA: Vision House, 1980.

McManus, Una. *Not for a Million Dollars*. Author's account of her years in Children of God. Nashville, TN: Impact Books, 1980.

*Mehta, Gita. *Karma Cola — Marketing the Mystic East*. New York: Simon and Schuster, 1979.

Methvin, Eugene H. *Scientology: Anatomy of a Frightening Cult* (May, 1980) and *Scientology: The Sickness Spreads* (September, 1981). Pleasantville, NY: The Readers Digest.

Mills, Jeanne. *Six Years with God — Life Inside Rev. Jim Jones's Peoples Temple*. New York: A & W Publishers, Inc., 1979.

* Mitchell, Dave and Cathy and Richard Ofshe. *The Light on Synanon*. New York: Seaview Books, 1980.

Patrick, Ted and Tom Dulack. *Let Our Children Go!* New York: E. P. Dutton and Company, Inc., 1976.

Reiterman, Tim and Jacobs, John. *Raven: The Untold Story of The Rev. Jim Jones and His People*. New York: E. P. Dutton and Company, Inc., $17.95, 1982.

*Rudin, James and Marcia. *Prison or Paradise*. Philadelphia: Fortress Press, 1980.

*Sargent, William. *Battle for the Mind: The Physiology of Conversion and Brainwashing*. New York: Harper and Row, 1971.

Sargent, William. *The Mind Possessed*. New York: Penguin Books, Inc., 1975.

*Schwartz, Alan. *The Way International*. New York 10017: Anti-Defamation League, 823 United Nations Plaza, 1982.

*Singer, Margaret. *"Coming Out of the Cults."* Psychology Today, January 1979.

Singer, Margaret and Louis J. West. *"Cults, Quacks, and Non-Professional Psychotherapies," Comprehensive Textbook of Psychiatry, III*. Baltimore: Williams and Wilkins, 1980.

Sklar, Dusty. *Gods and Beasts: The Nazis and the Occult*. New York: Harper and Row, 1977.

Sparks, Jack. *The Mind Benders*. Nashville, TN: Thomas Nelson, Publishers, 1977.

*Stoner, Carroll and Jo Anne Parke. *All God's Children: The Cult Experience — Salvation or Slavery?* New York: Penguin Books, 1979.

*Underwood, Barbara and Betty. *Hostage to Heaven: Four Years in the Unification Church by an Ex-Moonie* *and the Mother Who Fought to Free Her.* New York: Clarkson N. Potter, 1979.

Verdier, Paul A. *Brainwashing and the Cults: An Exposé on Capturing the Human Mind.* Los Angeles: Wilshire Publishers, 1977.

*Wallenstein, Herbert J. *Final Report on the Activities of the Children of God to Honorable Louis J. Lefkowitz, Attorney General of the State of New York.* Charity Frauds Bureau, September 30, 1974.

Wallis, Roy. *Road to Total Freedom: A Sociological Analysis of Scientology.* New York: Columbia University Press, 1977.

West, L. J. and Richard Delgado: *"Psyching Out the Cults' Collective Mania."* Los Angeles Times, October 26, 1978.

White, Mel. *Deceived: The Jonestown Tragedy.* Old Tappan, NJ: Fleming H. Revel Company, Spire Books, 1979.

*Williams, J. L. *Victor Paul Wierwille and The Way International.* Chicago: Moody Press, 1979.

Wood, Allen Tate with Jack Vitek. *Moonstruck: A Memoir of My Life in a Cult.* New York: William Morrow and Company, Inc., 1979.

Wooden, Kenneth. *The Children of Jonestown.* New York: McGraw-Hill, 1981.

*Yamamoto, J. Isamu. *The Puppet Master: A Biblical Perspective and Inquiry into Sun Myung Moon.* Downers Grove, IL 60515: Inter Varsity Press, 1980.

*Yanoff, Morris. *Where is Joey? Lost Among the Hare Krishnas.* Athens, OH: Ohio University Press, Swallow Press, 1981.

Zimbardo, Philip G. and Susan M. Andersen. *"Resisting Mind Control."* USA Today, November 1980.

Some additional works of interest in more specialized areas:

General Works:

Andres, Rachel and Lane, James (editors). *Cults and Consequences: The Definitive Handbook.* Los Angeles, 1988.

Catoir, Rev. John T. *World Religions.* New York: Christopher Books 1985

Cialdini, Robert. *Influence: How and Why People Agree to Things*, New York, Wm. Morrow & Co., 1984.

Conway, Flo & Jim Siegelman. *Holy Terror*. New York: Doubleday, 1982.

Halperin, David A. (Editor) *Religion, Sect and Cults*, Psychodynamic Perspectives on. Boston: John Wright, 1983.

Hassan, Steven. *Combatting Cult Mind Control*. Rochester, Vt.: Park St. Press, 1988.

Hunt, Dave. *The Cult Explosion*. Eugene, Ore: Harvest House, 1980.

Kahaner, Larry. *Cults That Kill*. N.Y.: Warner Book, 1988.

Langone, Michael and Ross, Joan Carol. *Cults: What Parents Should Know*. Weston, Mass: American Family Foundation, 1988.

Larson, Bob. *Book of Cults*. Wheaton: Tyndale House, 1982.

Nevins, Rev. Albert J. *Strangers At Your Door*. Huntington, IN: Our Sunday Visitor Publishers, 1988.

Whalen, William J. *Strange Gods*. Huntington, Indiana: Our Sunday Visitor Publishers, 1981.

Fundamentalism:

Keating, Karl. *Catholicism and Fundamentalism*. San Francisco: Ignatius Press, 1988.

Stravinskas, Rev. Peter M.J. (Editor) *The Catholic Answer*. Huntington, Ind. Our Sunday Visitor Publishers, monthly magazine published since 1987.

New Age Movement:

Adler, Margot. *Drawing Down the Moon, Rev. Ed.* Boston: Beacon Press, 1986.

Butterfield, Steve. *Amway — The Cult of Free Enterprise*. Montreal, P.Q.: Black Rose Press, 1986.

Cumbey, Constance. *The Hidden Dangers of the Rainbows*. Shreveport: Huntington House, 1983.

Cumbey, Constance. *A Planned Deception*. Shreveport: Huntington House, 1985.

Deparrie, Paul and Pride, Mary. *Unholy Sacrrifices of the New Age*. Westchester, Ill.: Crossway Books, 1988.

Farrar, Janet and Stewart. *The Witches Bible*. Two Vols. New York: Magickal Childe Publishing, 1984.

Hunt, David. *Understanding the New Age Movement*. Eugene, Ore.: Harvest House, 1983.

Groothus, Douglas. *Unmasking the New Age.* Downers Grove, Ill. InterVarsity Press, 1986.

Hunt, Dave & McMahon. *The Seduction of Christianity.* Eugene, Ore: Harvest House, 1985.

MacPherson, Pauline Griego. *Can the Elect Be Deceived?* Denver, Colorado: Bold Truth Press, 1986.

Vinson, Synan. *In The Latter Days.* Ann Arbor, Mich.: Servant Books, 1984

Satanism & related problems:

Aranza, Jacob. *Backward Masking Unmasked.* Shreveport: Huntington House, 1983.

Hart, Lowell. *Satan's Music Exposed.* Huntington Valley, Pa. Salem Kirban, 1981.

Larson, Bob. *Rock for Those Who Listen to the Words and Don't Like What They Hear.* Wheaton, Ill.: Tyndale, 1986.

Martin, Malachi. *Hostage to the Devil.* New York: Harper & Row, 1987 (originally published by the Readers Digest Press, Pleasantville, N.Y. 1976).

McDowell, Josh & Don Stewart. *Demons, Witches and the Occult.* (A pocket Guide). Wheaton: Tyndale House, 1986.

McIntosh, Christopher. *The Devil's Bookshelf.* Wellingborough, Northamptonshire: The Aquarian Press, 1985.

Michelet, Jules. *Satanism & Witchcraft.* — the classic study of medieval superstition. Secaucus, N.J.: Citadel Press, n.d.

Peters, Dan & Steve. *Rock's Hidden Persuaders.* Minneapolis: Bethany House, 1985.

Peters, Dan & Steve, and Cher Merrill. *What About Christian Rock?* Minneapolis: Bethany House, 1986.

Schwarz, Ted and Empey, Duane. *Satanism.* Grand Rapids, MI: Zondervan, 1988.

Unger, Merrill. *Demons in the World Today.* Wheaton: Tyndale House, 1986.

Warnke, Mike. *The Satan Seller.* So. Plainfield, N.J.: Bridge Pub., 1972.

The books listed here do not represent the entire spectrum of available works. Not all of these works necessarily represent the Catholic Church position, but do provide good explanations of the particular problem.